Young Writers 2005 Creative Writing Competition for Secondary Schools

From Kent
Edited by Steve Twelvetree

Disclaimer

Young Writers has maintained every effort
to publish stories that will not cause offence.

Any stories, events or activities relating to individuals
should be read as fictional pieces and not construed
as real-life character portrayal.

First published in Great Britain in 2005 by:
Young Writers
Remus House
Coltsfoot Drive
Peterborough
PE2 9JX
Telephone: 01733 890066
Website: www.youngwriters.co.uk

All Rights Reserved

© Copyright Contributors 2005

SB ISBN 1 84602 221 5

Foreword

Young Writers was established in 1991 and has been passionately devoted to the promotion of reading and writing in children and young adults ever since. The quest continues today. *Young Writers* remains as committed to engendering the fostering of burgeoning poetic and literary talent as ever.

This year, *Young Writers* are happy to present a dynamic and entertaining new selection of the best creative writing from a talented and diverse cross section of some of the most accomplished secondary school writers around. Entrants were presented with four inspirational and challenging themes.

'Myths And Legends' gave pupils the opportunity to adapt long-established tales from mythology (whether Greek, Roman, Arthurian or more conventional eg The Loch Ness Monster) to their own style.

'A Day In The Life Of …' offered pupils the chance to depict twenty-four hours in the lives of literally anyone they could imagine. A hugely imaginative wealth of entries were received encompassing days in the lives of everyone from the top media celebrities to historical figures like Henry VIII or a typical soldier from the First World War.

Finally 'Short Stories', in contrast, offered no limit other than the author's own imagination while 'Hold The Front Page' provided the ideal opportunity to challenge the entrants' journalistic skills, asking them to provide a newspaper or magazine article on any subject of their choice.

T.A.L.E.S. From Kent is ultimately a collection we feel sure you will love, featuring as it does the work of the best young authors writing today.

Contents

Robert Game (13)   1

Barton Court Grammar School
Clara Mooring (12)	2
Howard Clapp (11)	3
Max Stonier (12)	4
Lily Barr (12)	5
Hollie Dobson (12)	6
Cameron Veitch (11)	7
Beverley Newing (12)	8
Dominique Kiss (11)	9
Lewis Johns (12)	10
Remi Richards (12)	11
Joshua Fletcher (12)	12
Ursula Bishop-Harper (12)	13
Sam Marner (12)	14
Zaira Clarke (13)	15
George Davis (13)	16
Lauren Bishopp (13)	17
Oliver Power (12)	18
Laura Whitlock (13)	19
Lamorna Manning (12)	20
Jessica Lane (12)	21
Toby Green (13)	22
Samantha Healy (12)	23
Jame Geroli (12)	24
Ellie Simmons (12)	25
Timothy Riding (13)	26
Thomas Wiffen (14)	27
Alys Barr (14)	28
Charlotte Rowland (14)	29
Ben Cable (14)	30
Grace Benka (14)	31
Laura Young (13)	32
Thomas Higham (14)	33
Katy Tipping (14)	34
Paul Miller (14)	35
Vicky Forrester (13)	36

Christine Mills (13) — 37
Bethany Greenfield (12) — 38
Grant Bailey (13) — 39
Kathleen Mansell (14) — 40
Russell Laughton (12) — 41
Jack Heath (14) — 42
Maria O'Connor (14) — 43
Hannah Steadman (13) — 44
Sam Dent (14) — 45
Emily Murdoch (14) — 46
Thomas Dash (14) — 47
Rachel Oscar (14) — 48
Nic Vaz (13) — 49
Robert Sanders (14) — 50
Kevin Kendaru (14) — 51

Cranbrook School
Olaolu Olorunnimbe (13) — 52
Lucy Nelson (14) — 53
Susie Sohn (14) — 54
Oli Scheuregger (14) — 55
Toby Gower (14) — 56
Eddy Griffiths (14) — 57
James Hewitt (14) — 58
Edward Brown-Humes (14) — 59
Christian Davies (14) — 60
Abi Bishop (14) — 61
Alicia Cooper (14) — 62
Tomas Young (14) — 63
Eleanor Gill (14) — 64
Ellis Haberland-Schindler (13) — 65
Seb des'Ascoyne (14) — 66
Charlie Patrickson (14) — 67
Alice Marshall (14) — 68
Theresa Davies (14) — 69
Hannah Heap (14) — 70
Luke Pain (14) — 71
Chloe Edwards (14) — 72
Lewis Musk (14) — 73
Felicity Hayes (13) — 74
Myles Harvey (14) — 75

Victoria Burrington (14)	76
Hazel Hewitt (14)	77
Emily Hislop (14)	78
Chris Digby-Rogers (14)	79
Natalie Callan (14)	80
Lucy Snow (14)	81
Josh Cottington (14)	82
Rebecca Horner (14)	83
Matt Atterton (14)	84
Madeleine Hirschler (13)	85
Clemmie Home (14)	86
Lucy Conington (14)	87

Gravesend Grammar School for Boys

Peter Clements (11)	88
Daninder Singh Nota (12)	89
Lawrence Bricher (12)	90
Chris Daniels (12)	91
Grahame Johnson (11)	92
Manvir Khera (11)	93

Oakwood School

Tom Dowling (14)	94
Samuel Prideaux Clare (13)	96
Darrel Laing (15)	98

St John's Catholic Comprehensive School, Gravesend

Louise Wilcocks (13)	99
Sinéad O'Rourke (14)	100
Lucy Quigley (13)	101
Kasey Argent (12)	102
Nicola Hylands (13)	103
Louise Harman (12)	104
Sami Gosling (13)	105
Simran Bhogal (13)	106
Shaunnie Money (13)	107
Lauren Webb (13)	108
Ella Luscombe (13)	109
Ryan Gillingham (12)	110
Alex Brett (13)	111

Gemma Bradish (13)	112
Abbie Hooper (13)	113
Kayleigh Gourlay (13)	114
Abbie Twaits (13)	115
Chris McCann (12)	116
Charlotte Ide (13)	117
Chloe Barden (15)	118
Alex Clarke (14)	120
Hannah Hughes (13)	121
Lucy Brett (13)	122
Hayley Blackwell (13)	123
Isobel Pieroni (12)	124
Jasmine Reilly (13)	125
Thomas Toulson (13)	126
Thomas Rogers (12)	127
Thomas Shepherd (14)	128
Molly Brookes (13)	129
Christopher Furlong (12)	130
Rebecca Berry (13)	131
Ashish Sharma (12)	132
Jessica Tame (12)	133
Michael Evans (12)	134
Craig Ring (13)	135
Lorna Regan (13)	136
Laura Webster (13)	137
Liam Barnes (13)	138
Verity Theophanous (13)	139
Ashley McMaster (13)	140
Antonio Esposito (13)	141
Beth Gwynne (12)	142
Elise Apps (12)	143
Claire Comiskey (13)	144
Zoe Burton (13)	145
Joseph Coates (13)	146
Nathan Cronin (12)	147

Sir Joseph Williamson's Mathematical School

Michael Sears (14)	148
Michael Jelley (14)	149
Harry Brown (12)	150
Matthew Woodcock (14)	151

Liam Sammon (14)	152
Alexander Fisher (14)	153
Matthew Salt (14)	154
Thomas Ward (14)	155
Alexander Thring (14)	156
Robert Smith (14)	157
Matthew Hilton (14)	158
Harry Stevens (13)	159
Benjamin Chandler (13)	160
Charles Creese (12)	161
Nicholas Walding (13)	162
Thomas Mo (13)	164
Liam Borner (12)	165
Jack Conn (14)	166
Alexander Siamatas (14)	167
Ashley Collins (14)	168
Daniel Herbert (14)	169
Jamie Degiorgio (14)	170
James Hall (14)	171
Benjamin Lee (14)	172
Andrew Turbine (13)	173
Jack Baker (14)	174
Simon Howton (14)	175
Thomas Foreman (14)	176
Lloyd Horslen (14)	177
Jacob Roberts (13)	178
Haroon Latiff (12)	179
Tom Brookes (13)	180
Alexander Mold (13)	181
Grant Field (13)	182
Richard Stockwell (12)	183
Callum Bowie (13)	184
Jonathan Prenczek (13)	185
Kierran Boden (12)	186
Iain Hopkins (11)	187
Samuel Dixon (11)	188
Jatinder Singh Dosanjh (15)	189
Harry Jennings (15)	190
Daniel Barrett (14)	191
Max Cambridge (14)	192
Sam Huggett (13)	193
Michael Davies (14)	194

Greg Ceely (14)	195
Kurt Robinson (14)	196
Christopher Lee (14)	197
Harry Clarke (14)	198
Freddie Morgan (13)	199
Joel Calder (12)	200
Andrew Brown (12)	201
Matthew Thomson (12)	202
Gavin Hyder (13)	203
Edward Brookes (13)	204
Karl D'Souza (13)	205
Lee Maingard (14)	206
Ryan Badham (12)	207
Alex Jarvis (13)	208
Stephen Rowe (13)	209
Nicholas Simpson (14)	210
Sam Day (14)	211
Alex Cochrane (11)	212
Douglas Ebanks (12)	213
Joseph Dodson (12)	214
Joshua Heyes (14)	215
Timothy Hampton (14)	216
John Kallend (14)	217
Lee Bell (12)	218
Michael Lewis (14)	219
Tom Brown (14)	220
James Dance (14)	221
Jonathon Very (14)	222
Matthew Ainsworth (14)	223
Christopher Rossi (14)	224
Jason Cornish (14)	225
Michael Hutchings (13)	226
Remy Holmes (13)	227
Nicholas Hanchet (13)	228
Chris Shaw (13)	229
Andrew Bowdery (13)	230
Ryan Evans (13)	231
Ryan Dowsett (12)	232
James Black (12)	233
Ryan Smyth (12)	234
Cai Jarvis (12)	235
Jamie Aldred (13)	236

Nicholas Harlow (13)	237
Alastair Cole (14)	238
Josh Hoskins (13)	239
Ryan Bryson-Payne (13)	240
Daniel Routledge (12)	241
James Spencer (13)	242
Aaron Dimmick (13)	243
Michael Puddy (13)	244
Mihaz Bokth (15)	245
Robert Tear (15)	246
Daniel Sams (15)	247
Ben White (14)	248
Simon Yau (15)	249
Lloyd Sceats (15)	250
Edward Jarvis (14)	251
Alexander Souter (14)	252
Halvard Green (14)	253
Lewis Moran (13)	254
Ben Dance (12)	255
William Friend (12)	256
Jaspreet Sangha (11)	257
George Anderson (12)	258
Jack Paulley (12)	259
David Gay (12)	260
Cameron Bishop (11)	261
George Wright (12)	262
Daniel Forster (12)	263
Jamie Taylor (12)	264
Tom Warway (12)	265

Temple School
Jake Baker (15)	266

The Bradbourne School
Tanya Waghorn (12)	267
Georgia Donovan (12)	268
Rachael Fletcher (11)	269
Rebecca Moore (11)	270
Chandni Patel (13)	271
Sarah Barden (15)	272
Hannah Boyden (15)	273

Allanda Byrom (12)	274
Helen Trim (13)	275
Natasha Williams (13)	276
Amy Critcher (12)	277
Sophie Williams (13)	278
Phillippa Rowland (11)	280
Kate Rivers (11)	281
Laura Seare (12)	282
Nicole Young (12)	283
Alice Jamieson (11)	284
Helen Hayes (11)	285
Georgia Satterly (13)	286
Emma Cooper (13)	287
Rhonda Trevillion (14)	288
Abigail Allfrey (13)	289
Natalie Howie (13)	290
Laura Little (13)	291
Emma Brereton (12)	292
Ellena Pitt (12)	293
Alex Harradine (113)	294
Tamanna Miah (11)	295
Jasmine Hood (12)	296
Georgina Poacher (13)	297
Sophie Brooker (13)	298
Amelia Sharp (13)	299
Georgia Hart-Fisk (12)	300
Kiri Cramer (13)	302
Chloe Brown (11)	303
Deborah Launchbury (11)	304
Leanne Bashford (12)	305
Kirsty Brown (12)	306
Alex Lynch (12)	307
Laurie Monshall (13)	308
Stephanie Lee (13)	310
Helen Jenkins (13)	311
Sarah Fleet (12)	312
Rosie Cooper (13)	313
Amy Ashworth (13)	314
Charlotte Hazard (11)	315
Laura Powell (12)	316
Zoë Duffey (12)	317
Megan Haysom (11)	318

Hazel Ewens (12)	319
Abbey Warner (11)	320
Katie Foreman (12)	321
Chloe Checkley (11)	322
Megan Johnson-Hodges (12)	323
Lisa Surry (12)	324
Olivia Williams (12)	325
Katie Ray (11)	326
Sophie Kelly (12)	327
Daisy Hook (11)	328
Emily Maddox (11)	329
Shani Collins (12)	330

The Grammar School for Girls Wilmington

Natalie Price (12)	331
Laura Spitter (15)	332
Alysha Bennett (12)	333
Claire Martin (12)	334
Paige Smith (12)	335

The Thomas Aveling School

Katie Dodsworth (12)	336
Jodie Fraser (12)	337
Craig Evans (12)	338
Kirstin Bicker (12)	339
Amy Dettmar (12)	340

The Creative Writing

The Teacher

The teacher woke up, slumped in his chair, and looked at his watch worriedly. His fears had been confirmed. He was late for school, the second time that week. He wolfed down his oatmeal, downed his coffee and combed his hair carefully. It was unlikely that the pupils would notice, but perhaps the head teacher would recognise desperate pleas for promotion. As he hurriedly made his way to the Ford Anglia parked in his driveway, he realised that he had forgotten the worksheets for the day's chemistry lesson. He looked at his watch and realised that there was no time. When was the last time pupils had brought something to school for him, he mused.

Once his car had managed its arduous journey to school, he had morning registration. It did not surprise him at all that only half the class had come to school. He was not looking forward to the four free periods that morning which would be spent marking exam papers. He soon realised that all his efforts had been in vain as he observed the battlefield of red crosses strewn across the pages.

When the fifth period started, thirty pupils strutted into the room. 'Today we will have a *silent* revision session,' he told them. He did not mention the forgotten worksheets. It was not a successful lesson. The pupils did nothing but talk and rock on their chairs. *And on top of that,* he thought sulkily, *no one had remembered his birthday.*

Robert Game (13)

One Boy

Generally we British have a good society but there's always a few flaws. Not everyone's perfect.

I suppose what I'm trying to say is not everybody can con an innocent man and keep a straight face, be quick on their feet and play mind games on people ending up with them giving you their wallets and house keys without even noticing. So far in my book there is no one who can do all these things but, there is one boy who has the potential to reach this high standard - with the help of me and my grifters.

We were planning a big con, the best! The target - 55 45 gram diamonds from the Institute of London's biggest jewellers - Crust!

But back to my pride and joy, Morgan Tye. I knew almost everything about him except his hobbies and when I found them out he would be getting a little surprise in the post the next morning - a free holiday camp leaflet.

'Hello people and welcome to the keen surfer's camp, I hope you enjoy yourself!'

Morgan had a funny feeling about this camp, but he made some new friends and started to enjoy it. He learnt some new skills and was nearly at the top of the group. They were going to the nearby beach to do some proper surfing. Meanwhile I was watching his every move with my binoculars.

They say he disappeared after that but I'll leave it to your imagination.

Clara Mooring (12)
Barton Court Grammar School

Lord Of The Onion Rings

The Fellowship of the Onion Ring left Living Hell at 7 o'clock on a Sunday morning. Legless ran after them. Grandelf listened out for any spies of evil. Springly jumped over the Fellowship and ran on ahead. Frodo Baggypants pulled his trousers up once again, as he felt the wind blow onto his stomach.

The Fellowship eventually reached the Twisty Mountains. They clambered up and up until Nippin and Terry became tired. Ham Loungy lent against the cliff and Narrow Horn ripped off a sharp rock and started to sharpen his horn. Jolly Beer lent over to let Frodo have a drink. Frodo accidentally dropped the Onion Ring and Jolly Beer snatched it off the floor.

'It's strange how we can suffer so much over such a tasty thing,' he said.

Suddenly a flurry of snow landed on the Fellowship.

'This climb is difficult, can we travel through Moria?' Frodo panted.

'I suppose!' Grandelf yelled.

So they did.

As they entered Moria the entrance collapsed. A horde of Dorks jumped out at the Fellowship! All of them were dead before they had touched the floor.

The Fellowship eventually reached the Great Hall; suddenly thousands of Dorks surrounded them! Then a disgusting stench floated into the room. The Dorks fled!

They ran to the bridge of Kazahdum. All but Grandelf ran out of Moria. He fought the mighty Warthog.

'You shall not pass!' he roared. Then Grandelf forced the fearsome Warthog off the bridge, but it dragged him down with it.

Howard Clapp (11)
Barton Court Grammar School

Loch Ness

Danny looked in the mirror at his new zit and sighed. He couldn't really complain. His life was already messed up enough to make one zit not matter. It had all started going wrong when he was born. His mum left saying she couldn't handle him. Dad had always blamed him for scaring his mother away. So Danny's dad had thrown him in the worst school he could find and made Danny do everything for him. So he couldn't really let one zit get him down could he?

Danny took a short cut to school as he was late again. The short cut took him through the forest and along the shore of Loch Ness. He could hear a distant moan that sounded like a beached whale and decided to check it out as he couldn't be any later could he? When Danny got to the clearing where the sound was coming from he couldn't believe his eyes, he closed them and opened them again … but the 'thing' was still there, the 'thing' Danny decided to call the Loch Ness monster. So he visited it every day and took it food at the same place for a year.

One day after he had fed 'Lochie' he told his friends to meet him at the clearing in the loch, but didn't say why. Danny was late again and he was running through the woods towards her wailing sounds until they suddenly stopped.

Danny never saw Lochie again, or his friends.

Max Stonier (12)
Barton Court Grammar School

A Day In The Life Of A Superstar

5.30am - woken up by a loud ring, it was my agent on the phone checking if I remembered about the interview/photo shoot and press conference, today. The interview was about if I was doing a movie which I had been offered the main part in. It was all very exciting!

7am - off to London for my interview with 'OK!' magazine, in my expensive, flashy car driven by my chauffeur Mike. It would take a while to arrive.

8.40am - time flies by and before I know it we've arrived. The interview goes really well and I am pleased by the way the photos turn out.

1.30pm - time for my lunch break and afternoon off, shopping in London. I don't usually get to do this sort of thing, as my life is pretty hectic. I buy some cool shoes and jewellery to go with an outfit my stylist had chosen for me to wear for an awards ceremony later on in the week.

4.30pm - time to fly to Barcelona. Flown on my private jet. One hour and several diet bars later, I arrive.

5.30pm - the press conference goes very well, though I am worried on how the reporters will change my story into something totally different.

7.30pm - time to fly back to London.

8.30pm - arrive in London, grab something to eat, head back to my big house.

10.30pm - fall asleep and wait for my busy day to start again. Thinking of the day gone by, what a busy life I have!

Lily Barr (12)
Barton Court Grammar School

The Day In The Life Of A Spy

It was just two days ago that I was given this assignment and today I was going to complete it. I had just two hours until I was going to steal the Jewels of Ammesa ...

And those two hours went very quick I can tell you that. I was all ready, dressed in my black catsuit with my long rope and my emergency gadget pack. It was 22.00 exactly and if I was correct there should only be one guard at the back entrance. I was right, there *was* only one guard, it would be easy to get past him. I got a smoke bomb out of my backpack and threw it at the guard. He started to choke and I was sure he couldn't see anything, so I made a run for the door.

To my disappointment the door did not open! I tried to knock it down but that was hopeless and then before I knew it the guard was back on his feet trying to hit me. I quickly tackled him, he fell to the ground. I took the key in his left pocket and opened the door, there was a long dark passage in front of me and a door at the end. I walked straight for the door. It wasn't open but I could use the keys from the guard.

The weirdest thing happened, the Jewels of Ammesa weren't there. Had they been moved or had they already been stolen ... ?

Hollie Dobson (12)
Barton Court Grammar School

Glowing Fog

'But Benjamin, you must never take the boat out alone.'

'I promise Dad,' Ben replied.

Benjamin's father was a fisherman. He hoped Ben would be one too.

Benjamin had just finished his first sailing lesson when his father told him this. It was a shame he didn't listen.

A few days later, up in the quaint little town where Ben lived, he asked to go out on a walk. He walked briskly down through the town. Finally he reached the beach. Looking out to sea he saw a slight glow growing stronger then fainter, it looked like a ship but he couldn't see due to the closing fog. A great battle raged in his head as he fought his dilemma. He knew the fog was dangerous, but he was intrigued by the glow.

Benjamin was gaining on the vessel. Suddenly the heavens opened. Ben was drenched within a few seconds. The waves began to get bigger and bigger, Benjamin was feeling vulnerable in such a small boat. A sudden shockwave of icy fear rushed over him as he saw the boat engulfed in a wave of freezing water …

… Ben had just finished 'bailing out' when he saw it. The glow was there, right behind him; it was a ship! He turned the smack around and followed it, all the way to the beach.

As he got into bed he told his parents, 'I wouldn't have managed if it wasn't for the glowing boat.'

'What glowing boat?'

But Ben was asleep.

Cameron Veitch (11)
Barton Court Grammar School

A Day In The Life Of A Dog

9am - my pet wakes me up and shoos me outside into the cold. When I have checked outside I bark at the door and I am let into the house, where I go and take up my comfy seat on the sofa by the fire.

10am - I decide I want my walk and bark at the worktop my lead is on until my irritable pet comes out and puts my collar on. I decide to go on my walk across the fields and turf out a few pheasants. Then my pet starts to turn back, looking worn out, which is ridiculous as we have only walked a few miles and there was a nice-looking mud puddle coming up.

12pm - when we get back my pet just flops down on the sofa! It needs more exercise, so I pick up my ball and drop it in the pet's lap. Outrageously, it chucks it on the floor! I curl up and fall asleep on the sofa in disgust.

4pm - after my refreshing nap, I get up and eat all of my food. My pet gives a big sigh, puts down its paper and refills my bowl. I then drop my ball at its feet, which it picks up and throws a few times.

7pm - I had fallen asleep again from boredom. Lucky I've woken up. There's some good TV on for the next 2 hours. I'll watch that, after a snack.

9pm - I'm going to my basket now. Bye.

Beverley Newing (12)
Barton Court Grammar School

The Secret Of Brian

Brian Jones was an ordinary man who lived in an ordinary house with an ordinary wife and kids. But Brian had a secret. A secret so deadly, no one could believe it unless they thought about it for many hundreds of years. Brian knew the meaning of life, the ultimate answer to absolutely anything.

A great, huge, corporate, million dollar company in downtown San Francisco Bay heard of the secret from sources deep from here in the UK. Wanting yet more money, the company sent agents to England to bribe this overpowering secret out of what the company knew as 'Target One'.

'The agents,' the fat multi-millionaire paused, 'should be arriving just about now …'

The doorbell rang. Brian opened the door to a barrage of words.

'Hello, I'm here from Smith, Smith and Smith from America to interest you in selling your big, big secret for big, big bucks! All you have to do is sign here, hand it over and we'll be off back to America where we will sell the secret and give you half the dosh, while still making millions, as a sign of goodwill. So what do you say, huh, huh, huh?'

'Lousy sunnava … so he won't sell … hmm … you're fired!' The boss was peeved.

The phone rang.

'Hello! Mr Jones! You're going to sell.'

Later the company was printing the meaning of life. Well, that's what they thought and the rest of the world, except Brian who knew the real answer!

Dominique Kiss (11)
Barton Court Grammar School

Lord Of The Rings, The Mysterious Head

As Grandelf left his humble cave, the sun went in. 'Curse the weather! Yes, I curse at you, *****!' He stood for five minutes swearing at the sun (that was not there) as if it were. He left the cave and went on his way to see Frodo frog. On his way he saw Legless who was searching in the bushes for something. 'Ah, Legless may I assist you in finding what you have lost?' Grandelf was in a better mood than previously in the story.

'It is not what I have lost Grandelf …' Legless replied, 'but what I see. I swear I saw a head pop up from the bush, laugh at me then pop back down.'

'I'd swear, but this story writer won't let me!' Grandelf explained with an expression of doubt upon his face, at that exact same moment the head popped up again.

'Ha, ha, ha, you smell!' Then it disappeared, soon after a digging team was called in, they dug all night and most of the next day, but still they kept on digging.

Soon after they stopped digging the head appeared again and laughed, *'Ha, ha, ha,* you smell even more!' Just as it was going Grandelf leapt on it and pulled it out of the tree from which it came.

Frodo frog wanted to eat it, but Grandelf said, 'No, you don't know where it's been!'

Lewis Johns (12)
Barton Court Grammar School

When Wizards Call

One day Bobalo was walking to school when he fell down a manhole. 'Argh!' he cried out. 'Bloody hole!'

He stopped short as he realised he was in total darkness. He started to climb up the ladder, but where the top should be he felt a sort of oily substance. He was terrified and fell back down. He climbed back up again and went through the oily stuff.

There were men all around him who had the most suspicious dress sense. He gasped as he found himself in a round room which must have been four acres large.

'We are wizards from the Mostly Seen But Not All University of Mhaaathrewwp,' shouted one in mauve.

They all walked towards him and dragged him into a small room.

'You are needed,' said the same one as before. 'My name is Humpdydumpdy.'

'Why am I here?'

'You are needed to do something which none of us can do.'

'Okay, what?'

The wizards explained what he had to do to him, that he had to help in a ceremony, of death. All he had to do was lie down and be quiet. He was quite stupid and didn't realise that in death ceremonies there was a sacrifice.

He lay down on a wooden bench in the middle of a big room. He saw a large knife coming towards his chest, then felt a pain where his chest used to be.

Bobalo was a stupid fool and deserved what he got. And remember, to run when wizards call.

Remi Richards (12)
Barton Court Grammar School

A Day In The Life Of A Roman Guard: What If Hannibal Attacked Rome?

Julius Brutus woke up; a voice was bawling through the door. He found himself and began slowly and methodically buckling on armour. It was then he heard the words coming through the door, it was then he sped up.

Out came Julius running as fast as he could. He heard the door shudder and his sergeant rallying many men at the gate and positioning them in formation so as to stop them coming through. More archers he now saw running along the walls only to disappear into a bloodied red mass by a catapult. It had started.

Now only the smash of the battering ram and the catapults were heard. Then they heard a voice from a man ... and a whisper from his sergeant, 'Hannibal.'

Cracks were beginning to appear on the door so he ran over to the gates and joined the horde of men waiting there, silent. Then a shout was heard, 'Elephants.'

Ten minutes later ...

He was on the front line now and as the gate fell he charged, his spear finding its way into an elephant, slaying it instantly. He then began stabbing in an insane fury at all the elephants around him until they were all dead. There was a marching column of pike men closing in on him. He waited for them to arrive and suddenly some boiling water came pouring from above causing the pike men to break rank. As he charged an elephant appeared out of nowhere and, as he lifted up his spear, it fell down dead, squashing Julius in the process.

Joshua Fletcher (12)
Barton Court Grammar School

The Perfect People

There were five of them. Ema, Kitty, Jenna, Ella and Onyx. The Famous Five, some people called them. Or just perfect. Nothing bad ever happened to the perfect people, their lives were perfect to match their perfect good looks and their perfect grades and their perfect houses and families.

Until Ema moved away and Kitty was in a car crash. Jenna's perfect mum got seriously ill. Onyx's brother started beating her up. Suddenly life wasn't so perfect and no one at school could talk to or trust anyone except Ella.

The new popular group was formed, Roxy and Michaela and Lauren and Chelsea all became 'perfect'. A scared Kitty and a nervous Jenna and a bruised Onyx mourned what they once had.

Until the day. The day Onyx finally fought back and got pushed down the stairs. Jenna's mum died and Kitty was turned down for plastic surgery for her scars. It was the day Ella was finally tipped off the spot of queen bee. It was the first day anyone ever saw Ella do something stupid and the last day anyone ever saw her.

Ursula Bishop-Harper (12)
Barton Court Grammar School

A Day In The Life Of Julius Canter

'All men to the walls!'

Julius Canter slowly opened one bleary eyelid and yawned. He suddenly jerked up in his cloth-covered, hay-filled bed after hearing a huge crash from outside. He jumped out of his bed and ran outside, to see people running around screaming and corpses strewn over the street. Part of Rome itself was burning. Julius ducked as a huge ball of fire hurtled over his head and crashed into the barracks that he had just come out of. He ran towards the armoury, only stopping to take cover under a market stall as a volley of arrows thudded into the ground around him.

When he finally got to the armoury he slipped on a coat of plated armour and dextrously tied the knots on the front section, then put a short sword into his sheath and picked up a large shield and javelin. He rushed back to the walls and slowly climbed the rickety ladder to the top. When he got to the top he almost fell off the wall as he saw the sight before him. There were four huge long columns of Carthaginian pike men with a row of six elephants in front. Julius heard a cry from the gatehouse, 'They're breaking in!'

Julius ran along the wall and was almost knocked off when a huge boulder hit the top of the wall and sent a group of archers flying down into the street below. Julius came to his senses and continued running along the wall.

When he finally got to the gatehouse and down the ladder, Julius joined the ranks of thirty other soldiers. The gate shuddered as the battering ram hit its thick wooden surface. Then the gate jerked back out of its hinges and fell to the floor. Hordes of Carthaginian infantry with their short swords and moon-shaped shields charged through the gate, but were instantly cut down by a hail of javelins.

Then a huge trumpeting sound filled the air as a huge war elephant charged through the gate and sent lines of Romans flying. Julius held up his shield, but was thrown backwards by a sharp elephant tusk. He flew through the air for about thirty metres before hitting the wall of a villa and hearing the sickening crunch of his own bones shattering against the hard wall, Julius crumpled to the floor. Everything went black.

Sam Marner (12)
Barton Court Grammar School

A Journey To Nowhere …

A coach was rattling along a winding deserted road. All Jasper could see was baking desert sand and all he could hear was the drone of the engine lulling him to sleep …

'Hey, get up!'

Jasper jolted awake. It was the miserable bus driver.

'This is the end of the line,' he barked.

'Wh-when's the next bus?' stammered startled Jasper.

'Next week,' replied the driver and with a screech of tyres he was gone.

Jasper was left at the edge of an eerie village that looked like the set of a western when all the cast have gone home. He spent the rest of the day exploring, but there was no one. Anywhere.

He was going to investigate an abandoned factory when …

'Who are you?' a haunting voice inquired.

Jasper whirled round. Standing in front of him was a deathly pale boy with unnaturally bright blue eyes.

The boys soon started talking like they were old friends. The boy's name was Tarquin Thompson; he was 14 and had lived in the village his whole life. Everyone had had to leave the village due to a deadly plague, but he had been left behind.

Over the next week the boys became good friends, although Jasper always felt there was something odd about Tarquin.

At the end of the week, Jasper was walking through the church gardens to get the bus when a wave of fear washed over him. He was looking at a gravestone with the inscription: 'Tarquin Thompson 1870-1884'.

Zaira Clarke (13)
Barton Court Grammar School

Sergeant Major

Bombs were ticking, bullets were clattering, people were screaming. One of our privates was trapped under a large piece of rubble, we thought we would lose him. Then we heard a little whisper from inside a bombed-out house. The Germans were negotiating. The Russians were our allies, but we did not know anymore.

I was Sergeant Major Wycliffe, with corporals Smith and Weir and ten privates. We had just been involved in D-Day three days earlier. We had moved into a little Belgian town called Diegem then into Kortrijk, where a bunch of stukas had shot down both of our lieutenants and one plane's wing had trapped our veteran private. We were on a very important mission, we couldn't let one man keep us down and he was going pale. Corporal Smith had an idea.

'Sir, we can't bomb the building, we need to draw them out or we'll blow up the secret documents.'

'Good plan, right …' Private Brick screamed. A German shot out the window. The glass shattered over Brick's face. He screamed again. The German turned the door handle. *Click!* My heart was pounding. The only thing I could do was hide. One of our privates ran into a house to the top floor.

'What are you doing?'

'I'm saving your bacon!'

The Germans ran out. One fell to the floor. We ran out with our MP-40s.

'There'll be a lot more Germans in Heaven now.'

'Sir, do you want these?'

'Cheers, Smith.'

George Davis (13)
Barton Court Grammar School

The Horror

She screamed as loudly as her voice could. Her eyes hypnotised by the cold, shrilling stare. There was nothing she could do, no matter how hard she tried. The deed was done. The streetlamp flickered on, distant noises could be heard. She panicked. What had she done?

The blood began to ooze beneath her. Never had she seen such a horrid sight before. Footsteps behind her …

'I didn't do it,' she cried. 'Believe me … *please*, you must!' Her face turned redder, sweat dripped from her face, she could not move.

The stranger quickened his pace.

Thoughts were running through her head, over and over.

She had to be home 10 minutes ago, but all sanity had escaped her, she had lost the concept of time. How could she go home now, after what she had done? Strands of her coal hair began to fall upon her face, the crescent moon shone in her deep green eyes. She turned; nobody in sight, the streetlamp flickered once more. She looked up, feeling confused and dirty.

Slowly her eyes reverted back, her foot lifted. It looked even more horrific than she had remembered. Eyes opening wide, a shrill scream let rip … Beatrice Floganom had killed a worm.

Before she could think her heels turned and she ran off into the night.

Lauren Bishopp (13)
Barton Court Grammar School

Newspaper Report - Earthquake Hits Canterbury!

At 4pm yesterday, one of the biggest earthquakes ever hit Canterbury, Kent causing a huge fault line to open across the UK! Experts are saying that it measured 9.6 on the Richter scale. Apparently a new fault line has opened up running right up England, making Canterbury a new earthquake hotspot.

At precisely 4.13.24 today a huge earthquake rocked Canterbury, buildings were destroyed and roads buried, huge fissures opened up out of the ground, swallowing houses and lava streams flowed slowly through the street destroying everything in their way. The city has had no experience of quakes and it was unprepared, a serious earthquake has never hit England and the people were helpless. There was nothing the services could do but evacuate the area to get out of the way. But they are going to have go get used to it, Canterbury will now be experiencing several big earthquakes a year!

Specialists say that the new fault line will mean that stronger buildings must be made and people must be taught what to do in the case of a quake.

No one quite knows where the fault line came from, but it passes through Kent. Scientists believe it to span the entire length of England, going through several major cities. Experts are saying that it may have been caused by the recent oil dredging that has been taking place off the coast of Kent. However scientists say there are still many other plausible causes for the fault. We will keep you updated on the crisis in following issues.

Oliver Power (12)
Barton Court Grammar School

The Elegant Happy Lady

One day a beautiful woman was travelling across the country just to show off her elegant looks. The men were mesmerised by her beauty but the women just sighed in disgust.

On her journey through the green countryside, she passed an old woman, she was wrinkled with age.

'Please help me …' cried the beggar.

'Why would I help you, you filthy louse!' Cassandra snapped as she just kept on walking.

'Fine, then you will suffer …' and then beggar was gone.

Cassandra returned home but no one was to be found. 'Hello, is anybody there?'

No one replied. Then a strange creature emerged from her house. 'What are you?'

'My name is Sophitia, but I am also known as the Harpy lady.' This creature that stood in front of her had an elegant face with long red hair; her arms had blue wings on the side and talons for hands. Her legs were purple and she had huge talons for feet.

'Why are you here?' panicked Cassandra.

'I have come to teach you a lesson …' and as this was said the Harpy charged, wings outstretched and talons ready.

'Leave me alone!' cried Cassandra.

'Well, maybe next time you'll help people in need!' With a slash of her talons Sophitia cut Cassandra's face and then flew off.

The next day Cassandra walked through the town, but her beautiful face was shredded and the men and women laughed at her, so Cassandra ran away from the town and never showed her face again.

Laura Whitlock (13)
Barton Court Grammar School

The Tigers

The group of gigantic fiery tigers loped through the night. Rivets of sweat ran down their warm flanks and the ground shook as they travelled. Their leader was the biggest and strongest of them all, with huge sharp claws and teeth like carving knives. They were a formidable sight as they drew near to the city.

The young princess was waiting for them, as arranged. Her long hair shone in the gloom. 'King Sabre-Tooth,' she said, her refined voice echoing in the darkness. 'Please accept my many thanks for coming to us in our time of need. I promise that this great deed will always be remembered.'

The tiger king purred and the terrific noise was heard throughout the city. 'Princess Thirrin,' he replied, 'your thanks are accepted with love and respect.'

Sabre-Tooth saw that her eyes were troubled and sad. His ferocious tribe milled around him, towering above the young girl. The king saw her grief and let her ride on his back.

'I can tell you have news,' he said gently, 'please let me know if you are ready.' He heard the princess take a deep breath and felt her soft hands grip his warm fur. After a moment, she spoke and her voice was choked with tears.

'My father, the king, has been killed in the battlefield earlier this very day. That means that I am now Queen Thirrin and your tribe and mine are facing our first battle.'

Lamorna Manning (12)
Barton Court Grammar School

Darkness

The torch illuminated only fragments of the black cavern. Sharp shards of light fell across the dusty ground, breaking up the darkness momentarily until it swept on to explore other corners, allowing it to be replaced with the same suffocating darkness. The dame darkness that fills the chamber to the brim, spilling into passageways and caves, the same darkness witnessed only at death. It is here that no light can ever penetrate, where no gentle fingers of sunlight can stretch to caress the forgotten blackness. Here, settled in a place where looming shadows and gloomy corners cease to exist because there is no glimpse of light, silent misery awaits a foolish explorer who dares to venture within its grasp, brave enough to stop and feel its icy breath. Until today.

Anna Yokes carefully wielding the torch, crawled eagerly into darkness' clutch and then faltered … with a flash of red hair, invisible in the dark, Anna flung her head round, trying to pinpoint the direction of the sound. *Click, click, click.* The sound of death striding its way towards her. The torch fell to the floor as Anna struggled to run, flickering once and then dying. The darkness grew more menacing as the walls began to close around her. The clicking stopped.

'Anna, you naughty girl! Get yourself out from underneath your bed this instant!'

Jessica Lane (12)
Barton Court Grammar School

Heatwave Hits Kent

The people of Kent are taking refuge from the incredibly high temperatures from a heatwave in the south east of England. In these early days of June, scientists are saying temperatures are sure to continue rising. Many people have theories as to what has caused this disaster but nearly all seem impossible.

Very few people are found on the streets of Kent now as temperatures reach heights of 40 degrees centigrade. Residents are not encouraged that things will get any better as scientists are saying over the next few months, before they sort out what actually has caused this disaster; temperatures will keep rising and may exceed 55 degrees.

Temperatures like this are only ever reached in one other place in the world. This is Death Valley in California in the USA. The British terrain and residents are not suited to this sort of weather and they don't have the sort of protection against the sun factor and intense rays. Over the last few days we have seen tar on the roads melting and poor old Blean Woods has gone up in flames.

Kentish citizens are urged to stay inside as our British skins are simply not strong enough to withstand the intense rays and heat. Although there is not a theory which everyone agrees on, the strongest theory is that there is a large whole in the ozone layer directly above us.

Toby Green (13)
Barton Court Grammar School

A Quest Into Death

As Carsineus fades away the king shouts, 'Bring back my queen or else!'

Carsineus begins to travel across stormy seas and dangerous water searching to find the island. Many different obstacles get in his way such as dangerous animals and mysterious islands.

He begins to see the island, but there is only one trouble that would stop him from getting there, Carsineus spots a storm ahead of him which means he may have to change his course.

The storm hits the sea just as he is within metres of the island. The storm is as strong as a blue whale. The waves come up as tall as the Eiffel Tower crashing down on the boat at full speed, with full force. The boat smashes into smithereens sending Carsineus into the air and down to the bottom of the deep sea.

Carsineus swims to get to the surface to take a breath, he pops his head up and out of the water and gasps for air, swallowing saltwater as he struggles to swim. He struggles to find the energy to swim to the island, but he just about makes it.

Carsineus tries to get to the queen, but his strength just keeps on getting weaker and weaker. The guards spot him crawling into the island and charge. They are armed with many dangerous and lethal weapons. They start to attack Carsineus, tearing him to pieces. Blood is everywhere. He dies in a puddle of blood.

Samantha Healy (12)
Barton Court Grammar School

Theseus And The Minotaur

The Minotaur was half man, half bull, he was the most fearsome monster in ancient times. The Minotaur lived in the labyrinth. This was a great maze with winding passages on the island of Crete. Each year seven children and seven ladies were sent from Greece to feed the Minotaur.

Theseus, the greatest Greek hero, said that he would go to Crete and fight the Minotaur. He told his father to let him go as one of the victims. Theseus claimed he would go there and kill the Minotaur and free Greece from a life of being scared. Theseus thought about when all the other people said they were going to slay the Minotaur, but never came back but he still insisted he would sail there with black sails to represent doom. He told his father Aegeus that when he returned he would hoist a white sail to represent that he had killed the Minotaur.

When he arrived in Greece he fell in love with the princess, she said that even a hero would get lost so she gave him a ball of thread and said, 'Unwind it and then follow it back.'

As he walked in he could hear the bellowing of the Minotaur. The further he got in the louder the roars, until he reached the centre of the maze. As the Minotaur turned its back he plunged his sword in it.

He was so excited he forgot to hoist the white flag, so his dad jumped off a cliff in despair.

Jame Geroli (12)
Barton Court Grammar School

A Day In The Life Of Caesar

I woke up to the sound of screaming and yelling coming from outside of my window. I got up and put on my dressing gown and then I rushed over to the windows and tugged them open. 'What is going on?' I boomed and all went quiet.

Then a small voice from the large crowd squeaked, 'It is the tigers Your Honour, they have escaped from the amphitheatre!' And all was quiet again.

'What!' I exploded. 'Get me five of my most fierce warriors and then send them out to find them, and if I don't get those tigers back, then something dreadful is going to happen!' With a sweep of my dressing gown, I disappeared into my room.

After a morning of pacing about my room, I heard an uproar coming from outside so I ran out to see what had happened and saw two battered men. 'Where are the tigers?' I boomed.

'We couldn't find them, Your Honour,' one battered man said.

'Argh!' I screamed, but it was drowned out by the loud roar which came from behind me. I spun around to see two white tigers growling. 'That's it!' I cried and picked up the nearest spear and threw it at one. It missed, and the tigers turned on me and started to come towards me. I ran down the hallway, trying to get away, but I could hear them gaining on me. Then suddenly I had an idea. I turned round and just stood there knowing what was about to happen to me. Just as the tigers came towards me I shouted, 'Cages!' and down came two huge cages which landed straight over the tigers. I heard cheering outside and I looked out of the window and saw that everyone was watching and they all looked impressed. Once the tigers were taken care of I went outside and all I could say was, 'All in a day's work!'

Ellie Simmons (12)
Barton Court Grammar School

Nuclear Missiles

He shuddered as he looked onwards. Every inch of land was left barren and dead. The few plants left were old, void of leaves and they tilted towards the ground. They were clinging to life with extraordinary determination, but it was obvious that the landscape was winning.

He looked around for some sort of life, but there was none to be found. Not even the lizards and reptiles that usually infested this sort of environment could be seen. He looked up at the sky, but that too was void of life. There were no clouds, for water did not exist in his harsh land.

Taking a swig from his bottle, he started walking. The air seemed heavy with loss and heat and the wind on its own told a tale that once there was life here. The further he walked from his car, the worse it became, until he stopped again, he had seen something, right in front of him.

Crouching down, he carefully removed it from the sand. He was pretty sure that it was just a bit of one … but he had to be careful. Wiping the sand away, he saw printed on the rusted metal: 'BCOAA'. The Bomb Community of the American Alliance. It was only a bit of it, a chunk from the real missile.

The man sighed and looked up. This had only been a small missile. Most of the bombs that were tested in this desert were nuclear.

Timothy Riding (13)
Barton Court Grammar School

The Stone In The Sword

Many years ago, deep in the mists of time, an old lady died of a deadly disease that was then unknown to man. Her body was lain in a crudely carved wooden coffin and next to her was lain a silver sword encrusted with many semi-precious stones of every colour imaginable, the hues changing with each turn, like a colourful kaleidoscope.

Years later a beautiful maiden fell from her horse, her long, cascading, brunette locks flowing behind her like a waterfall in spring. As she fell the short distance to the earth the ground gave way beneath the weight of her body and she found herself face-to-face with the skull of the long-buried corpse. She screamed a high-pitched scream and scrambled from the grave. Her heart beating fast, she remounted and rode to her home.

The open grave was discovered six months later by a noble gentleman out walking to relieve his mind after his wife's untimely demise. As his eyes alighted on the yellowed skeleton he caught his breath in his throat. But soon the shock receded and his vision drifted to the sword that was still as shiny and fresh as the day it was first cast. Over the years many honourable gentlemen and gracious ladies held and caressed the sword and over the years each picked off a stone to keep for themselves. Yet there was one stone that would not come off: one stone that would stay there eternally.

Thomas Wiffen (14)
Barton Court Grammar School

Not Her Fault

She stood quietly, shaking with fear. The man stood beside her, a firm grip on her arm. So firm, her arm was now red and streaky where his fingers tightly gripped her, not letting go. Looking at her, he snarled nastily, the cold light making his head look shiny and greasy, just like his long dark hair. Glancing around the dirty, smelly room that was supposedly her home, she let one small tear clumsily roll down the side of her face. She gently wiped it so as not to catch her cuts. She hated calling it her home. It wasn't a home at all; it was more like a prison. She looked around and started to sigh, but abruptly stopped and closed her mouth. She couldn't risk it. The man roughly changed his grip and half dragged the weak girl up the stairs.

'You'll sit it in ya room, until I next wanna see ya!'

The girl nodded, she knew what was going to happen to her later, as she had heard the same words every single day for the last three months.

Shuffling into the gloomy room, she carefully placed herself on the hard bed and winced with pain as she caught one of her bruises. The door clicked shut and there was a rustling as the man pulled the key back out of the door.

Curling up into a ball on the bed, she thought about how it used to be and what she had done wrong.

Alys Barr (14)
Barton Court Grammar School

Don't Come Out!

He was scared and started trembling with fear. The nerves gradually flowed around his body. What was going to happen next? He looked around the room, it was cold and bare. There was no light, no wallpaper on the wall, just a bed in the corner and a pole to hang all his clothes on, so that they wouldn't get ripped and his dad wouldn't get found out.

His name was Billy, he had just had his thirteenth birthday exactly one week ago. All poor Billy received was a colouring set and a pad of paper that looked like it had been taken out of the junk box in the attic.

He had a rough time at home, with his dad treating him like he was nothing. He had to scrub the floor on his hands and knees and do all the washing up. There were seven people living in the house and they were all messy.

Billy used to put up with his dad picking on him and telling him what to do, but it was when he had got into a row with him that he knew it had to stop. Unfortunately for Billy, he said 'no' to something his dad told him to do. His dad hated the word 'no' and went ballistic, grabbing him by the arm and smacking him as hard as he could. As soon as Billy could break free he sprinted out the house and hid.

'What have I done to deserve this?'

Charlotte Rowland (14)
Barton Court Grammar School

Train Dodging

Many had been here before them.
 Many had risked their lives before them.
 Now, it was their turn.

Jim and Mark stood waiting by the tracks. It was cold outside, rain was trickling down the side of the tunnel, though both boys felt hot. Both were sweating with fear. The surrounding area had once been home to the homeless, it was easy to tell due to the smell of urine and the empty beer bottles that littered the place. It was the perfect place.

Two weeks previous a couple of friends had introduced them to a sport they liked to call 'train dodging'. This involved waiting till the last minute, before jumping out of the way of an oncoming train. Of course the sport was dangerous, many had died or lost limbs trying, even the best of them had failed.

The boys were brought back to reality by the sound of a train's horn, still far into the distance. They took their places on the track and waited for the familiar sound (they had tried before but chickened out) of the humming of the tracks as the electricity began to flow through them.

In the distance a light appeared as the train came around the corner making its way down the long tunnel towards them. It gradually came closer and closer by the second.

At this point the driver could still not see them.
 At the last moment Mark jumped out of the way.
 Jim was not so lucky.

Ben Cable (14)
Barton Court Grammar School

A Day In The Life Of Dr Who

The tardis had landed in the middle of a stony road in the year 1520. The Doctor and his sidekick, Rose, stepped out and looked around.

'According to my time watch, it is the year 1520, the year in which King Henry the Eighth was king. Shall we go and take a look?' remarked the Doctor.

His sidekick silently nodded.

So, down the cobbled road they went, looking around at everything they passed.

'What the hell is that?' asked Rose, but it soon became clear to her that it was a castle and as you can probably guess, it was the king's.

'How about we take a look inside?' smiled the Doctor.

'C'mon!'

They raced up to the big double gates and knocked. There was no answer so Dr Who used his sonic screwdriver to open them. They tiptoed down the passage silently as they knew their presence wasn't requested. The king spotted them soon enough, though the Doctor got away. Rose however, didn't.

'Well, well, well, you're a pretty thing aren't you? How would you like to be my wife? But I am warning you now, this is not a question. Just think of it more of a command.'

Rose nodded not knowing what to do. The Doctor watched all of this in a far-off place and wondered whether he would always get stuck with rubbish sidekicks. The trouble is everyone knows it is always wrong to mess with time . . .

Grace Benka (14)
Barton Court Grammar School

A Day In The Life Of The Care Bears

It was another usual day at Care-a-lot and all of the Care Bears and Care Bear cousins were enjoying care-tea and star biscuits whilst they had their morning meeting.

'Right, how is everything going down on the ground today then? Are there any troubles that need attending to?' Tender-heart asked.

'Well, there have been a few problems but they are all sorted and we shouldn't have any more trouble for the rest of the day if my calculations are correct,' Cheer-bear spoke.

'Ah well, it is splendid to hear that Cheer-bear! Well, if we do not have any troubles to fix today then everyone can have a fun day,' Tender-heart shouted.

'Yeah!' All of the Care Bear and Care Bear cousins cheered.

Immediately, everyone rushed out in the cloud play area and started to enjoy their day of fun. Cheer-bear and Love-a-lot started playing on the rainbow seesaw and were having the time of their lives. Lucky-bear played with Sunshine-bear on the cloud slide. Then, not long after, Brave-heart joined in with them.

Everyone was having a blast except for one lonesome Care Bear. Poor Grumpy-bear was all on his own in the dark and depressing clouds where he spent most of his time. 'No one cares about me. I'm just a cheerless bear.'

Then suddenly Cheer-bear came along. 'What's wrong Grumpy-bear? Why are you all alone? Come on, let's go and enjoy the rest of the day.'

Grumpy-bear smiled and together they went off to the rainbow seesaw to enjoy the rest of their fun day.

Laura Young (13)
Barton Court Grammar School

The Mystery Of A Magic Man

Goldwin, a mage studying at the wizardry college of Branspatch, was walking about in never-ending thoughts. What he was thinking, no one would know. How he became a mage, no one knows. And how he ever came upon this mystical place in the hills of Timbuktu, no one knows. The only thing that people will ever know is that he is no ordinary mage. Spells which ordinary mages can't perform, he can. He is a mage who goes up to the level of all of the great ones from the history of Branspatch.

Walking, he eventually arrived at the misty doors of his classroom. The teacher magicked the door open, and Goldwin, along with all of his other friends, walked into the classroom, each one more eager than the next to learn some magic. But, with all of this eagerness, Goldwin still stood out. There was a certain glint in his eye, as though he was powered up, ready to perform the spells, but he just needed to learn them, and then he would be perfect. It would be a sad thing if he was to leave the art as soon as he graduated.

'Everyone, wave your hands in the air and chant with me,' shouted the teacher. 'Gangrene through the desert snow, turn the tables round,' the teacher started the chant.

'Gangrene through the desert snow, turn the tables round,' chanted everyone repeatedly.

On the tenth chant, one table started to turn around, the one of the magical Goldwin.

Thomas Higham (14)
Barton Court Grammar School

The End Of The World!

The world was dying, moaning from millions of years of pain and suffering. This was it, the end of humanity in the year 2055!

There was panic throughout the world, people screaming, running away, trying to escape from the firm world beneath their feet. They could not escape from the Earth, it had a firm grasp on its murderers and was willing to take their lives too.

Alistair was sitting by the river, his most favourite place in the world. For some reason he was drawn to the small, trickling, mysterious river, it made him feel close to his father. He wanted to be near his dad one last time before the end, before almost all of humanity came to the same sticky end that his father had.

He was trying so hard to forget about the terrible decision he was going to have to make, because he was the richest man in the world. He and one of his chosen passengers would be spared from the wrath of the world and survive on another planet in space. The only problem was who would he choose, his pregnant wife or his 3-year-old son? He loved both of them with all his heart and could not choose. The dilemma was excruciating. Either way, a part of him would die from the loss.

Katy Tipping (14)
Barton Court Grammar School

Addicted To Thrills

Entering the first turn, cold tyres scrabbling for grip, championship leader Rob Liddle swung into the apex of the corner, clipping the curb with perfection, setting himself up for the long straight ahead.

After a perfect start from 8th on the grid, Liddle had carved his way through the field of Caterham kit cars and whizzed up to the front. At only 18, Rob was the hottest driving talent around and victory today would mean championship glory and a stepping stone towards a career in the British Touring Car Championship, maybe more, and so far all was going to plan.

Lap 24 out of 50 and the first round of pit stops had just been completed. With no problems detected, the race was back on, Rob now back in 4th after the pit stops, but biting at the heels of the top 3 places. After a series of amazing overtaking moves, the top spot was back in his grasp and with the last lap in sight, adrenaline and excitement flowed through his veins like an addictive drug.

But something was not right. Full power wasn't getting to the rear wheels …

'S***! Drive shaft's gone. Let's hope I can creep it home though.'

An early instant had taken its toll. The team sat nervous but finally their man rounded the final turn, rolling across the line. Cheers went up, relief and champagne flowed and motor racing showed its bright side, for a change.

Paul Miller (14)
Barton Court Grammar School

The Haunted House

It was Hallowe'en. Sam and Abi were rapidly changing into their costumes as the anticipation of trick or treating was boiling up inside. They both ran so fast down the stairs you could barely see them. Sam was a blood-sucking vampire, whereas Abi was a spell-casting witch. After grabbing their gigantic goodie bags they dashed outside. They both gazed around …

'Where shall we frighten first?' Sam asked in a creepy voice.

'How about Montague Lane?' cackled Abi.

'Perfect, let's go,' Sam replied and off they headed.

As they raced towards the first house they heard some passers-by say to each other that the old house gave away loads of sweets and money.

'Please can we go there?' Abi pleaded.

'Yes let's go,' replied Sam, already starting to walk.

They slowed down as they approached. Just looking at the house sent shivers down their spines. Whilst linking arms they approached the door, spiders' webs and dust covered it but Sam slowly reached his hands out to knock but the door swung open whilst creaking loudly. They crept in, all around were spiders' webs, dust, rats and very scary-looking statues and paintings. Suddenly the door slammed and a statue opened up. Out burst a mummy!

'Run!' shouted Abi as she grabbed Sam.

They ran but the door wouldn't open. Crying with panic they slumped down in front of the door as the mummy approached, it took off its mask to reveal it was their dad playing an evil trick!

Vicky Forrester (13)
Barton Court Grammar School

The Ghost Stalker

He won't leave me alone. I see him everywhere. I'll be in the bathroom getting ready to go out. The mirror would be steamed with the hot air from my warm shower, and as I'd be doing my hair in front of it, he'd be behind me. The whole time. Just in the mirror, I could stare at him all day, but if I turn around to face him, he won't be there. He's just a reflection.

I only really cracked when I was in the library. But then I saw him again. My eyes were intensely fixed on the keyboard, tapping slowly at the keys, making sure I worded every sentence correctly. Then I glanced at the screen. Notepad opened. It was typing by itself. First of all, the words made no sense. Then, it wrote, very slowly, a letter a second 'I'll have my revenge'. The screen flickered and a faint image of his face appeared, his face sullen and features distorted. He had blue bags under his empty eyes, his skin which was once full of life, was now dead and pale, so dry that it was peeling. He's angry. He's coming.

I can't take it anymore. Every night I'll lie awake in bed, restless, knowing that he's out there. So now I've come to it. A simple fizz of a pill in my water is all it takes. One sip and I'm gone. I have no troubles anymore. You see, the truth is … I killed him.

Christine Mills (13)
Barton Court Grammar School

Six-Year-Old As New Prime Minister

On Sunday 9th May the votes flooded in.

Little did we know that day, that our poor, unsuspecting country was in for a shock. This morning it was announced that little Tommy Clark was going to be in charge of England.

The new Prime Minister has already set about making some new laws. We managed to schedule a meeting with the six-year-old, (who promptly informed us that he was six and three-quarters), and below are some of his views:

'Everyone has to pay a lollipop tax!' our new Prime Minister commanded.

He even attempted to change our National Anthem to the tune of the 'Tweenies' but officials refused.

Tommy's opposition is furious.

'I can't believe I lost to a six-year-old'! wailed Labour representative Tony Blair. 'Why would the people do that to me? Why?' cried the ex-Prime Minister.

But our current Prime Minister has only one thing to say to Mr Blair and that is, 'Ner ner! I won! Ha ha!'

The Daily Gossip interviewed some voters. Kate Green, 31, says, 'It's a disgrace. Why did people put such a vulnerable child in charge?'

However, Yaya De Zegra, 24, disagrees, 'His policies are much better than any of the other candidates'!'

Although there may be disagreements, we all agree that the next four years are going to be fun - and definitely something to remember.

Bethany Greenfield (12)
Barton Court Grammar School

What Goes Around

The Wild Swan Hotel sat between Auroras Casino and the laundry shop. Night had weaved inconspicuously across the sky and a fine mist covered the city in a concealing blanket of eerie fog. Rain began to fall, tiny droplets smashing to harmless shards on Tommy's well-pressed suit. He looked down into his scarlet-laced pocket. He reached into it, hand quaking with adrenaline, and pulled out his gun just so that the glimmering trigger could be seen. He took a deep, long puff of his cigarette and walked through the gold-trimmed doors.

The reception desk was empty; silence was all that greeted him in the cold, marble-laden lobby. He went behind the desk and carefully removed the key from room 326 on the second floor. He chose to take the stairs, the safer option in his mind, in case any unwanted surprises blocked his route. He climbed the flight of stairs silently, removing another cigarette from his waterlogged jacket. The nicotine calmed his nerves; soothed his pain.

Many things had happened that he couldn't change, couldn't stop from happening. But this was one thing he could control, although it was one thing that he thought he would never have to do - seek vengeance.

He was nearly at the top of the stairs now, bursting with primal rage. He was so close that he could hear the voices of those that had tortured his soul.

The door swung open revealing his victims. They screamed as he took aim …

Grant Bailey (13)
Barton Court Grammar School

Evacuee

It was strange; scary even. Harry didn't know quite what to make of it all. His mother kept telling him not to worry, it was for his own good - but somehow he couldn't quite bring himself to believe her. If it was to benefit him, it would make her happy. Why then, could she never look straight at him anymore without her eyes suddenly welling up and her having to leave the room? It seemed awfully confusing.

After these seemingly random bouts of sobbing had been happening continuously for a few months, Harry arrived home from school to find his small, rather grubby, old suitcase in the hall. He knew the time had finally come. The war had been going on for three weeks now, and already it was clear it would not be anything like the previous one. It was not safe for anyone in the large towns such as this.

A few moments later his mother shuffled through, looking faintly dazed.

'I'll miss you,' he said slowly, struggling desperately to swallow the lump rising in this throat.

His mother abruptly burst into tears. 'I love you so much. Be brave. Write to me … every day …' she trailed off, choked by her overwhelming grief.

And all of a sudden they were at the train station, being bustled about by other forlorn-looking children and their numbers. Harry was bundled onto the train, losing sight of his mother and her tender, tear-streaked face. He didn't understand he would never see it again.

Kathleen Mansell (14)
Barton Court Grammar School

Local Man In Shark Attack!

Two days ago, David Hale was peacefully living in Townsville, East Australia. However, yesterday he was viciously attacked by a 14-foot long great white shark.

David, 36, was at the Townsville beach with his wife Jill, also 36. He was snorkelling in waters around 7 feet deep when the killer shark swam at incredible speeds towards him and bit off his left leg.

Witnesses on the beach said they saw David thrashing around in the water then the water turned red with blood. Lifeguards aimed at the shark with a shotgun and fired. The bullet missed but the shark swam away in fright.

David was saved by a lifeboat and is now in a critical condition in the Townsville hospital. Authorities are hunting the shark last seen just after the attack by fishermen off the coast.

Jill, David's wife, said, 'I looked up to see David thrashing about in the water screaming for help. People on the beach were screaming. I was screaming and crying for help'.

Jill burst into tears shortly after the interview. Our thoughts are with David and his family at this time.

Russell Laughton (12)
Barton Court Grammar School

A Day In The Life Of A Pound Coin

I can't believe this has happened, I thought to myself, *how did I end up here again?* I'll tell you how, it all started this morning …

It was a lovely, typical day and I was just on the table, when Sarah grabbed me and shoved me in her pocket. (It used to happen a lot, but I've been at Sarah's almost a week now.) I assumed we were going to McDonald's so I could be traded in for a cheeseburger again. But I was in her pocket for at least two hours.

We walked into a store called 'Superdrug' and Sarah got me out of her pocket and exchanged me for a tube of lipgloss! I was placed in the till with many other coins. I quite liked being in there, everyone was friendly.

'Excuse me,' said an old 50p, 'what did you get traded in for?'

'A tube of lipgloss,' I replied.

'Oh, that's low,' he said, and then just didn't talk to me.

I could hear people chatting outside of the till and buttons beeping, whilst the cashier was trying to open the till.

'That will be 4 pounds,' I heard the cashier say. She opened the till and lifted out a five pound note and myself.

I heard a familiar voice say, 'Thank you,' and I was put in somebody's hand and then placed in a pocket.

That's when I realised I was back in Sarah's pocket. (I'd much rather belong to the Queen.)

Jack Heath (14)
Barton Court Grammar School

Kylie's Shocking News

This week Kylie Minogue revealed that she has been diagnosed with breast cancer.

The wonderful Kylie Minogue, who has been singing and touring for many years, has been forced to pull out of her world tour to receive treatment. Kylie says, 'I was so looking forward to bringing 'The Showgirl' to the Australian audience, and am sorry to have to disappoint my fans'.

Australian concert promoter Michael Gudinski says, 'She is a pretty, fit, strong girl. I'm hoping and praying because the doctor found it so early that everything will be OK'.

At only 36 years old who would have thought that she would be diagnosed with cancer.

Due to the amount of fans sending Kylie emails wishing her all the best and sending their condolences, the website has been temporarily closed down, but should be up and running again soon.

Meanwhile, while in Melbourne her partner Olivier Martinez, the French actor, is at home comforting her along with friends and family.

Her sister Dannii Minogue has been said to have gone back home to see her sister.

Kylie is due to have her operation some time this week.

According to a breast cancer research charity, Kylie having breast cancer is devastating but it opens people's eyes to the risk of it: 'We hope that by people seeing what is happening to her that women will check themselves for a lump. It may just be nothing, but it is better to check than leave it until it's too late'.

Maria O'Connor (14)
Barton Court Grammar School

Guilty

Guilty? No, not me.

I'd had to put up with it for years and then one day I snapped. I'd been pushed to the edge ever since I was little. I remember the days when all that filled my house was love and no one would ever have thought of hurting me.

It was my 14th birthday and I tiptoed downstairs just to get a glimpse of the cake, but I was caught by her again. I ran straight back into my room, I was trembling with fear and hatred, I could hear that dreaded sound, Daddy was home again and was trudging up the stairs to my room. I huddled up in the corner of my dark, gloomy box and cautiously fiddled with my shabby blanket that Mum had knitted for me in the good days.

Daddy breathed heavily and sweat was running down his neck. He took one look at me, grunted and then hesitated slightly.

I stood up abruptly as he pulled my hair and flinched as I caught one of Daddy's usual punches to the back. And then it was over, Daddy stomped out the room, back down the hall and started to run a shower.

As I crawled to my bed I carelessly let a tear drop down my face and I started to tingle as I felt blood rushing out of my arm again.

And that's when I thought, *what have I done to deserve this? It only happened once.*

Hannah Steadman (13)
Barton Court Grammar School

Child's Play

Bddmm … bddmmbddmmbdmm, I heard the painful screaming beat of my heart grow faster and faster, my chest heaving, ready to rip with anger away from my trembling body. 'Calm yourself,' I told myself, 'they can smell that stomach-churning smell of fear, you can't let them find you or it's over. Curtains!'

I heard footsteps of evil, the pitter-patter of pure darkness; I scrambled to my feet tearing my back from the dusty, choking wall. I was running before my feet, almost stumbling to the floor. Not yet, it's not time, a foolish way to go down. I sprinted round a corner when my eye caught a wonderful sight like a net catching a butterfly … a tree. Just about climbable. I grabbed the lowest branch before I realised what I was doing, like a wild monkey I swung with such agility. I climbed, hiding myself among the green forgiving leaves …

'Shhh!' they told me, hiding me away. It worked, I saw the shadows slither across the ground looking, scanning every nook and cranny in the ground. I was safe. Slowly, with caution, I stepped down from the tree on tiptoe. I crept away, ninja of the shadows.

I headed back to an exit from this place of war when it struck me like the sharp lash of a whip cracking across my brain … *you can't escape.* I saw someone from behind and I gave up. What was the point of running? They approached me nearer, nearer …

'It!'

Sam Dent (14)
Barton Court Grammar School

King Arthur

Sometimes, when the skies get confused, when stars predict that they don't exist, and fortune tellers pack up their stalls, things go wrong - very wrong. In fact, once in a while a person exists who shouldn't, or is moved through time.

And so, in the middle of a coronation, a very long, boring and tedious affair in the 12th century, when most of the crowd had fallen asleep, something went wrong - very wrong.

So when the crown was lowered onto Prince Fred's head, a small popping noise was the only indication that something was wrong. And even the Archbishop could not explain why the words, 'I crown you King Fred', changed into, 'I crown you King Arthur.'

The crowd felt nothing. It was always meant to be like that ever since the words left the Archbishop's lips. They saw no change. Only the Archbishop noticed something amiss.

The king wasn't wearing the normal clothing etiquette. He wore a strange cap with a front part, an extremely baggy top with 'innit' written on it, strangely large blue trouser things and shoes that looked a few sizes too big. He looked slightly out of place and the weird black glasses on the hat confirmed it.

But, as the Archbishop told himself, he must try to move with the times. After all, nobody else seemed to have noticed. Mentally shrugging his shoulders, he helped the king to his feet.

'You got a fag?' quoted the 21st century teenage king with a sneer.

Emily Murdoch (14)
Barton Court Grammar School

Over The Top

The battle between the rebels and the government waged on in the unforgiving sun as the rebels were defending the gateway into their home; Sector 32 X-1.

The rebels didn't believe in the government's dream of communism, but they were soon fighting purely for their lives, as they had recently got news of a squadron of bombers heading towards their location, and they had to go over the top or die.

Eyedis Demora, the general of the rebel army, had ordered her troops to obtain all able civilians and to arm them with weapons.

The army rounded up as a sudden cry of 'Charge!' rang through the ears of the soldiers. They poured out from the trenches, opening fire on whatever moved in front of them while sprinting forwards with all they had.

They had made it around halfway when Eyedis noticed that there were only around 50 friendly troops left. Nevertheless, she carried on running at the enemy, when she felt a sharp pain in her stomach. She froze, motionless in the middle of the battlefield. Everything went silent, and her grip loosened on her rifle and it clattered to the dusty ground. Another sharp pain hit her in the chest and she fell to the ground, looking up into the cloudless blue sky. A tear ran down her left cheek as she knew that all she had once fought for had been lost and the bombers blotted out the sun.

Thomas Dash (14)
Barton Court Grammar School

Haven't I Been Here Before?

Have you ever felt like you're reliving a moment in time constantly? Do you know the unnerving experiencing of doing something you think you have done before, but you really haven't? Well I do, and it really isn't fun when you relive someone else's life as well.

So far I have almost been killed, found lost treasure, travelled to Egypt, Greece and Italy, been buried alive, almost forced to marry a demon and then killed him and my stepfather. Only, I didn't do this as me, I did it as Catya.

My life is full of reoccurring moments from mine and Catya's life. This is because if I don't get it right the first time, or second, or third I have to do it again until I do get it right. This is a definite burden to live with, although I've got to admit that I do like the travelling side of it. The worst part is reliving Catya's life in a different country when people still see me in England as usual. This means that I have no idea what I have done that day as me, but in special circumstances I'm told about that day by my guardian.

Apparently, this is my job in life; I am destined to keep Catya and me alive, until we have fulfilled our life duties but knowing my luck that might take thousands of years. Or has it already?

Rachel Oscar (14)
Barton Court Grammar School

Vengeance

As he held the candle up to the darkness, he saw it. The object he had searched tirelessly all his life for. He picked it up and held it, in awe of its beauty and the light it let out. Suddenly a large man crept up behind him with a pistol. He swung round with the orb in his hand, screamed and fell as a bullet embedded itself in his stomach. He dropped the orb and it smashed. 'A wasted life …' were the last word he breathed.

Three days later in New York his son was given news of his death and given a form to fill in for the return of his body. He filled it in and went back inside. He felt so guilty; he had never told his dad what he worked as. His father had assumed he was unemployed. He could not have been much further from the truth. He was known as 'The Raven', a big time Mafia hitman and he knew who had killed his father.

He lifted up the trapdoor under the fridge, took out the 9mm pistol, got in his Cadillac Impala and drove to his favourite shop.

Upon arrival a team instantly got to work putting a bomb in the car. He drove to a secluded woodland area and primed the bomb. He looked into the air and screamed, 'I'm sorry Dad.' He shot himself through the roof of his mouth and the car exploded.

His father's death had been avenged.

Nic Vaz (13)
Barton Court Grammar School

Perseus And The Gorgons

Perseus dragged himself through the delicate plains of grass and scrub, moor and maple. The waxy moon wheeled above three times before Perseus reached any sign of hope or destination.

A light, quavering gently on the dusk-taken horizon. A silver thread, it wove itself into some recognisable shape. A woman with waterfalls of damson hair stooped high into the sunset. Perseus felt an overwhelming yearn to bow to her, as she radiated an aura of respect and might. He knew she was immortal - a goddess of the Old Ways. Her winged sandals fluttered over the earth towards him, and she spoke, a watery voice with the echo of a million canyons.

'I know of your task,' she said to the wind. 'The monsters of legend are waiting for thee not far from here.' She pointed a sharp, curling fingernail towards the west where the sun still massaged the clouds with fingers of citrine beauty. 'But you will not take them alone. The trio you search for are enemies of us above, we come to you now with midnight magic.'

A spear of gold materialised in her left palm, a shield in her right. Perseus felt their strength upon him.

'Blessed be, mighty warrior, and let the speed of the winter blizzard be upon your back. And with that, her blossoming aura sank back into the earth and she was gone.

And thus he travelled to where the sun slept, to Their lair.

Robert Sanders (14)
Barton Court Grammar School

Hidden Trigger

Galente sat in silence in the sedan, his mind relaying back and forth his conjured master plan. The time was nearing one but five miles east, New York was very much awake.

'Three minutes, Caro.' Roy Twain, a devoted Englishman, seemed transfixed with the clock on the dashboard.

The road was quiet; the Italian Embassy was hardly used past midnight. According to Galente's plan, the decoy on east-side Manhattan was now underway.

Carlos Galente's father, also named Carlos, had links with the American government and gave them confidential information through clandestine communications. One night, the last ounce of his life took a breath filled with the essence of guilt and bewilderment; the man stood over him with a barrel pressed against his temple was his own son, the self-proclaimed Caro Galente.

Three police cars sped past the sedan, sirens piercing the night sky. Galente, Twain and Breza exited and forced their way into the embassy in search of the documents, a list of illegal Italian immigrants that had been fed to them by Caro's father. The building was empty; Breza and Twain had been watching it for weeks and informed Caro of the different shifts. Caro found the documents and started to turn, only to be met by a bullet from the gun in Breza's hand.

Betrayed. So close to finding freedom. With his bloody head finding peace and death as his floor, Galente knew he only lacked his companion's loyalty. His family had failed the Italians.

Kevin Kendaru (14)
Barton Court Grammar School

The Sword Of Nedrub

I'm Talon and this is my life, my story, my burden. I was born in 2005. On my thirteenth birthday, my parents bought me a lifelike dagger with impressive impressions of a sapphire, a ruby and an emerald. That night, I was woken up by a bright light coming from the dagger. I touched it and then I fainted. I woke up in an alternative reality where monsters exist and only the toughest survive.

Presently, I'm being nursed back to health by the white wizard, Werop, and his trainee archer, Eagleye. Soon I shall master the skills of my dagger and become a fully-fledged knight of Nedrub. But there are secrets of this dagger which Werop would not tell me. I, however, have noticed one thing - as I grow with maturity, skill and age, so does the dagger; so much so that it now looks like a sword. Tomorrow I shall begin to learn the secrets of the jewels encrusted within the sword. Now I'm feeling really sleepy but I can't wait till tomorrow.

I woke up this morning feeling quite excited and then I remembered why - I was going to learn the secrets of the sword. I began my training around noon. The training began by Werop telling me that if he shared the secret, I must remain his servant until I was released by him. I readily agreed. He told me first that the sword was called Nedrub because it was burden spelt backwards. Now I understood - this sword had become part of me; it had become my burden. Werop then told me that I had to learn the power of the jewels on the sword to become a Nedrub master.

Olaolu Olorunnimbe (13)
Cranbrook School

A Day In The Life Of A Dog

It started as usual; she came downstairs after a late night, all boggy-eyed and tousle-haired, still in her pyjamas. I feel quite sorry for humans sometimes; they have to wash and get dressed and some of the time they spend ages choosing what to wear. We dogs don't have that problem; we just wake up when we wake up and give ourselves a quick lick and we are ready for the day. None of this choosing an outfit; we have a permanent, stunning, glossy coat that doesn't need that much attention.

I sat in my bed watching her stumble around the kitchen looking for the coffee pot, then realising that there was no milk and would have to settle for black coffee. She makes me laugh sometimes!

After watching her for a while and giving her the famous 'puppy-dog eyes' she remembered that she hadn't given me my Bonio or let me out to smell all the rabbits that had taken over the garden while I was dreaming of them. When I came back in I went back to bed as there was not much going on downstairs, my pet should have done the same by the looks of it!

When everyone came back downstairs, it was time for the school run. At first they weren't going to take me, but I just sat on the doormat staring longingly into their eyes. They soon gave in and off we went down High Street on our way to school.

Lucy Nelson (14)
Cranbrook School

A Day In The Life Of …

It was a late Monday night, the time of the week when the stress levels of humans are at their peak. I was in an off-licence, sitting on one of the shelves behind the counter inside the warm packet with all of my brothers when a mature teenage boy by the name of Jamie strolled in through the doors and requested a packet of cigarettes. After scanning the shelves, I felt the shop assistant pick us up and hand us to the boy. He took us gratefully as he handed over the cash. After the transaction was done, he left the shop with us in his pocket, whistling.

We rounded a few street corners to arrive at the local park - Jamie sat down on a vandalised wooden bench. His hands unwrapped our packet, introducing a breeze of fresh, cold air into our filters, then whipped out a lighter from his other pocket, and his fingers then dived into the packet to take hold of one of our heads to set light to its feet. We frantically tried to pull him back down, but unfortunately we were average cigarettes and did not have arms.

I watched in helpless agony as five more of my brothers, courageous and honourable to the end, were put to ashes by chain-smoking Jamie. As I watched the massacre, I asked myself, *why do millions of people around the world risk their lives for ours?*

On this thought, I felt my feet being alight in the clammy fingers and my body slowly disintegrating into nothing. A cigarette as perfect as me did not deserve this. No one did.

Susie Sohn (14)
Cranbrook School

The Day I Died - The First Chapter

I awakened from my deep sleep with a feeling in my stomach that meant something terrible was due to happen that day. It took my brain several seconds to get sorted out and remember what disaster was to take place.

It was only when I turned my face to look through the iron bars that I came to terms with what lay ahead of me that day.

Dread and fear ran over me like a cold shower, draining any happiness that may still be left inside me after fifty long, harsh years. Nearby footsteps told me Officer Tweety was fulfilling his usual duty of wake-up call. Officer Tweety was a kind yet fair man with short brown hair that he constantly fiddled with. His black jacket sat neatly on his broad shoulders while his trousers barely fell below his bony ankles.

'Wakey, wakey!' he called in his soft, deep voice.

A few seconds later the officer was standing in front of my cell and gave me a warm smile. 'How are you this morning?' he asked. 'Is there anything I can get you today? Any special meal you would like before …' He broke mid-sentence.

This was usual for people to eat their favourite meal or do something special on their last day, but I felt nothing could make my day go quicker or feel like it was a happy one. Today I would die.

Oli Scheuregger (14)
Cranbrook School

The Tale Of Iban

The battle was over. Lord Iban stood on top of a cart and surveyed the desolate landscape which had once been green fields. It was now littered with bodies of his enemy, King Luthas. Iban won many a battle after this, slowly becoming more obsessed with death until it was like a drug to him. Iban was a tyrant of death, seeking it where he could, making his own battles. Then, one day he was hit in the back by an arrow when retreating to regroup. When he lay there bleeding, his blood killed the grass around him and burnt the people who touched it.

His body was left as a scar on the landscape, draped in his robes and his armour still on. Lord Zaros, an evil warlock, saw this as an opportunity to cause chaos. He went to the grave of Iban and cast a spell bringing Iban back with supernatural powers, inhuman, like he had taken a transformation through this spell. He was more beast than man now.

Zaros and Iban stormed the lands heading for their one goal - King Luthas II. King Luthas himself had died many years ago. The war had been finished. No one was ready for an attack so great. After the third week of war it was decided that the only way to win was if Iban was captured in his sleep and imprisoned.

That night, King Luthas II and his best men snuck into Iban's camp and knocked him out. They put him in a mobile prison and started their journey deep into the mountains. They left Iban in a huge cave in the heart of the mountains and blocked him in. This is the last that was ever heard of him.

Toby Gower (14)
Cranbrook School

A Day In The Life Of A First World War Soldier

Just been woken up at the crack of dawn by the sound of a German shell exploding about fifty metres away from our trench. I am so nervous. Actually it's not nervousness - it feels more like fear, knowing that this may be the last thing that I do. In the trenches I don't really try too hard to make friends because the chances are that they will die and then I won't miss them quite so much as if I had liked them.

I know that we are going over the top today. What's the point? We're just sending more and more men off to their deaths each day. We are sitting in knee-deep mud and we are sharing it with rats the size of badgers. I looked out over no-man's-land yesterday and saw the corpses of my fellow soldiers scattered all over the dug-up soil which had been soaked with blood and shook by the countless bombs leaving great craters.

I can smell the fear among the men who are going over the top today. Most of them definitely will not be coming back. We are just moments away from that fatal moment when the sergeant blows the whistle and sends us off towards the Germans.

The whistle goes and we all run over the top of the trench and out onto no-man's-land. Running and shouting we try to scare the Germans but generally it doesn't work. Firing shots randomly everywhere, just hoping and then …

Eddy Griffiths (14)
Cranbrook School

A Day In The Life Of My Cats, Missy And Mel

Yawn! Ooo, it feels good to stretch! I'm hungry. Good, at least there is food. Now, what to do. Let's see. I know, let's go upstairs. Now that we're awake everyone else should be. Oh good, Katie's door is open. Up on her bed. She looks strange in her sleep, urrgh! Miaow, miaow! Good, I've finally got a reaction. Yes, that's it, stroke me, ow, not that hard. Oh, get off now. Great fun you are.

(Walks off disgruntled)

Let's try Nick. He better be awake and prepared to give me some attention otherwise someone's going to be grumpy today.

(Everyone else's door is shut and both cats walk, already stressy)

Off down to breakfast. What's wrong with them? They all look half-asleep, people, so dopey.

Now, that's just great.

(Most sarcastic expression)

They've all gone out for the day. I don't think anyone even realised I was here. Good to see I'm loved. So now they will just have to have dirty sheets. I can go outside and get messy.

(Both cats go outside and come back in filthy. They head upstairs and leave pawprints everywhere)

(Sleep)

(More sleep)

(Yet more sleep. How can cats be so lazy?)

(More sleep. Are they dead? They haven't done anything.)

Oooh! *(waking up)* I'm already exhausted. At least they're finally back. I will kill them if they don't give me any attention. Honestly, the life one leads being a cat; so energetic yet deprived, the hardships. At least there's lots of food!

James Hewitt (14)
Cranbrook School

A Day In The Life Of A Slave

We were herded onto the ship like cattle. I had been taken away from my village only yesterday. It felt like a part of me had died. I scarcely have the energy to do anything, yet I have been forced to walk a whole day with no rest, food or water. We were forced to walk, tied in chains so we didn't escape. I had a giant metal collar as well.

As we approached the ship the stench was horrific. The stench of faeces radiated from the lower decks.

The ship was very ominous-looking; it was black like soot and the fear then drilled into me. There were at least 400 of us, yet as we walked up the gangplank I couldn't believe they were going to attempt to cram us all onto one ship. However, my fears were confirmed when one of the white men spoke.

He said, 'Cram as many as you can on, they're just cargo with voices.'

As I entered the lower deck, all the light disappeared, but the stench was overpowering. I was shoved to the floor by an invisible hand. I was still in chains and I was in such a confined space I couldn't move. The stench of sweat from the heaving mass of bodies now engulfed me. The floor was composed of excrement and had become like quicksand. Children were crying, calling for their mothers that they had been snatched from. I was alone in the worst environment imaginable. I didn't deserve this; I can't have sinned much, after all, I'm only 10 years old.

Edward Brown-Humes (14)
Cranbrook School

A Day In The Life Of A Child In The War

One day I woke up early, about six in the morning. Mother looked anxious and worried. I asked her what was wrong, but she didn't say anything. Father was already in the bomb shelter. I kept asking her what was wrong, but she kept her mouth shut. Then the air raid siren went off - the siren of death.

As I sit here in my rocking chair, smoking a pipe, pointlessly retelling a story which brings tears to my eyes; I still hate the sound of that siren.

Mother and I hurried into the shelter and realised Father wasn't there. Neither was Spike, our dog. We put two and two together and realised Father was outside, rescuing our dog. I rushed to the door, but Mother held me back. I kept trying and screaming, but with no success. Later that day I heard a terrible scream. I still hear that today; it sends a chill down my bones. It was the scream of my father.

I'm not sure if I heard it, but I think I heard Spike barking and then the barking got quieter.

When we eventually came out of the shelter at eight o'clock, Father and Spike were nowhere to be seen.

Christian Davies (14)
Cranbrook School

The Legend Of Lake Louisa's Big Fish

If you lived in the mountainous parts of Canada, it is unlikely you have not heard of the famous town around Lake Louisa. The reason it is famous is not because of its delicious, fresh catches, but its poor, slithery morsels currently being put on the market.

There are stories going around that in certain places there is the most enormous fish an eye has ever encountered. Said to be as big as a fishing boat in body, it is questioned whether it could even be a shark. Whether this is word of mouth, I don't know, but I have chosen to believe that it exists.

Could it be that this monster is going about, devouring every little fish it can find in order to grow even more? I like to call it the Lake Louisa Legend.

This immense fish, in my imagination, is 5 feet long and 3 feet wide, with a tail more powerful than a windmill. It has whiskers protruding from its monstrous mouth that are longer than my legs. Its rows of pearly white teeth are menacing and it snaps them viciously, to warn anything in its path of destruction. It's a tank at war with any living thing. Its aim is to wipe out even the tiniest of fish.

So, whether the fishermen want something to believe for their poor results, or whether or not this is true, I will never know. Until I am unfortunate enough to come across it one day. If so, I doubt I will survive to tell the tale of the Lake Louisa Legend!

Abi Bishop (14)
Cranbrook School

A Day In The Life Of A Complete And Utter Drama Queen!

I wake up every morning feeling so emotionally drained. OK, you won't really understand unless I tell you the whole story, so let's go back to the beginning.

It all started on the first day back at secondary school. I wanted to let everyone know how much little Molly Barton has changed into Miss Molly Barton! I wore my best skirt and my best shoes that, if I may say so myself, really showed off my calves which I have to say are utterly my favourite feature, and I mean I really don't look nice in that many skirts, it's so pink and fluffy and, OK, sorry, I'll focus.

I was doing the short walk down the steps to the entrance of the school, those marvellous steps that were going to go down in history as having had Miss Molly Barton walk down them. People from all over stopped and smiled with glee. It had finally worked, all that exercise had paid off, so many people walked past and laughed with ultimate pleasure. It wasn't until my total best friend, Josephine Henagar, came up to me and dislodged what looked like some dirty tissues which must have got stuck there when I was at home. Oh, how can I explain it? It was utterly the most embarrassing moment in my life! How could I go on? I mean, how? I might as well die! You don't know how much I had looked forward to that day and it was just completely ruined. Although I don't really want to die, I guess I could just wait until next year to woo the crowds of secondary school. I actually don't belong in that school anyway. I mean, I'm only seven!

Alicia Cooper (14)
Cranbrook School

The Lesser-Known Adventures Of Robin Hood

Once upon a time in a land far away (well up north a bit) lived Robin Hood, super do-gooder, stealing from the rich to give to the poor. It was his turn to cook for his merry men but, as I'm sure you all know, there were not many supermarkets in medieval Nottingham and even going to a normal market is hard if you are an outlaw and have a huge price on your head, so, as per usual, Robin had to organise a raid of the sheriff's land.

The target was one of the smaller outlying farms of the sheriff's private estate. In the centre of one of the fields was a barn that was stacked high with corn, dried meat and the merry men's favourite ale!

It was the middle of the night when the small band of merry men decided to attack. Like panthers, they crept up the heavily-shadowed path to the store house. When they got there they were surprised at the number of guards they faced. They had predicted five well-armed men to be there, but it seems they were wrong because there was only a very tired-looking dog between them and unlimited amounts of booze! Quickly they set to work with a horse and cart. They moved every last ounce of food and drink within a few hours and long before anyone else was awake, so in the end they got a damn good meal and a fine drink.

Tomas Young (14)
Cranbrook School

The First Story

It was the first Monday of November, 1940. Up in Scotland there were three children playing by Loch Ness. Wrapped up in their games, they were oblivious to the war continuing around them.

Willie, Mary and Glen sat on the bank of the loch, a mile from their homes; nobody knew where they were. You see, this was their spot; not a soul ever came but them.

It was a huge loch in the middle of a cold country, in the middle of a cold time, in the middle of winter.

Glen was always in charge of what happened and what they did. He was, of course, the eldest being 11. Then there was Mary aged 8, making her the youngest and her brother, Willie who was 10.

Mary was standing in the water, about two metres from her comrades, who were eyeing her every pebble-throwing movement. They were very protective of her.

Willie spotted an extraordinarily shaped cloud so he and Glen lay on their backs to watch it for a while. Then there was a splash. They turned to see, but Mary was already gone.

Willie and Glen, aware and terrified of the 'paranormal' forces at work surrounding them, saw flashes of a fin and what looked like an abnormally long tail, but the imagination plays tricks.

The next day, a group of men from the nearest town were sent to Loch Ness to search for Mary. She was never found, but her tough, indigestible shoes were.

Eleanor Gill (14)
Cranbrook School

Opening To A Mysterious Story

The wind was blowing; trees were almost bent in two. The sky was black; rain thundered down and the sea beat angrily against the cliffs. A dark figure floated towards Katie, hooded and cloaked. She couldn't move. She felt shivers going down her spine. As the figure glided towards her, her brain was frantically trying to get her to get as far away as possible but she couldn't; something inside her was stopping, holding her back. The figure was now so close she could smell its putrid breath. Katie gazed in horror at the face underneath the hood and screamed. She screamed so long and hard that rocks started falling from the cliffs. The thing started laughing at her terror. It was a loud, cruel laugh that could even be heard over the screeching storm. A rotten hand emerged from beneath the cloak and wrapped itself around Katie's throat. The more she screamed, the tighter the figure squeezed. The long, hard nails were digging into her skin, making it bleed. Suddenly the hand let go and the rocks started falling on top of Katie. The creature laughed even harder and Katie woke bathed in sweat, the laughter still ringing in her ears.

That was the fourth time she'd had that dream this week. It was becoming more frequent and more and more vivid. At first she couldn't see the creature but now she could see it as if it was real and something inside her told her it was.

Ellis Haberland-Schindler (13)
Cranbrook School

Cassius Clay

My name is Cassius Clay. I am the best boxer in the world. Well, I will be once I beat Sonny Liston. Now, I have finally got my chance. I have been training all my life for this fight; skipping, sparring - you name it, I've done it. Not only have I trained physically, but also mentally. I've been thinking about what I'm going to do, and when I do it.

As I walk up to the ring, I'm feeling confident. I see him in the ring. I'm not afraid. The next thing I hear is the bell. For the first round I just dodge all his punches, studying his movements. He doesn't get a single punch in.

The next round is my round. I run to the middle of the ring and throw my hardest punches. He doesn't know what's hit him. 'Float like a butterfly, sting like a bee', that's my motto. He just survived that round.

The next round is the hardest. He punches me so hard that I can't see out of the corner of one eye. Nevertheless, in the dying seconds of the round, I unleash my fury. I've got him against the ropes, punching and jabbing him until he is on the floor. He can't get up again. I know I have won and jump on the ropes to celebrate, shouting at the cheering audience. This is the best day of my life. I am the heavyweight champion of the world!

Seb des'Ascoyne (14)
Cranbrook School

A Day In The Life Of A World War I Soldier

July 16th, 1915

Jesus Christ, this war's been going on for a year. What happened? Their countless numbers won't stop coming. This isn't an easy laugh. It's a depressing slaughterhouse. The insane death cannot be put into words. The overwhelming stench of the mangled, trampled, disfigured corpses is actually unbelievable.

    The corpses aren't just left alone; men, living men, must then disgrace the dead by making a suicidal dash into oncoming fire. For a short moment they stare into the grim, crushing eyes of Hell itself. We're charging over friends only to meet with them in a few minutes. Why must this insane, stupid, pointless war continue?

Charlie Patrickson (14)
Cranbrook School

Danger In The Desert

The wind whipped across the barren dunes, sending waves of sand into a golden, rippling sea. A lone figure was riding in the midst, their craft a camel. A white robe was draped over the person's body, covering the face, leaving a slit for the eyes as protection from the peppering blast of sand. The person was a woman, but whether native, foreigner, enemy or friend - impossible to tell. However, she was familiar with the lie of the land and rode steadfastly southwards.

With night approaching fast, she slowed to a halt. Recovering a bundle from her bags, she set about constructing a tent. The wind eased considerably, and once finished, she swept off the material concealing her face. She was young with sun-singed hair tumbling to her shoulders. She had deep dark eyes and tanned skin.

She breathed deeply, taking in the cold night air. After tethering the camel, she ate some fruit and bread. She had been riding since early morning, fleeing what had been her home. The town had been attacked by enemy tribes, the townspeople massacred, so she fled, abandoning her family, her losses heavy in her heart. She was forced into the desert; the brutes were intent on exterminating the people together with their secrets, especially the one she carried. She must survive at all costs. The provisions she had were limited, the future uncertain. She was being pursued, and when she saw the looming figure racing towards her, she knew she had made a mistake.

Alice Marshall (14)
Cranbrook School

Chasing Fame

'Today, Chasing Fame is offering you the chance to make it as a dancer. Just call the number for your chance to be part of our open auditions'.

This is the advert my gran saw and of course she entered me. I never thought I would be chosen but I was, so before I knew it I was making my way to London to try and make it as a tap dancer.

Within seconds, Gran had packed my bag and I was on the train up to London. I was lucky to get one. It was lightly snowing but I arrived on time. I made it to the dance studios and got ready. I slipped on my tap shoes and waited at the end of the corridor to be called. There were girls all around me, stretching and warming up, looking really professional. I felt really intimidated; I felt like I should just turn around and go home. My hands were dripping wet; I was so nervous. My legs were shaking and that's when they said it. That's when they called my name.

'Toby Chiswick.'

I stood up and looked down the corridor. I started walking. Everyone was looking at me. I was starting to think that this wasn't such a good idea. My tap shoes were echoing in my ears as I walked. I stepped through the door, stood in front of the judges and the music started to play. My feet started to go with the music. I was away.

Theresa Davies (14)
Cranbrook School

Storm

It's cold outside tonight. I have been listening to the wind thrust branches at my window for about an hour. It's times like this when I wish that Sam was still around; he would have comforted me. I know I still have Mum and Dad, yet sometimes it just isn't the same.

Do you believe that God has signs, you know, to tell us when He's mad at us? Perhaps this weather is an omen to warn me that God knows what I did. That is another reason I wish Sam was around still because he would know what to do about clearing my conscience.

Tomorrow I am going to the creek come rain or shine. I always go there to empty my mind; it feels so peaceful to me. All my friends think me brave to go near such deep waters on my own, but they don't know what I know. Maybe one of these days I'll take them down to the water's edge and share my secret with them. They would probably be shocked so much that they would fall in - that could be a good thing though.

For now I'll just try to get through the storm. Maybe to pass the time I will look through my photo collection; they had so many memories for me, some good, some too awful for others to know about …

Hannah Heap (14)
Cranbrook School

Lethal Breakout

We've been heading here for some time since the chaos began. It must have been for six hours now. The power's down and the signal on my mobile has gone. All contact I had with the outside world is now down. I have no idea where my family is or whether they're still alive!

It started this morning at about 8.30am. I remember it clear as day. The creatures broke out; they broke out from a military base. These things must be extremely intelligent; they outwitted the top level security and all the guards. Watching the news this morning horrified me. They had managed to unlock a 38-pinned door, after that they just flooded out in their droves, killing every security guard in the area. One of these monsters was wounded in the breakout and unable to move. Watching the TV they showed the path of the creatures as they spread across the country. Then it dawned on me. The catastrophe was going to reach me, and soon.

Luke Pain (14)
Cranbrook School

A Day In The Life Of A Doctor

Saturday 6th November, 2005

Well I've just finished my night shift, 7pm until 5am, and it has been so busy! As you may have guessed, yesterday was Guy Fawkes night, so there were extreme cases from all the incidents of inappropriate use of fireworks and dreadful displays of burns from fires.

I sometimes feel like I can't cope anymore; I have a really sensitive nature you see, so I take most things to heart. Like if a patient dies under my supervision, I feel awful as it was down to my hands and I failed. Especially last night when I alone lost 5 patients; this was all in the same accident, a big explosion at a house party, involving a box of fireworks and cigarettes, not a good combination.

I saw all sorts of cases from massive burns to amputations of legs, but I guess I must look at the positives - well, that I saved many and they were very thankful for their satisfaction from me. It's my job, and it's what I chose, so it's my duty to make them better! My worst case so far has been the death of a recently born baby who had a blood clot in her heart; unfortunately there was nothing any of us could do to help as it had already formed well before birth.

Got to go now. Must sleep. Got the next day ahead!

Chloe Edwards (14)
Cranbrook School

Legend Of The Brothers

During the time of the god wars, few stood against the might of the hordes of Zamorak. Six of these few were known as 'The Brothers' and they fought with the might of 100 men. During their campaign to the heart of the barren plains, they fought like no others had before; one hurtling powerful magic at the enemy, four using their mighty weapons to gouge the enemy to shreds of what they were, and one to fire crossbow bolts into the few who came near him.

During the campaign, a stranger started to appear and stare at the brothers, and then walk off at dawn, back in the direction they were all heading. The only time you would see the brothers uncertain was at these times, and they would often draw weapons if the stranger got too close.

One night, the monstrosities plagued the camp. Their rotting flesh and bloodied bodies swept through the camp like a swarm of flies. The brothers rushed to the aid of their comrades and fought the bravest and strongest they had ever, disregarding their injuries and fighting on to save the ones who were still left. By dawn, what was left of the force fled faster than any man could follow. The brothers fell to the ground, their wounds were found swelling and bulbous, with a rotting smell coming from them. The physicians couldn't find a cure, and at dusk they all sighed and went into eternal sleep.

Lewis Musk (14)
Cranbrook School

Unreal Day

We ran through Shillingdon Hill Forest, down to the dank and grimy river at the bottom of the hill. The single, not-so-grimy place here, was the bridge.

Anyway, as we made our way through the undergrowth, I was just beginning to enjoy my day when Sam (my younger idiot of a brother) began moaning. Apparently he'd lost his penknife, so he continued whining until I gave in and said we could start trekking home again to look for his stupid knife.

Eventually, he got up from his hands and knees and said it didn't matter. About a minute after he'd given a speech about not even needing it anymore, I noticed the shining object under the bush. Sam became very excited, thinking I *had* found his long-lost penknife after all. But *thankfully*, it wasn't.

As I bent over to see what the 'thing' was, my ears pricked and tuned in to hear an eerie whistling hum. I stretched out an arm to feel around for the object. As I bent further forwards, I saw something glistening in the early evening sunlight. I held what looked like a horn in my hand and gently began tugging it free from the brambles. As I gradually noticed the body of this creature, it occurred to me it wasn't just a creature but one that, until now, was supposed to be only a myth. Sam nearly toppled over backward from disbelief. It was, of course, a unicorn, a unicorn close to death.

Felicity Hayes (13)
Cranbrook School

A Day In The Life Of A Soldier At Pearl Harbour

As far as I can remember, days were never quite as loud, disturbing and tragic as this one. 0815 hours, December 7th, 1941. A day when, for once, I was scared and almost in tears.

It struck on the fifteenth minute of the eight hours of the morning, the first bomb, and I was asleep in my hammock inside the dorm. I rose, along with twenty other men. We rushed out as the blue siren sounded and circled through the ship.

As I clambered out and grabbed a rifle from the gun room, I saw the hole in which the bomb had struck. It was huge and I could see my fellow friends dead and some unconscious.

This part of the ship was knee-high in water and we fought our way through the fires and the spraying water to the deck. Here I had never seen such a sight. The sky was black from smoke and only small bits of orange from the morning sky shone through. Japanese planes buzzed overhead; machine guns blaring as we tried to shoot them down.

Shooting made no difference and as we shot away, a devastating attack occurred when a plane crashed into the ship. I was thrown into the water. All I saw was a collapsed motorboat, so I pulled myself aboard, soaking wet.

I was in total shock. I had trouble placing the key in the ignition, but as I did I could not hear the motor from all the warfare. Pedal to the floor, the boat skimmed across the murky water as I accelerated to shore.

Myles Harvey (14)
Cranbrook School

A Day In The Life Of Nicole Kidman

'Nicole's new fella!'

Another lie spread across my kitchen table. I'm used to it; the papers are continuously spreading lies about my life.

I had sat down to read my paper, eat my toast and drink my cup of tea - instead, I sat and read about how I've been sleeping with Liz Hurley's ex. It all stemmed from me going out to dinner with friends; harsh, but I'm used to it. This kind of thing makes me feel bad for those kids who dream of a life of fame, and hunger for the media's attention. But the spotlight of the media is a cruel one, crueller than the light from the car that freezes the innocent rabbit on the road at night.

Today I'm going to forget about the downsides of being a celebrity. I'm going shopping to spend a little bit of my fortune. This is a true benefit. I see something I like, I buy it without even looking at the price. Or I can phone one of the top designers and get something unique made that nobody in the world has. Then I'll go and have an expensive lunch, keeping an eye on the calories. I need to keep thin because wherever I go, cameras will follow and they don't want pictures of me looking good, they want pictures of me looking fat. To be honest, nobody wants to browse through a magazine to find a picture of their rolls of fat or cellulite.

Victoria Burrington (14)
Cranbrook School

Memories Of Arthur

In the days of old, Arthur rode with his knights seeking their freedom which had so long been denied to them, for they were the remainder of the Sarmation army sent to destroy the Roman legions. At the end the only men left standing were the remainder of the famous Sarmation cavalry, these men were admired by the Romans for their bravery and rewarded with their lives in return for the service of themselves. It is unknown to them that they must face one last challenge before their freedom can be granted.

They are asked to save a Roman family trapped by the immanent Saxon invasion. Marius Honorius is their lord and master.

On reaching the estate of Honorius, they find the buildings burning fiercely. Feeling the flames on his face Arthur is taken back to a memory of his childhood. An attack on a village, the screams of an innocent woman as a cart is rammed across her only escape route. A boy runs to the house crying, 'Mother!' He sees the burning house and runs to the burial mound of his father, where the sword Excalibur is planted in the grave. He pulls it free and runs back to the house only to find the scorching flames licking the chimney of the house, and he knows that she is dead.

As Arthur feels the flames on his cheeks he vows to his knights to save the family and rid the land of the animals that murdered his mother.

Hazel Hewitt (14)
Cranbrook School

The Box

I was there that day - that fateful day. I witnessed the entire thing - from a distance of course, but I was there, make no mistake. Watching helplessly, without any power to change what was happening. I watched her lift away the white cloth and open the box - even after she had been warned, warned of the consequences of her actions, she still did it. I watched as the innocent little voice got to her; breaking her down until she gave in. It seemed eternal that moment, as she slowly opened the lid; for a moment it seemed the box was empty but it was not, oh no. Floating shapes seemed to rise from the box, spreading like steam into the air.

They lingered for a moment; then were gone - a sudden whoosh and they flew out of the house faster than my eyes could follow. Although it seemed that they were gone the world felt different after they had been released; greyer. People suddenly changed - hunger struck, jealousy arose, hardship ensued. She slammed the lid when they had gone, as if trying to re-trap them but it was no use. They were out in the world now and could never be returned to that box - the box that had been the sole barrier between the hardships of the new world and the innocent who are now suffering into eternity because of the foolishness of one woman - the woman who condemned mankind into a painful eternity - my mistress: Pandora.

Emily Hislop (14)
Cranbrook School

The Fall Of An Empire

A wave of panic flooded over the defending troops. They saw their last hopes crushed in the shadow of death, any possibility of glorious triumph was gone.

When the attack had begun, the Verdantian stronghold had been hopeful at best but morale had quickly deteriorated with the defeat of the berserker forces. They had been the first to leave the stronghold and try to take on the invading wall of Iron Shields. They had been the first to die. As they had advanced the Iron Shields had continued, paying them no attention. While the berserkers had hacked at the wall, it gradually closed over them, locking them from sight. The screams of rage faded, one by one, until there was just a deathly silence. It seemed like an eternity, but finally, a scream rose from the walls.

'For the empire!'

Arrows were loosened from their tense imprisonment, released in a barrage of piercing edges, aimed upwards, while quickly gaining momentum downwards, crashing into the raised shields. Then the gates opened, and tides of barbarian warriors surged forth. Charging into the narrow gap between the stronghold and the shields, they found that knocking away the shields heralded an unmerciful blackness.

Warriors rushed into the gaps, war cries echoing from the seething shadow, all sight lost, Then, another silence, deeper, more final than that of the former, as the Shadows drifted over the tired mortar of the stronghold, devouring the remains of the warriors, and then absorbing their spirits.

Chris Digby-Rogers (14)
Cranbrook School

The Daddy's Girl

Thursday 17th May

People say that school is the best time of your life. When you are free, when there are no limits, there isn't anything you can't do. I read that in a magazine today in the car home with Liam (the dreamy new chauffeur). At first I thought, *what a load of rubbish,* but then people at school have happy fulfilled lives, not much to worry about, they are all really lucky, all wrapped up in their little lives. All they have to worry about is 'when is my homework due?' or 'my life is so over, Dave has just dumped me'. Ceci Gibbons for example, she has millions of friends, she is pretty, with blonde hair cascading over her shoulders, intelligent blue eyes. Her family is together, a united front. But despite her bags of money and all her advantages in life she only seems to get any sort of pleasure from two things - getting round every boy in the year and picking on me.

I admit, I'm a little cleverer than her, in fact in some aspects prettier than her. With my large brown eyes, dark hair and olive skin. People pick at the scars in my life. Ceci knows where it hurts, she was once my best friend, well almost.

Things changed when Lauren, Alex and Mum died in the fire. I thought at first people avoided me because they didn't know what to say or because of the scarring on my hands. But it was Ceci who told people things about my life, how I needed counselling, how my dad became a workaholic and of course, his pay cheque. My father is a movie director and earns more in one movie than Ceci's dad earns in a year. When I went to confront her about this she turned everyone against me. It made me sick when she told everyone that I was taking my brother, sister and Mum's death out on her. I went mental and slapped her. My once Ceci Gibbons existence (plenty of friends etc) became something else, I was now invisible, I was no longer Molly Keats-Brown. I was only seen when the time of verbal and physical abuse came. They circle round me chanting, shoving, hitting.

Today was no different. Invisible until break time then unlike most normal people I'm counting down the minutes for the bell to ring, where's a good friend when I need one … ?

Natalie Callan (14)
Cranbrook School

The Secret

As soon as she put her key in the lock she knew there was something wrong - something had happened. The whole family had been emitting an uneasy feeling for months, a feeling of secrecy and mystery. It had made Molly feel most uncomfortable.

And now, as she pushed open the front door, she knew it was all coming to a head.

She entered the kitchen, where her parents sat, her mother's hands wrapped around a big mug of coffee she was intently staring into.

'Hi love, how was your day?' her father asked, with transparent brightness.

'Um … it was OK,' she replied.

An awkward smile followed, only interrupted by the sound of her mother anxiously sipping her coffee.

'There's something we need to tell you Mol … ' said Dad, deliberately and slowly.

She looked over at Mum who was still staring at her mug, refusing to make eye contact.

'Mum?' Molly said questioningly.

'You're adopted Molly,' said Dad, sadly.

And Molly's whole world turned upside down …

Lucy Snow (14)
Cranbrook School

A Day At The Beach

It was not usually like this. I had been to this beach many times as a child and I had never imagined it could be in such a horrific state like this.

I remember I used to build sandcastles and knock them down with pebbles.

The beach looked different. It was June the 6th 1944, D-Day. The Normandy beaches were stained with the blood of simple men and the blood of complex nations. Men were lying motionless on the bloodstained beach. Men who were sons, brothers and husbands, were all dead or dying. The enemy were all the same. We were all simple people in the most unusual situation you could place someone in.

I stood in the landing craft shaking from cold and fear of the enemy. Men were killed before even landing on the beach. It could have been a good thing; they did not know the horrors we would be facing. People were seasick and praying. All the prayers in the world wouldn't save us. We could die any moment. Every second could be your last. It was a daunting feeling knowing you may never see your family, your friends or anyone who you cared for. I felt empty inside, we all did, none of us could feel any happiness at all.

The craft juddered to a halt. We lurched forward. I stumbled across the beach trying to find any form of protection. I did not. There is a bullet with your name on it.

Josh Cottington (14)
Cranbrook School

A Day In The Life Of Maximillious Ambrosius The Nineteenth

Also known as 'Tim', I am Maximillious Ambrosius the Nineteenth, wheel-runner extraordinaire and personal pet to my owner, Kaleigh.

Life in this humble hamster cage has always been very - hang on … ooh carrots! I love it when Kaleigh gives me carrots, they're so crunchy. Anyway, life in this humble hamster cage is very luxurious, with all my little tubes to run around in. Kaleigh's packing her bag to go to the big teaching place now; she took me there once. Rows and rows of tall people, all dressed the same. I was terrified.

'See you later Timmy. Don't forget to exercise!'

Isn't she wonderful? I'm telling you, she's wonderful. Sometimes she lets me run, play in her hair … so silky and gold … and hey! I always exercise. I'm the wheel-runner extraordinaire - self-proclaimed, but for a good reason. Well, maybe later. Time for a nap.

What time is it? I didn't really sleep all day, did I? Oh great, Kaleigh's home. Wait, she's crying. Why that's not good at all.

'Oh Tim, why are those girls always so horrible to me? Why don't they just leave me alone?'

Not again, those stupid bullies are always making her upset. Stuck here, with no way to help … I'll get them one day, then they'll regret it. Poor thing, she should go to bed and get some rest, I know it'll cheer her up, or I'm not Maximillious Ambrosius the Nineteenth, wheel-runner extraordinaire. Well, maybe I'll run tomorrow instead - I'm tired now …

Rebecca Horner (14)
Cranbrook School

A Day In The Life Of A Housefly

Hi, my name is Leo the housefly. I live here with the lovely Joneses in a small terraced house. Here's a day in the life of me.

My day starts at nine in the morning with a quick early morning flap down to the kitchen, just to get a snack and then it's back up to the attic, but being careful to avoid the spider's web in the stairs otherwise Boris, the average house spider, will eat me.

You then have to wait until ten to get out, as that's when the humans go out to school and work. Then you can do whatever you want; I like to pester the cat by landing on its nose and then just as it goes to swipe me, I move and then it hits itself. It's so funny to watch. Ooh Leo, you cunning devil you.

Next, at eleven am, you take a leisurely flutter outside through the blue tit's nest. It's always fun to get outside and have a stretch as that's the only time I get to socialise with other flies. Boris ate my last friend that lived in the Jones' house.

Whilst out I get lunch, just a bit of nectar is what fills my belly. And then with such a full belly I go back to the house and sleep it off until the morning.

After that it all starts over again. Thanks for listening and bye.

Matt Atterton (14)
Cranbrook School

A Day In The Life Of A Celebrity

Being a celebrity may seem very easy, relaxed and fun but trust me, it isn't. Normally I have to wake up quite early in the morning, at about five-thirty, due to the fact that I need to fly out to a country I am going to be staying and working in that I have never heard of until I get there. When I'm not working I will wake up whenever I want to, around ten o'clock. I will stay in bed and have breakfast brought up to me by Henry the butler. After eating, I will normally have a nice hot bath with herbal remedies which either Charlotte or Isabella has prepared for me. By then it is about eleven-thirty. I will then get my make-up done by Alan. This is the relaxing part of the day when nothing and no one bothers me.

Seeing as I make so much money I will normally decide to go shopping for hours on end. You are probably thinking, *what is so bad about that?* Well the fact that the shops close just for me and the owners help choose my outfit is fabulous, but the paparazzi part of the trip is awful. Everywhere I go, they go, hundreds of them asking for my picture.

After the fun but annoying shopping trip, I am chauffeured driven in my Hummer back to the mansion. For the rest of the evening I will sit at home, eat dinner with my two sons and husband, and relax!

Madeleine Hirschler (13)
Cranbrook School

A Day In The Life Of A Monkey

Why do they look at me like that? I'm a monkey trapped in a cage of doom with a million people gazing into my eyes and saying how cute I am. I do like being thought of as cute, but when little children scurry along and start teasing me by pretending to give me a banana but don't, it is just cruel. Here come a crowd of kids now, looks like a birthday party.

What are they doing? They are probably trying to get my best friend, Martha, to go near them. Fat chance! Martha isn't stupid and hides in a corner and only reappears when the coast is clear, which isn't very often.

Why do they come to see us monkeys? There are many more animals to look at but oh no, they follow us like a pack of wolves.

Now there is a little girl staring at me. What do I do? I think I'll just act cool and have a swing on my trapeze.

OK, it's twenty minutes later and I am still swinging around. Why haven't they gone yet? My arms are going to drop off.

Finally! I do love it when the zoo closes and all the people have to go home. It's such a delight to be able look through the bars and not see some hideous human. Now there is no one to disturb me, I'll take refuge right here and have a lovely, long sleep. Goodnight Shropshire Zoo.

Clemmie Home (14)
Cranbrook School

A Day In The Life Of An Afghan Girl

12th August 1998

This has got to be the most terrible day of my life. I feel so overwhelmed all I can do is write.

We were all laughing when several Taliban soldiers burst through the door. Palwasha was the first to react. The slam of the door shocked her and she screamed. Mother leapt to her feet and in an instant, Palwasha and Nahid were shrieking and crying behind her legs. Petrified of what might happen, I just sank lower and lower behind Chador. I had heard that quite often young women were stolen from their homes by soldiers and never seen again.

I sat frozen while the giant soldiers towered over me with their piled high turbans making them look even bigger. Their ghastly green uniforms marching around like green poison instilling fear. They grabbed Father. Mother screamed to leave him alone but instead they smacked him across the face. Blood poured from his nose onto his white shalwar kameez, his face crumpled in pain. Mother then jumped on the soldier and started pounding him with her fists. One soldier raised his rifle and smashed it on her head, I looked away. She fell instantly to the ground. I can remember so clearly, the piercing screams of Palwasha after every blow.

I looked up to see the soldiers dragging Father out. He looked me in the eyes with a desperate expression and said, 'Look after everyone for me.'

Lucy Conington (14)
Cranbrook School

A Day In The Life Of A Napoleonic Soldier

Dear Diary,

This may be the last time I ever write on your pale creased pages. The French scum are tracking us, they have tracked us for weeks now and the group's morale is extremely low. Our supplies ran out back in Calais, it has been two weeks since then and our stomachs now cry out for food. My uniform is dirty, I am parched of thirst and my stomach growls like a bear. I miss my family dreadfully, especially my daughter Elizabeth, oh I do hope they are all OK. We have even run out of ammunition and our guns are rusted and bowed. If we are attacked all we will be able to use are our rounded swords.

   I have a very bad feeling about this tracking we could be ambushed at any point. I hear voices in the bushes at night now as though people are watching us all the time. I see eyes everywhere now, people staring long empty stares with wide ghostly eyes. I could be going mad but I am sure we are being watched constantly.

   Oh Diary, you are the only one who listens to me, my commander doesn't listen to me, neither do my fellow soldiers. I am the only one who is suspicious of being ambushed because apparently Sir says we are well camouflaged. He isn't wearing a bright red uniform!

   Diary, I hope I write on your sweet pages again.

Yours
Edward.

Peter Clements (11)
Gravesend Grammar School for Boys

A Day In The Life Of The Queen's Corgi

Dear Diary,

After waking up from one of the worst sleeps ever, on a bed made with velvet and studded with emeralds, Prince Harry took me to have my breakfast. Habitually I would adore breakfast but today was a Monday and on Mondays I have to eat muesli.

'Come on Foofoo Dennis McGrill,' the Queen ushered. I hated the puerile name but I couldn't speak so I couldn't change it.

After the muesli the Queen decided to take me for a walk in the palace grounds. I despise walking. All I desire to do is to watch 'The Story of Rin Tin Tin' from my 100-inch wide plasma television.

Taking no notice of my continuous whining, the Queen grabbed me by the collar and took me to the grounds. I plodded across the gold-plated fountain examining the Queen feed her horses. I miss my brother Pharos, as I have no one to play with anymore.

Suddenly I saw Florence, Princess Anne's Corgi killer of a pet. Her psychologist, Mr Mugford, accompanied her. With him around she couldn't lay a single paw on me. I have incessant nightmares about the whole ordeal and I vowed that I would get my retribution on that bloodthirsty fiend that Princess Anne calls man's best friend.

Appreciatively, today had been a lacklustre day and consequently, I was relieved that I was away from Florence. I was carried off to my football pitch of a bedroom, dreading the instance when I knew I would remember my brother's massacre.

Daninder Singh Nota (12)
Gravesend Grammar School for Boys

A Day In The Life Of Godfrey Mayfair

Dear Diary,

If you could give me an answer to any one question in the world, it would be; why the devil did I do it? I mean, who would want to be a maths teacher? Today I had the dreaded 9D. They are nothing short of barbaric and today was no exception. As I plunged into the delights of algebra, their focus slipped somewhat. Ryan Jenkins was shouting, 'Sir's gay!' when he knew I could hear him, he carried on anyway. I gave him a lunch time detention but he didn't show up. Ross Taylor's no better. He drew a pair of breasts on the whiteboard. I confronted him but he just blamed Tyrone. I mean, I try with that form, I do, but they just throw it in my face like a … a … throwy thingy. I try to be hip and cool by playing McFly and Busted but Shane suggested Outkast or Shim Slady. Vicky says that Shim is a 'rappa'. I've heard of rappers and they're a terrible influence what with their references to girls. Even McFly disappoint me with numerous mentions of girls. Lads should not think about girls till the age of 17 at least. Anyway, I'll go now. Boiled cabbage and cinnamon and still no one to share it with. I'll turn it in … dear, oh dear …

Lawrence Bricher (12)
Gravesend Grammar School for Boys

The Unsuccessful Lion Tamer

The lights were burning me, I could feel them. I was sweating and shaking but I kept smiling. The smile would hide the truth. There were people in the crowd now asking parents, 'Mummy, why isn't the man in the silly costume scared?' But I *was* scared, I was absolutely petrified, which was understandable since I was about to step into a cage with the most mean-looking lion imaginable and maybe that had ever existed.

I was the worst lion tamer the world had ever and would ever see. I almost fled the cage in fright before my act was finished. This was my last chance; if I failed this I would be fired.

I was standing in the cage and adrenaline was pumping in my ears. I looked timidly at the ring of fire and then back at the lion who gave me possibly the worst look that ever existed, not a 'you think I'll do that, you need your brain examined', but a 'try and make me do that and I'll rip your face off' look. The difference is small but incredibly important for obvious reasons. I gulped in an extraordinarily large gulp of air and muttered, 'Symba through the ring.'

It felt like I had swallowed a whole bucket of ice-cold water. Symba calmly stepped towards the ring of fire and roared. The ring of fire was instantly extinguished. Symba stepped through the ring and leapt towards me …

Chris Daniels (12)
Gravesend Grammar School for Boys

A Day In The Life Of A World War II Soldier

December 1941

I had hoped it would be another normal day. The fiery red sun began to rise over the snow-covered mountains near the Russian city of Stalingrad. The Volga river shimmered in the morning sun as snowflakes fell onto the tranquil water.

The last of my men began to appear from their tents. The whole camp became a complete buzz of activity, for I heard an attack was being prepared against the Soviets. At noon the glimmering sun was high in the deep blue sky, and me and my squad mates crammed onto a small landing craft painted vividly with a light grey. Over the river, above us, were waves of aircraft darting from one point to another. Some were even bellowing smoke from their behinds. At last the mist gave way and ahead I could see Stalingrad engulfed in flames. On both our sides jets of water threw themselves into the air.

By 4 o'clock we had fought tooth-grinding, close quarter battles. All around me was the smell of blood and piled along the floor were dead men, hundreds of them, and the rattle of machine guns whizzed from one building to another. Back at our camp that night were fewer people than had crossed this morning.

That night, after I got back, our base came under heavy attack. I couldn't escape …

Grahame Johnson (11)
Gravesend Grammar School for Boys

A Day In The Life Of A Vietnamese Soldier

As another day goes by of war and misery, I am confused. We have seen nothing from the American soldiers. I slit a Vietcong's throat today, but that's all. Some say the Americans have gone back after a new president was elected and pulled them out. I, for one, do not believe it. They are on the verge of victory, they would not pull out. They killed my family and I'm not going anywhere till I avenge them.

My eldest son was only eight. They killed him and his brother who was seven, regardless. As for my wife, there is no sign of her. My best friend was taken to a prison. I cannot stand it. I will have my revenge though. Soon we are going to cross the 17th parallel. That's when I'll find him. However if he is dead, the person who killed him I shall skin alive.

First we are to block the Ho Chi Minh trail. After that we shall move in on Diem Bien Phu. The fools who have attacked and tried to starve us for so long will never live to see another day. Every now and then I must put my head out of these tunnels. Those fools know nothing of our underground systems, I may die tomorrow so I must go now and save my people.

Manvir Khera (11)
Gravesend Grammar School for Boys

In Loving Memory Of Toby Dowling, My Friend

One day there was a dog called Toby and he was a friendly dog. When he was a small puppy he was very loving but his owner entered him into dogfights and that changed him. This made Toby vicious towards other dogs.

One day a kind and friendly man, Sam, met Toby's owner. The cruel owner gave the dog to Sam because he did not want him anymore. So Sam took Toby home with him and his wife, who already had a dog that tore up the furniture, who was pleased to have Toby.

A couple of months after they got Toby their old dog had puppies. When these puppies were ready to leave home, Sam's friend was given one of them.

One week later Sam and his wife went out to have a drink. When they came back Toby was sitting on the furniture and Bow, one of the puppies, was sitting under the settee with a hole in his foot with a little bit of blood on the floor. They took the puppy to the vet for treatment and then gave the puppy back to his friend because Toby had come to the family first - if one had to go it had to be the puppy.

As Sam didn't know what had happened in Toby's earlier life, he thought it would be best to take Toby out early every morning so as he would not bump into other dogs and cause fights. Some people would also take their dogs out early in the morning though. Because it was really early Sam would let Toby off the lead and if another dog came around the corner he would have to go before any trouble started.

Over the years Sam took him for walks. When he had enough of these walks he let Toby out in the back garden because they now had a baby.

One and a half years later another child was born. The first baby was a girl and the second was a boy. Because Toby was left to do what he wanted, he started finding different ways of getting out of the garden. Sam used to look for Toby and find him fighting other dogs, but sometimes he found his own way home. He had a group of dogs that were his friends, one big mongrel and one medium-sized mongrel and two smaller dogs.

As Toby got older he stopped getting out of his garden and slowed down a lot. He stopped fighting other dogs, he was sleeping a lot of the time. One of his friends got run over and died. The big dog was taken away by the RSPCA and the small dog died of old age. One of Toby's friends is still alive today. Toby died after having a stroke. Before he died the vet told Sam to take him home for a week and see if he improved a little. When Sam saw that there was no improvement he thought that it would be kinder to put him down than to see him suffer like he had. The family were very upset that they had to lose Toby but they were very happy that they had had him for so long.

Three years after the death of Toby, Sam got a new dog and he called him Harvey. Harvey is still alive today and he is a beautiful dog.

Tom Dowling (14)
Oakwood School

Untitled

Through the thickness of the trees, we could see a bright but faint beam of light penetrating the overhanging branches. Ecstatic with excitement, we began to run towards it, not caring about the thorns and branches scrapping against our exhausted bodies. But, no matter how far or how fast we run, we didn't seem to be getting any closer, more like further away. Finally we stopped. Gasping for breath, we sat down on a nearby stump of freshly overturned tree, peering through the branches to see if that light was still there, but it had gone.

The fresh dew of the early morning air was what woke me, but if it hadn't, me and my friends would have certainly been trampled on by those horse-looking things. They had piercing white fur coats and two blood-red horns were placed just behind their ears.

We quickly scurried up onto a nearby wilting oak tree, and peered down, watching those creatures hustle along underneath us. Suddenly, one of my close mates, Ben, had an outstanding idea. He said that them creatures must be running from danger and be going somewhere safe, or be going somewhere safer. So with that, we all jumped into their dust-filled path and began to follow them through the bewilderness.

Exhausted and dehydrated, we finally came to the end of the path and into a clearing, in which was centred a dazzling, sparkling pond with an extraordinary life-like statue of what looked like an overgrown troll, which had three hands and in one was clasped a menacing-looking club with protruding spikes coming from it. We sprinted down to the pond and began guzzling down handfuls of water until something caught my attention, a piece of rock had just plopped down into the water just in front of me. I looked up and at the same time so did Ben and Luke. This statue had come to life, swinging its arms ferociously about. We all started to sprint towards the opening of the forest, but as we got there, the branches of the trees swung themselves into a wall enclosing us in this clearing. I turned sharply around and I saw the troll's club come swinging towards me, frozen with fright, I just stood there and if it hadn't been for Luke pushing me out the way, I would have been hit. But for him to do this he, in return, got hit by the club. Now knocked out and spread up the tree's wall, it was just Ben and I; we had to take on this troll by ourselves.

When I awoke, it was still early. The sun had not yet risen fully and Ben and Luke were still asleep. I sat there; thinking about what had happened the day before and why we were here. But that was no use, I couldn't remember, the same as Ben and Luke, they couldn't remember either. So, until they awoke I decided to climb the tree. I did, and when nearing the top I heard an almighty roar! Shaking with fright, the roar seemed to be getting closer, so not thinking I jumped out of the tree and landed on a nearby bush. I bounced off and tore off towards my friends. Shaking them and shouting at them they finally woke up. As I told them of what I had just heard, it happened again. With no hesitation we all ran in the opposite direction of the noise. Sweating, gasping for breath and worn out, we came to a bubbling, murky, green swamp. It stretched out to the left and right of us as far as we could see, and was about 100 metres wide. So how were we meant to cross it? With the roar of that creature coming forever closer, we had to get across.

Looking around for something to use, or something to float across on, frantically searching for something, Luke spotted an overhanging branch that reached about halfway across, but how were we meant to get across the other half? We didn't care, that was our only option, and so we climbed up and onto the branch. At the end of this branch we could see the other side of the swamp, there was a kind of hole, a manhole but it was closed.

We had all forgotten about that roar. I looked round and saw a large beast, it was the troll, but much, much bigger. It looked at us and then started to shake the tree with its powerful arms. With that the branch began to break, terrified we all fell into the swamp. Waiting for us to smash into the swamp, all we did was land softly upon a floor, surprised, but thankful, we weren't in that swamp. Looking round to see where we were, not knowing what to expect …

Samuel Prideaux Clare (13)
Oakwood School

The Angels Are Looking For Their Feather

One dark day the heavens opened and the rain came down. The angels were upset so they made it rain. They could not find their feathers; they were missing. Someone must have stolen them.

They looked on their security cameras and they saw a green, ugly, bold troll, sneaking the feathers away. Alarm bells rang because they did not know how he'd got in and were there more?

They had to get the Angel Army out. The head angel called an emergency situation and an emergency meeting was held. He told them what had happened and all the angels cried. All the angel tears caused a flood on Earth. The angels were devastated because they needed their feathers for strength to help and to help them fly. How would they be able to fly around now and help all the people on Earth?

The Angel Army dipped their wings in goodness because that was their only weapon against evil. They then flew from Heaven to the unknown land of the troll. From the sky they could see the troll and the head angel shouted to the other angels to do their work. They could see the entire troll community jumping up and down on all their feathers. This caused a lot of damage to the feathers and to the hearts of the angels.

The angels had to act quickly. As they flew over the trolls they sprinkled goodness over the ugly, fat, green midgets.

Suddenly all the trolls froze. They looked up at the magnificent angels and they started to glow. They glowed with goodness and all the evil disappeared.

There was no more evil in the land of the trolls and the angels could have their feathers back.

Darrel Laing (15)
Oakwood School

The Thing

On the outskirts of town there was a dark forest, a mysterious forest which no one had entered for about a century. There were rumours of mysterious creatures that made strange noises and only came out at night and knowing this, without thinking, I accepted a dare to camp out, alone, in the wood.

It was sunset and everyone had come to see me off and say their goodbyes and I was off.

I had just got to sleep when I saw a warm glow come through the holes in my well-used tent. I thought it was just the guys coming to spook me but the light was coming from a distance.

I clambered out of my tent, grabbed my torch and took hold of a very large stick and went exploring. I soon came to another clearing and realised it was an old building, a mill I thought. It stood tall with the light shining out of one of its few windows. Grasping my stick I slowly opened the crumbling door and realised there was no person but a small fire in the centre of the room.

Then out of the shadows came something I didn't recognise, half man, half beast, it communicated in strange howls. At that moment my instinct told me to run, that I shouldn't be there. I ran all the way home leaving everything, still grasping the stick, and to this day never told anyone of my encounter.

Louise Wilcocks (13)
St John's Catholic Comprehensive School, Gravesend

Eos' Night Light

Dawn goddess, Eos, had always feared the dark. Her father, Hyperion tried everything to banish her dread of the night. He gave her pet foals that Helios' geldings had recently birthed, who shone with the sun's radiance. But their comforting glow would diminish with the setting of the sun, and Eos' chambers would be swamped with shadows. She was appointed the role of dawn-bringer - some hoped she'd find dispelling the darkness empowering, but her fear continued to plague her.

She confided in her mother, Theia, who was mending some torn muslin. After intense contemplation, Theia had a flash of inspiration. She rummaged through her vast caches of jewellery, emerging with as many gems as she could carry. Theia crushed them, mixed the powder with a brew of krystha-root and wind-blossom, making an unusual dye. She left the fabric to soak in the dye-filled pot, whilst green and rose-coloured waves of light washed over the material.

Finally, Theia nimbly leapt into the sky and secured the shimmering canopy to the stars above Eos' bedchamber. Eos rejoiced - no longer would she ever fear the dark. Eager to share her happiness, she summoned her children, Austra and Boreas. However, when the young wind gods gasped in awe of night light's beauty, their breath tore it in two, and swept one trembling half to the north, the other to the south. Now, should you see the Aurora Borealis or Aurora Australis sway and billow overhead, you'll know how they came to be.

Sinéad O'Rourke (14)
St John's Catholic Comprehensive School, Gravesend

A Day In The Life Of Annie

Monday, the day dreaded by every child across Britain, no, the entire world. Today has been hanging over me all weekend, science first lesson and the idea of facing Mr Wormwood, (one of the most 'unique' specimens on this planet!) didn't really excite me too much.

I'll tell you something about Mr Wormwood. Every morning he strides into school sipping some of his lemon tea and his glasses, oh the glasses, they're like magnifying lenses! Trust me you will never meet another man like him. I'm wearing my dreaded uniform, (blue and orange skirt, yuck!) and walking in the pouring rain.

Oh God, here I go, just walk in there, try not to be noticeable! *Not noticeable!*

'Annabelle Farm come here immediately!'

Oh no.

'Explain to me why you decided to spill acid all over my desk and then decide to run out of my classroom!'

'What?'

'Maybe if I put it like this, you decided to 'leg it' without even telling anyone. Imagine the fright that Jeremiah Klarks got when he sat on the chair.'

'Well ...'

'Go ahead and give me the pathetic excuse I know you're dying to tell me.'

'What do you mean, you wrinkly old trout, if you let me get my words out ...'

'Get out!'

So I ended up sitting outside the principle's office, I've got two weeks' suspension and three weeks off after schools for calling Mr Wormwood a wrinkly old trout but I'll never forget the look on his face. Ever!

Lucy Quigley (13)
St John's Catholic Comprehensive School, Gravesend

The Greekly Scroll

Zero To Hero

Hercules saves two children from hundred-headed monster!

Hercules, an ordinary man, saved two children from a massive rock slide by lifting up a massive rock weighing more than one hundred horses and men. But this huge disaster woke the monster that lives in the cave. That is when he pulled out his magnificent shining sword and sliced the monster's head off. When everyone thought the fight was over the monster grew back two heads instead of one, so Hercules sliced off the two heads but it grew back four heads, and just kept multiplying until the monster grabbed Hercules and with one huge opening of the mouth Hercules was nowhere to be seen. There was silence in the crowd.

Then the monster's stomach ripped open and Hercules stepped out and the crowd went wild. His enemies picked him up and carried him out of the gorge and back to the little town. Posters were put up everywhere and Hercules has become a great hero and I will make sure he is known forever.

Kasey Argent (12)
St John's Catholic Comprehensive School, Gravesend

The Beasts

Mist filled the air as haunting shadows hovered across the moon's surface. My heart started to quicken as the distant sound of beats drew nearer. The atmosphere grew extremely daunting as the freezing cold mist scattered over the iced waterway.

My feet seemed to sink into the mushy ground like weights as I tried to move. I could hear the bloodthirsty beasts' cries. I started to run through the looming trees, their branches blowing uncontrollably.

I felt an agonising pain across the back of my head. I went to touch it. As I looked at my hand, I saw blood! I began to feel woozy. I kept running!

The shrieks of the distressed animals seemed to be growing closer. My head was gushing with blood, but I still kept running. The wind whistled in my ears as I clambered over lightning-struck logs.

I tripped and fell onto the mawkish ground. I tried to get up, but I didn't have the strength. Blood was oozing, I saw a figure coming towards me. I couldn't make out what it was a figure of.

I didn't have the strength to keep my eyelids open any longer. I could hear the rustling of the mysterious character bending down next to me. I could feel it breathing across my face, then touching my cut head.

Next thing I knew I was in a cave. It smelt damp and moss-like. I heard grunting noises behind me. I turned to look, it pounced ...

Nicola Hylands (13)
St John's Catholic Comprehensive School, Gravesend

Warning!

The gloomy, dark Panoramas Forest loomed over the children, as they stared at it in suspense. The ghostly, whirling wind rustled through the shadowy trees. It had been reported that this forest was haunted and most people who went in there never came out, but of course, people always tried their luck!

'Come on, let's go in there, or are you a chicken?' asked James mockingly, his voice echoed in the misty air.

'OK,' spoke Becky with an uncertain, panic-stricken tone to her voice.

She and her brother walked hesitantly towards the mysterious, creepy forest, their silhouettes only to be seen. The sky was like a huge black blanket and the maze of trees in the forest were engulfing the children!

As they continued on through the eerie dark forest, a petrified look flashed across their faces. Perhaps this wasn't a good idea, but they couldn't stop now! They carried on. The huge monster-like trees seemed to be leering down at them, icicles hanging off the branches like claws. Their blood was curdling, their spines were tingling, and the hairs on the back of their necks were raised. Becky froze. Her jaw dropped. *What was that?* she thought to herself.

All of a sudden a dark shadow crept up on the children. James and Becky swapped each other a terrified look. *Bang!* Those children were never seen again. That was just two of the people who took a chance. I warn you, *never* go in that forest.

Louise Harman (12)
St John's Catholic Comprehensive School, Gravesend

Snowhara

As you read this article, the used to be Sahara Desert will look more and more like a shocking blizzard scene from the Arctic.

At 2 o'clock this morning it was reported that the usual scorching, blistering heat of the Sahara had been replaced with the sub-zero temperatures of the Poles. Scientists believe that this is another freak weather phenomenon, just like the fatal, grief-stricken Boxing Day tragedy.

So far nobody has been found, neither human nor animal. Two weeks before this incident scientists discovered that the herd of camels they were using for an observational study had been acting strangely. The camels were getting strangely unruly and restless. Also, they seemed to be more conscious of their surroundings, looking frequently at the sky while facing north. A scientist from Cambridge University, where the information was being used said, 'We think that the camels we were using for observational study could have almost certainly sensed the drastic weather was about to arrive'.

We have been informed that the camels have ventured out of the radar boundaries, which covers the whole of the Sahara Desert, which has now cleverly been dubbed the 'Snowhara'.

Early this morning weather experts were trying to find out how long this astonishing weather would be lasting and if the usual scorching temperatures would be returning to the Sahara Desert. They came to a conclusion that eventually the normal desert conditions will return, but when, they do not know.

Sami Gosling (13)
St John's Catholic Comprehensive School, Gravesend

A Day In The Life Of Bartholomew - A Disciple!

You think you know Jesus? A cross doesn't seem so exciting does it? Nails? Try being Jesus, doesn't seem so glorious does it?

The barriers of Jerusalem sealed with silence, we hid in the cellar, if you could call it that!

Matthew was growing impatient and anxiety ran through his body like a gush of sudden wind! John was irritating me because of his weird mumbling. We were all so annoyed Jesus was dead now! What were we doing just waiting, what for? I was trying to keep hold of my emotions but it seemed whatever I did, whatever I said whenever the word 'Jesus' was said my eyes filled up with salty tears.

Thaddeus stormed through the secret passage, he began to shout, 'The Romans are coming!'

We were so quiet we could hear the screeches of the eerie mice. They searched the grounds hoping to find us. We were OK this time but how long would we go on?

The room filled with solemnness, Jesus had died for our sins - why were we in fear for our own safety? We are so selfish! You never miss a good thing until it leaves, I finally realised that I needed Jesus so much! There was a sharp knock at the door! The room shook! My mind became split, was it Mary? The Romans? The Sanhedrin?

Walking towards the bolted door with fear - Mary emerged from the smudged vision. Jesus' body has gone ...

Simran Bhogal (13)
St John's Catholic Comprehensive School, Gravesend

A Day In The Life Of A Boy!

What the? I woke up, same as usual, but there was one difference, I was not in my room. I went into the bathroom, half dragging myself. Splashing water on my face, I gazed into the mirror. Screamed. I was a boy! An ugly one in fact! Wait, if I was this boy, that meant he was me. He'd better not ruin my life. How? How could this happen, a friendly, tanned face should be staring back at me. Wait a minute, this could work to my liking, this boy I now was had friends with the boy in Year 9 at school. This could work to my liking, so great in fact, I think I was going toenjoy this day.

    Scoffing down the breakfast the boy's mum gave me, I ran upstairs then stopped, facing the wardrobe. Oh my God! I had to get dressed, I didn't know anything about getting this body dressed. I closed my eyes and reached in the drawer and grabbed a pair of blue socks? I opened them up, eww! Gross, sick! Blue boxers. All through getting dressed, I had to close my eyes.

    I walked to school, somehow I knew the way. Getting close to the building, a boy ran up to me screaming, 'James, *James!*' I turned around and noticed that it was the boy I fancied. I felt like I was being hurled into the air. I landed on my bed, my mum was shaking me. It was a dream. Damn! I was enjoying my dream.

Shaunnie Money (13)
St John's Catholic Comprehensive School, Gravesend

A Day In The Life Of Rachel

6.00 - My alarm clock goes.

7.00 - I get up.

7.10 - I get in the shower and try to wash my hair but there is no conditioner so I have tangly hair - great! I get the blow dryer and straightening irons and plug them in.

7.20 - Try to hurry as the bus comes at 7.30.

7.30 - Just about finished blow-drying my hair. I'm running late!

7.55 - I'm all dressed, got to try and get Mum to drop me to school.

8.27 - Finished persuading Mum, now we have to get to school in 10 minutes.

8.28 - It's raining so my hair is ruined and that's the reason why I'm late, fantastic!

9.00 - In the middle of a lecture with the head teacher and I don't have an excuse because my hair is frizzy and wet - what a waste of a morning. I should have never got up this morning.

Lauren Webb (13)
St John's Catholic Comprehensive School, Gravesend

The First Day In Spring

My day started in a dear little park in the country where two middle-aged people slid up the bench to allow me to sit down. Whilst waiting for my grandson in the park I caught my eye on this lovely family who had hired some boats. The mother and father were in a rowing boat with their little infant child. However, their other two children were in canoes. The adults looked like they were struggling with rowing the boat, especially with a little boy anxious to row a boat. The two elder children were thoroughly enjoying themselves and they had races with each other to see who was the quickest.

It was getting rather warm on the bench so I decided to move onto a nice shady position if at all I could find such a spot. First, I needed to track down my grandson. *Now where is he?* I thought to myself, my old eyes moving from side to side. He was nowhere to be seen. There he was on the swings. I explained that I was in no hurry to leave and that I just needed to get some shade and if he would just take me over to the little miniature railway I could sit under the station shelter. He promptly sat me down and ran off in the direction of the park.

After a while of watching little children get on and off the trains my grandson came over to find me. I told him I'd had the most enjoyable time. We set off for home.

Ella Luscombe (13)
St John's Catholic Comprehensive School, Gravesend

A Day In The Life Of Paris Hilton

Paris Hilton was born on the 17th February 1981, she has one sister called Nikki and her father is the owner of Hilton Hotels. Paris spends most of her time modelling but she also has a music album coming out and she has appeared in some films. If Paris has any spare time she likes to party and get drunk. On her 21st birthday she threw not one, not two, but five parties for herself.

Not many people know that Paris also has two brothers called Baron and Conrad. Paris gets most of her belonging crystallised, she has had so much stuff crystallised the shop owner runs a special overnight service, only her and Lindsay Lohan get this special service. So if Paris gets a new phone she can ring the crystalliser and say, 'I've got a new phone, I'll be down there soon,' and the phone would be done for her the next day.

Paris owns a dog called Tinkerbell. This dog has to be the luckiest dog in the world because I have never seen a dog that has a $3,000 chain around its neck and Nike shoes on its feet. Paris' dog is a Chihuahua and that dog has seen more bars and nightclubs than most people because Paris takes Tinkerbell everywhere. It is like Tinkerbell is her fashion accessory.

Ryan Gillingham (12)
St John's Catholic Comprehensive School, Gravesend

Is This The End?

I opened my eyes to see the murky darkness of what seemed to be a stone prison. I sat for about 20 minutes thinking of what to do when light started to slowly pour in at the far end of what I could now see was a cave. I headed towards the light and could smell the fresh air.

As I reached the exit to the cave I could see trees stretching for miles, below the edge of the small, windy path down the side of a mountain. How could I have possibly got up here?

It was a glorious day, the sky was a stunning blue and there was not a cloud to be seen. I wandered down the rough, rocky pathway to the shady grass beneath a great oak tree.

After a five minute breather I wandered through the dense forest for hours upon hours in search of someone who could help me.

I emerged into a clearing and there stood a village. I followed a path down through the village but it was strange, the houses were smaller, about the size of bungalow but with 2 floors, whoever lived there sure was small.

I kept wandering and not looking where I was going clumsily walked into a small greeny grey troll-looking thing. The troll thing fell backwards and examined me with a nervous face before letting out an extremely high-pitched scream, I covered my ears but the scream was the least of my worries, I was now being surrounded by the troll things all brandishing sharp weapons. I could not go anywhere, I was trapped …

Alex Brett (13)
St John's Catholic Comprehensive School, Gravesend

Terror In The Tunnel

That morning Lyla woke up as excited as she could ever be. It was a gorgeous, dazzlingly bright morning and she had a great day ahead of her. Lyla and her mother were going to indulge in a dose of retail therapy in the city of London.

Later, as soon as Lyla stepped onto the tube to get there, a blanket of intense heat smothered her. The only fresh air her and the passengers were receiving was from the dashing breeze blowing into the moving tube. Suddenly however, the tube started slowing down. Concern overwhelmed Lyla and the other passengers until the train completely stopped.

No more fresh air.

No exit.

An announcement was made that there had been a power fault. After that the lights went out. They were plunged into a terrifying situation. Lyla couldn't see anything. There wasn't even a minute shaft light.

Suddenly there was a loud howl echoing around the tunnel.

'Hello,' one man cautiously replied. The sound came closer and closer. The lights started flickering on and off. Once that had subsided the carriage began rocking. People leaned back against the window. When they did, a sudden and quick pounding started on the glass pane. A sharp instrument poked Lyla in the stomach. She shrieked, 'Aaarrgghh!'

At last what seemed like a miracle occurred. The lights came back on. Once the ordeal was over, Lyla learnt that in that part of the tunnel where they were stranded, a ghost is said to lurk ...

Gemma Bradish (13)
St John's Catholic Comprehensive School, Gravesend

A Day As My Cat Shodan

Oh God I am so tired, even though I've just had 16 hours of sleep I am still tired. How do these humans do it? I know what I will do, I will go stuff my face with Go-Kat. Oh God she is there, my little sister Belle, every day she licks my ears while I eat, it is so annoying so I smack her on the head.

Yum! It's great having free food. I am gonna go out now, I hate it since they put that cat flap in. Yes it is sunny! I love the sun! Ginger who lives two doors down is in my *garden!* Right, you get out of my garden, go back to your own spot. That's it, get out of here. Look it's a mouse in position, get ready to pounce on the prey. Go! Got it, I will bring it back to my owners for my gratitude. I will leave it on the door step.

Hey Belle do you want to play chase? Good. I am so worn out, that was so fun.

The worst thing I think is being picked up. When someone picks me up I growl because sometimes I think I am a dog. Woof. Oops forgot my mouse, my gift to my owners. Right that's on the doorstep.

Belle give us a kiss. I love you. I am going to retire to my bed with my special black blanket with paw prints on it. Well good night.

Abbie Hooper (13)
St John's Catholic Comprehensive School, Gravesend

Philemon And Baucis

One bright shining day there were two Roman gods named Jupiter and Mercury. They were walking around looking for hospitality from mortals. But the rich, powerful, selfish mortals did not welcome them at all. Although they were not welcomed they carried on when they suddenly came across an elderly couple named Philemon (the husband) and Baucis (the wife). This couple were extremely poor, living in poverty with just a small bit of food and wine. They invited the gods in and shared their last grain of food and their last sip of wine, they gave the gods all the hospitality, love and care that was needed. The gods were very, very pleased and could not thank Philemon and Baucis enough. As for the other selfish mortals the gods pitied them and decided to punish them.

In thanks for their wonderful hospitality the gods told Philemon and Baucis to climb to the top of the nearby mountain, as they intended to flood the land and drown the people because they were not friendly or kind. Philemon and Baucis did as they were told and at that moment their home was changed into a temple by the gods.

Jupiter and Mercury asked the elderly couple if they would like anything else. They then requested that they serve as priests in the temple and that when their time is up they could die together.

So when Philemon and Baucis' time was up they began to sprout leaves and as they finally changed into trees they had one last chance to kiss each other goodbye. These two trees were entwined forever.

Kayleigh Gourlay (13)
St John's Catholic Comprehensive School, Gravesend

Girl Saved By Stray Cat

It was on the 14th March 2005 the kidnapper found his victim. The kidnapper was named as Brian Klesh, 24 years old. He'd already tried to kidnap once before but again did not succeed.

This time, Brian tried to kidnap Kylie Williams, aged 11, who goes to Turner Primary School.

Kylie was on her way home from a normal day at school, when on the way home she noticed a man following her. She felt very suspicious and scared.

'The man got closer', Kylie said, 'he pulled out a scarf and tried to tie up my hands. I tried to free myself and wriggle but there was no hope'.

Just as Kylie was being tied up and dragged to Brian's van, a cat was being chased by a big, scruffy dog. As Brian struggled, he staggered about. By this time, the cat was pretty near, and still coming at high speed. The cat came crashing into Brian and because he staggered he stepped on the cat's tail.

The cat was very angry seeing as he was being chased as well, so he scratched and bit Brian. He was in so much pain he fell down and shouted. He let go of Kylie so she ran away to her house and reported the attempted kidnapping to the police. Brian was left on the floor bleeding with a cat bite.

A neighbour witnessed the attempted kidnapping and said, 'This is a miracle, I was so worried. I was hanging out my washing when I heard the scream. I ignored it at first; I thought it was just some kids playing. The screams got louder and started to scream for help. I ran outside and witnessed the kidnapping. I called the police straight away. Thank God for the little stray cat!'

Abbie Twaits (13)
St John's Catholic Comprehensive School, Gravesend

A Day In The Life Of A Tortoise

I opened my eyes to the gleaming sunlight with its gentle rays softly touching me. The sky was a pure blue colour laying over me like a blanket.

I clambered out of my makeshift bed, my shell felt lighter than ever and I knew this was just the beginning of a beautiful day.

I slowly plodded down to the pond and jumped into its refreshing clear waters to wake myself up.

Now I felt thoroughly awake but I was absolutely famished so I went around, found a few leaves and sat on the patio to eat them. The taste was sensational and immediately satisfied me. I now felt energised and ready to take on the day's events.

I found a way into my owner's conservatory, it was like an oven in there it was so hot, I climbed up onto the cosy cushioned chair. As soon as my feet touched the cushion I was fast asleep.

I slept right up until dusk was closing in. I woke up wondering where I was but then I remembered I was in the conservatory.

Not too long after that it was time for my dinner and after falling asleep which meant missing lunch, I was ravenous. I nibbled on a fruit bush eating its fine, juicy summer fruits and its tasty green leaves. Despite the fact of my dinner and my sleep I was so tired so I thought I'd go to sleep, and wake up to another beautiful day.

Chris McCann (12)
St John's Catholic Comprehensive School, Gravesend

Tales Of Kia And Serena

'Shut up Kia,' Serena hissed, 'do you want the soldiers to find us you stupid dragon?'

'Sorry, but there's no need for name-calling, you try having wings,' said Kia hurtfully.

'Sorry, but stop being so melodramatic and die quietly.'

They waited for a while and they heard nothing but the whistling wind.

'I think they've gone,' said Serena scrambling out of the undergrowth, 'I'll go check, stay here unless I call for help.'

Serena walked out onto the path with a feeling of foreboding in the pit of her stomach. Serena had lived in the forest for so long she almost had a sixth sense, and right now it was warning her to get off the road ... but too late.

A cart came whizzing down the road with almighty speed and scooped the helpless Serena away.

Serena woke up in an unknown area, her hands were numb from the rope tying her and had cut off her blood circulation. She looked around to see a small fire surrounded by weapons of nearly every kind, and a horse grazing gently by the cartwheel, which she was tied to.

Serena's senses were telling her that her faithful Kia was nearby. The bush nearby rustled and a dirty man with an unshaven face appeared. He smiled wickedly at her and stroked her golden ringlets, saying, 'I won't hurt you, yet ...'

Charlotte Ide (13)
St John's Catholic Comprehensive School, Gravesend

One Man's Memories Of The Great War

Late at night, even now, 90 years on, I can still hear the stuttering of the German Lewis Gun. I've tried everything to get these horrific memories out of my mind but nothing seems to work. I suppose I should think myself lucky to be able to be here having such dreams when there were many like Jimmy Artright and Charlie Bridge who lived these nightmares. Poor old Charlie; he died his first day on the front line with me. I can remember the blow of the loud, shrill whistle and Charlie taking his first steps over the top, when a Jerry shot him. I never knew where he was shot; they left his body in no-man's-land; twisted like a screw with his wide, white eyes rolling like lifeless golf balls and blood trickling down his side, staining his mud-caked khaki shirt. He wasn't the only one to die like this, left unknown, unnamed with millions of others and no one there to grieve for them when they were gone.

I remember when I used to think joining the war would be a positive experience. I have never been so wrong! I was so naïve back then; I can't believe I was persuaded to risk my life by a poster! I can still remember it as clear as day; a big, dirty black gorilla with a small, limp writhing woman in its clutches. The desire to help this woman was overwhelming. I couldn't just sit back and let her be savagely attacked by this beast, I had to help her; *my* country, little old Britain, through her desperate time of need.

My brother, Harry, had been in the British Navy for five years already and in his letters he sounded as if he was having the time of his life. I had known I had wanted to be in the forces ever since he'd joined. There was one problem about me joining up though; I was only 16 and the legal minimum age for joining the war was 18. I was very tall for my age though, I always had been, but what if they could tell? There was always that fear, especially walking down Marble Street to the office where you were told to join up. I had no other fears or regrets; my dad had died when I was only five years old in an accident at his workplace but I knew he would approve of what I was doing. My brother was away at Scapa Flow but could be shipped off anywhere in the world because of this war. I had no love interest and my mum was so proud of her two boys helping in the Great War. So I joined up with no hesitation.

I did get a funny look from the doctor whilst he was checking me over, which I think could have been for many reasons. But apart from that I don't think any of the men at the office suspected me to be under eighteen years of age, this was a huge relief on my part.

Chloe Barden (15)
St John's Catholic Comprehensive School, Gravesend

A Day In The Life Of A Person In Africa

Thousands of my family and friends die every day. We are not as lucky as other people in other countries. We are not like other people. We have a different life.

I get all my family up for breakfast, I don't have a lot but at least it's something. I have a bowl of rice, it's the only thing we can get. I don't take my children to school. I wash everything up and have to get fresh water from the lake.

My children go to a factory where they are squashed and cramped on the floor. They make most stuff that is being sold in other countries. They earn little money, 60p a day. My husband does cleaning jobs.

I went down to the lake where I cut my foot. We don't have shoes and the ground is rough and has jagged rocks sticking out. I got back to the house and started to prepare the tea, some vegetables from crops which I grew.

The children were home, my husband is home. We all sat down together. We went straight to bed. There was nothing to do. I started to feel sharp pains in my heart and lungs. Clutching it I knew I was dying but what could I do. Nobody cares about us. I am just another one of those 8 billion people dying in the world every day. That was my last day.

Alex Clarke (14)
St John's Catholic Comprehensive School, Gravesend

Marijuana Mama!

An 87-year-old pensioner arrested for possessing and selling illegal drugs from her farmyard barn!

Yesterday police arrested 87-year-old Ethel Pithery from Slough, Berkshire. The pensioner was found high on drugs after neighbours were alarmed after sighting black smoke coming from the barn.

Neighbour, Neil Stoned, explained this, 'I saw thick black smoke rising from the chimney barn and dashed round to make sure the elderly lady was in no danger. When I found her she was flat out, laughing and rolling around with her eyes rolling in her head and I could not make out what she was trying to tell me. I grabbed hold of her clothing and pulled her from the barn, and that's when I called for the police'.

Sergeant Speed, informed us that Ethel has been taken to the local hospital and the discovery of marijuana 'pot' had been burning all morning inside the barn.

Police are continuing with their investigations on how the elderly lady could possibly be part of a syndicate. More marijuana has been found in the lining of the walls in her home and also in the cow shed and in the battery hutch.

Ethel Pithery is now facing the rest of her life in prison for the alleged trafficking of drugs to care homes. We tried to interview Ethel but police explained that she was in an unfit condition and could not be interviewed until further notice. We are still investigating this crime.

Hannah Hughes (13)
St John's Catholic Comprehensive School, Gravesend

Treat Others How You Would Like To Be Treated

Once upon a time there was a boy named Jack. Jack was disabled and was bullied every day by some horrible boys, Bradley, Charlie and Joshua. One day Jack was on his way into school and saw that the three boys were waiting for him at the top of the road. Jack was very scared and worried and tried to turn back when Joshua shouted, 'There he is, get him.'

All three boys ran towards him, *bang*.

Charlie was hit by a speeding car.

Everyone stopped and stared in shock as the little boy lay still in the middle of the road, there was not a sound to be heard when Charlie managed to screech out, 'Help!'

Jack took out his mobile phone and called an ambulance, they were there almost instantly and took Charlie off to the hospital.

Later that day Jack phoned the hospital to see if Charlie was OK, but unfortunately it was bad news, Charlie was paralysed from his waist downwards.

A few days later Jack went to visit Charlie in hospital, when he was there he asked if Bradley or Josh had visited and he just told him they were no longer friends.

As Jack went to leave Charlie asked, 'Will you forgive me please, I am really, really sorry for what I have said and done to you, now I know what it is like to be you, I would like to be your friend, will you please forgive me?'

As soon as Jack heard him say this he wheeled himself over to Charlie and said, 'You are forgiven.'

And to this day Jack and Charlie have been best friends.

Lucy Brett (13)
St John's Catholic Comprehensive School, Gravesend

Dragonheart

In the 10th century a legend known as Dragonheart was born and the heroic tale has now been reborn.

900AD, Einon a 14-year-old prince witnessed his father being slaughtered. Although a skilled swordsman neither he nor his protector, Bowen, could defend him on this horrific day of revolt resulting in Einon being severely wounded.

Einon's desperate mother, Queen Aislinn guided the dying prince, in Bowen's arms, to a dark cave. Here she invoked the Celtic religious belief in the divine omniscient power of dragons, as she pleaded for the supernatural intervention of a flying, fire-breathing creature to save her son's life. It was not until Einon swore that he would rule with mercy, that tyranny and bloodlust would be forever buried with his father, that the dragon severed his chest and gave half his life-force to Einon so he might live to fulfil this promise. Einon lived, but emerged as a far more evil despot than his late father. Bowen, believing it was the dragon's heart that poisoned his charge, vowed to spend the rest of his life ridding the land of dragons.

Twelve years later Bowen and the last remaining dragon, which he named Draco, put their feud and differences behind them and travelled the land together.

Bowen and Draco intended to take on the overwhelming forces of Einon himself. However, they soon discovered that victory over Einon came with its own heavy price, as the fate of the king is inextricably bound with the fate of the dragon.

Hayley Blackwell (13)
St John's Catholic Comprehensive School, Gravesend

Element Witches

The dragon suddenly lifted itself up with Ora in its forceful grasp. She managed to push her hand into her pockets and fiddle about. To her relief, she pulled out a penknife. She opened it out and started hacking away at the dragon's leg. It stopped, hovering in mid-air. It screeched in pain, shaking its leg vigorously. Ora dropped her knife. There was only one option left. She held back her head and threw it forward, digging her teeth into the scaled leg. The dragon dropped her.

She fell until she landed on and broke through a mountain. It was very dark so she couldn't see much. She took out her wand and recited a spell. Slowly, the tip of the wand worked from a dim glow into brilliant streams of light. She gasped. She had fallen into a crystal cave. Everywhere she could see shimmering points. Deeper in the cave, crystals had formed into a spiral with a globe settled on top. It contained a polished, circular stone. It was an emerald. Ora was aghast.

A legend said that there were five witch stones for five elements: earth, water, fire, wind and one to rule them all. She touched the globe. It smashed and the stone moulded into Ora's skin. She was an element witch. With her new-found confidence, she held her wand high and ventured deeper into the cave, towards the awaiting dangers that lurked ahead ...

Isobel Pieroni (12)
St John's Catholic Comprehensive School, Gravesend

Why We Have Stars

A wizard has always had a job. This job was to cover half the world at a time with a giant black blanket. This would be known as night-time.

Everyone was happy until the cloth snagged and a hole appeared. The wizard was a perfectionist at this point and was shocked at this dilemma.

'This can't happen,' he bellowed, 'it makes it look unattractive and scruffy.'

He thundered about until a moth, tired of being disturbed from bathing in the firelight, spoke up. 'Listen, if I make the blanket neater will you stop all that banging?'

The wizard was desperate for a solution. 'Yes if you just make it nicer,' he pleaded.

So the moth spread its wings and flew up to the blanket.

Half an hour later it flew back down and settled itself by the firelight again. The wizard was aghast.

'But ...' he spluttered, 'but how does it help?'

'Trust me,' said a voice from near the fire, 'just trust me.'

So the wizard did. Everyone was amazed.

The moth had bitten holes into the blanket to allow a bit of light in. It was spectacular. From then on we have always had the small bits of light shining down on us stars.

Jasmine Reilly (13)
St John's Catholic Comprehensive School, Gravesend

Blair Blown

Yesterday, March the 15th, the leader of the UK, Prime Minister Tony Blair, was assassinated by a reported Russian hitman. The attack took place at 3.16 while he was visiting a school. This attack shows yet another lapse in British security as the building the bullet was fired from was unchecked and provided a perfect spot to snipe from.

Later in the day John Prescott, the Deputy Prime Minister, issued a statement saying, 'We are gravely sorry for the Blair family for a devastating mistake and the Cabinet are now meeting to discuss a plan of action and decide who will be the next Prime Minister. I would like to issue a warning to the organisation responsible for the attack'.

The equipment used by the assassin was of the highest technology which means a major terrorist organisation must have been responsible.

The bullet hit Mr Blair in the shoulder and everyone thought he was going to be okay until the bullet exploded and Mr Blair died.

Thomas Toulson (13)
St John's Catholic Comprehensive School, Gravesend

A Day As Dr Jekyll And Mr Hyde

I woke up with a throbbing pain in my head. I tried to recall what I was doing last night, but I couldn't. I wandered over to the kitchen for my breakfast and I saw the box on the table full of potions. I now remembered. This urge was just too much for me now, I had to *be* him. I looked in the mirror and saw him, Mr Hyde. He tried to persuade me to take the potion. He wanted to leave my mind. I regret the day I made him. I must get rid of him.

I went for a walk today and I saw some troublemakers. I thought I'd leave them. Unfortunately they were terrorising. They threw a rock at me, my head was bleeding. My body trembled and I collapsed to the floor clutching my head with one hand and reaching for my pocket with my other. I pulled out my potion and drank it. I didn't mean to drink it but I had to. I couldn't resist taking it with me. I transformed into Hyde and he turned to face the children and smirked.

I can't believe he did it. I stood over a cliffside and thought about what he'd done to the poor innocent children. Four teenagers killed. I jumped. Now I've got rid of him forever. But as I hit the floor I thought, *he didn't kill them, I did.*

Thomas Rogers (12)
St John's Catholic Comprehensive School, Gravesend

A Day In The Life Of A Chair

Most people take us chairs for granted, you don't know what we go through. I'm a school chair, it's not good pay but I live. My best mate is a park bench, he hates it, cold, wet drunks using him.

I wake at eight thirty am, except for at weekends when I lay in. This is when my first shift begins. 'They' call it 'registration'. I have a small boy using me which is great for the morning. Usually I get graffitted, or that's what they call it. My clients sit on me and write all over me, it leaves a bad impression on me.

I get two breaks in-between my eight shifts. This gives my four legs a bit of rest. Many of my friends have been taken to 'the place' because of ignorant clients swinging on the legs. My legs start to ache by eighth shift, 'swinging on chairs', ends careers. After work I usually meet up with chairs and Hoovers in the cupboard for a drink, we watch musical chairs on 'Chair Sports'. Those chairs are real tough. Hoovers are nocturnal you see. When I sleep they clean the floor, but they don't work at weekends so we party.

Break is usually good, but I've heard from mates that people come into the room at break and throw them around. At the end of work I sit and read.

I hope you take consideration when you use us chairs as toys. *We have feelings too!*

Thomas Shepherd (14)
St John's Catholic Comprehensive School, Gravesend

Bluewater - Code Of Conduct Been Made

Bluewater bans youths wearing hoods and hats.

On the 11th May 2005 Bluewater, Greenhithe set a code of conduct. It was to ensure that Bluewater was a pleasant and safe environment for guests to shop in.

The Code of Conduct was made by many workshops, Bluewater staff and the Bluewater guests. The main reason why Bluewater made the Code of Conduct was because many shoppers felt intimidated by the groups of youths hanging around Bluewater, with their faces covered (eg hoods and baseball hats). Also the language they were using.

Some of the subjects brought up in the Code of Conduct were:

All groups of more than 5 that are hanging around and don't intend to shop will be asked to leave. This applies to the whole Bluewater Estate.

Wearing any item which restricts the sight of your face will not be allowed, with the exception of religious headwear.

Any act of vandalism towards Bluewater will be dealt with and the police will be informed.

Bluewater Portfolio Manager, Matthew Clements says, 'Ensuring that Bluewater is a safe and pleasant environment for our guests is of paramount importance to us. We continue to work with our retailers, guests and partners such as Kent Police to ensure that this is maintained at all times'.

North Kent Supt Martin Hewitt says, 'Bluewater has a deserved reputation for its pleasant and safe environment. By clearly setting acceptable standards of behaviour, this code will allow staff and police officers to work together in maintaining the quality of experience for guests'.

The Code of Conduct leaflets are available at the information desks. For further information call 0207 802 8111.

Molly Brookes (13)
St John's Catholic Comprehensive School, Gravesend

The Furlong Times

The mystery of the stolen football trophy.

On the 8th of May at 12pm, Manchester United's football stadium was broken into. Only one item was stolen and that was the FA Cup trophy that they'd won last year. We spoke to Alex Ferguson, the Manchester United manager, he said, 'Me and the team are shocked, as we do not understand why some buffoon would want to take this beautiful trophy. We are also livid that the FA has told us that we have to pay a 2.5 million pound fine to pay for a new cup'.

The police are looking for any evidence at all from anyone who saw something unusual going on that night. There is a £100 reward for anyone who can give a good description or tell us anything that will help us to find this man or woman, as the police have no leads at the moment. We plead with the person who took the trophy, to please bring it back as soon as possible.

This picture is the only picture they have from CCTV and it does not give them any clues. If you recognise anything about this call the police on 345674, or with any other information.

Christopher Furlong (12)
St John's Catholic Comprehensive School, Gravesend

All Alone

'Katie, get up!' screamed Katie's younger sister. 'You'll be late for school.'

Katie's sister Bex always got up before Katie and was always the one getting Katie up. Bex was ten, five years younger than Katie was. Finally, Katie got up, went down to breakfast and got ready for school.

After school, Katie decided to go for a wander in the woods. The woods were beautiful! It was just coming to the end of spring so the sun was shining. She hadn't walked in the woods for a while now so she had forgotten how pleasant it was.

With a flash of lightning and a rumble of thunder, all this pleasure ended and turned to fear and coldness. It wasn't raining yet so Katie kept walking and trying to enjoy it. However, it didn't work. By this time, she was trembling, and she turned cold. She quickened her pace, gripping her school books even firmer. It felt like eyes were watching her and she felt herself running. Soon it was chucking it down with rain and she was drenched. All of a sudden, she felt something grab her and she fell! She put her arms out to stop her hurting herself, letting her school books go flying. She realised she was falling and nothing was stopping her. She kept falling, falling, fall ...

'Katie! Katie!'

She opened her eyes to see herself lying in her bed in her own room with her sister standing over her, roaring at her to get up.

Rebecca Berry (13)
St John's Catholic Comprehensive School, Gravesend

Back In My Day ...

School Discipline

William Hague had criticised the government's record on school discipline saying that Whitehall interference is preventing teachers from bringing proper discipline to Britain's schools. How can poor discipline in schools be reversed? Labour say that they have invested £131 million in improving discipline and prevention of truancy. School exclusions are dramatically reducing under their administration.

The Tories are attempting to bring back the days of tougher punishments for truants.

The Lib Dems say individual behaviour plans for children with exclusion orders.

Money is being thrown at the problem but it's being wasted on bureaucracy. The shadow education secretary, Tim Collins, has signalled that serious studies are taking place which could result in the law being strengthened. This means that anyone who assaults a teacher will be given the same punishment for assaulting a police officer. Some parties, like the Conservatives would introduce the 'the teacher protection bill'. Other parties would cut class sizes or make an investment in professional teaching. What would you prefer?

Each year one in three 11-year-olds leave primary school unable to read or write properly.

A million children truant every year.

A teacher is assaulted every seven minutes.

Teachers are given approx twelve pieces of paperwork a day.

'Teachers are expected to be educator, councillor, social work, police officer and arbitrator every day'.

Ashish Sharma (12)
St John's Catholic Comprehensive School, Gravesend

Game On!

The green coloured letters of 'Game Over' came on the screen.

'No!' Tim shouted. 'I just wish I could defeat Metta.'

'Tim.'

Tim looked up and gasped. Simon, the game Planet Dark's hero, was standing right in front of him. 'Are you real?' Tim asked.

'Yes. You want to defeat Metta. Well, here's your chance.' Simon grabbed Tim's T-shirt and threw him into the TV.

'Wha-? Where am I?' Tim wondered.

'You're in a game,' a slippery voice spoke.

Tim looked up, and saw the part alien and part robot, Metta.

'You dare challenge me?'

Tim jumped up and smiled. Everything, from the walls and doors to the uniform that was on him, was all real and from the game, Planet Dark.

Square on the chest, Tim was hit with an energy blast. Tim didn't have a chance to look up, before he was being aimed at again. Whilst he was running, Tim noticed he had a handgun in his hand. He dodged and shot. The alien screamed and the battle raged on. Bullets and energy blasts continued to be fired across the room. Then with one final shot, Tim aimed at the middle of Metta, where the alien and robot parts joined. As Metta blew up, Tim ducked.

'Tim, will you stop playing that stupid game!' Tim's mother called.

Tim looked up. He was back home again. The controller was in his hands, and on the TV screen, the blue coloured letters of 'Metta Defeated' stood out.

Jessica Tame (12)
St John's Catholic Comprehensive School, Gravesend

A Day In The Life Of José Mourinho

I woke up in a bright mood and I felt as if I could win today. It was Saturday and it was an important match today as we were playing Arsenal and the kick-off was at 3pm. It was 7.30am and I was hoping for a good training session, as we needed to win. My butler brought my breakfast and got my clothes and car ready.

It was very warm in the car so we set off for training, this was mainly due to the sun but also because I was nervous, if we beat Arsenal today we would go top on goal difference and we would only need a draw next game as Arsenal have their last match today. I know if we lost, Man Utd could go second and Arsenal could be the Champions.

When I got to training most of the players were practising so I just watched. Our training session went quite well but I knew we would have to improve before the match today if we wanted to win. The next challenge of the day was to name the team. Luckily most of the players had no injuries so I put together the team - hopefully the winning team.

At 3pm the whistle blew. I sat in the dugout throughout the first half but as the first half came to a close I felt dreadful and disappointed. In the second half I brought on 3 subs but soon John Terry got injured and the keeper was sent off. The final whistle has just gone and we had lost 4-0.

It had been a long day and at home I tried to have dinner and watch the replay on television. I knew we had the squad but it just wasn't our day. It was 1am and I felt really tired. I knew we could have won if we'd put in a better performance but we didn't so we got what we deserved. I don't think the keeper should have been sent off though. I think today the best team did not win but lost and with those thoughts I drifted off to sleep.

Michael Evans (12)
St John's Catholic Comprehensive School, Gravesend

Will My Parents Find Me?

On the 25th April, 2001, I was walking down an alley from school. My name is Joe, I have blond hair and blue eyes. I was on my way down the alley just minding my own business when suddenly someone or something took me from behind and covered my head with a cloth bag. Little did I know it would be three hours before I got to see daylight again.

All of the kidnapper's clothes were black. One of the men was wearing a black hat that covered his whole head. I was in the back of a white van scared and worried. We stopped in a car park and the kidnapper was outside. I wondered what he would do with me, would he kill me or sell me to someone for slavery? I didn't know. I had to get away or something but it was impossible so I left a clue for someone. I found a letter and pen in my pocket from school so I wrote on the back of the letter, 'Help I am in the back of a white van, I have been kidnapped, ring this number 21203525919, tell my parents'.

The kidnapper got back into the van and started driving again. We stopped after about one hour so I left another clue, it said, 'I'm roughly about 4 hours from home and I have been kidnapped. I'm in a white van, help, ring this number if you get this message ...'

Craig Ring (13)
St John's Catholic Comprehensive School, Gravesend

A Day In The Life Of An Apple

'Ah Bert, this is the life isn't it?'

We were sitting in our cosy new fruit bowl, complete with kitchen towel for lining. Better than those cold supermarket shelves, people prodding you as if you had no feelings! Each time I'd yell, 'Put me down you animal and stop prodding my (newly) waxed skin!' But I was out of that hellhole now and living the good life in the fruit bowl! What was this I'd seen? A huge peach-coloured claw hurtling towards me! The next thing I knew, I was in the black crevice with colossal, pearly teeth gnawing into me like a piece of meat. I was being whirled around like when Bert and I were being delivered ... a time I'd rather forget.

Whoa! I was sliding down this opaque tube and I think I saw what they call a 'heart'. For a few moments I felt gleeful, until I realised I was still plummeting down to my death! *Boom!* I landed on something soft and supple, a cushiony thing. It was the stomach, where all the food goes. I once heard the pineapples next door calling this 'the last mile'. It didn't seem too bad to me, a snug bed to lay on and a splendid view of the belly button. I'd say five star! But yet again I was on the move. I felt myself being transformed, no longer being my rose-coloured self! Water surrounded me and I could see the light!

So here I am in this waste hole, waiting to continue my journey internationally!

Lorna Regan (13)
St John's Catholic Comprehensive School, Gravesend

Prince Charming

Once upon a time there was a beautiful princess who met a handsome prince. They fell in love and lived happily ever after ...

Then I grow up and realised that nothing is ever that simple. I should know. I'm twenty-two years old and I've only ever had two boyfriends; Jarvis Wilson, a big mistake in school and Dane Samson, my boyfriend of six years. Life with Dane was wonderful. He was so fun and kind, but nothing is ever that easy. He was cheating on me with my best friend. Nice!

'Rachel. I'm so sorry!'

I looked up from my diary to find a desperate man watching me. 'Dane! I've already told you! I never want to see you or Natalie ever again! Understand?' (Did I forget to mention I only found out yesterday!)

'I didn't mean to do it, it just happened!'

'So you didn't mean to date my friend for almost a year behind my back? Is that it or is this all somehow my fault? Everything else normally is!'

'I know it was wrong, but ... Rachel!'

I ran from my office. I needed to talk to someone. But if I can't trust my friend, who else is there?

I arrived home to find the solution at my door. I was getting a new neighbour.

'Mum, I've got a date! He's called Niall, he's twenty-four and he's just moved in next door!'

I suppose my fairy tale could end happily after all!

Laura Webster (13)
St John's Catholic Comprehensive School, Gravesend

Armageddon

It was the night before the war of Havoc. The two kingdoms of Foredor had to negotiate. The kingdom of Heatherford was in the east and Ardonia was in the west. Armageddon was about to take place. Judgement Day had arrived. The armadas were ready as the centre was isolated, an army of ten thousand men on each side had arrived.

The sun was rising, the sky covered with black clouds, the rain poured down. Heatherford took control of the castle as Ardonia surrounded them. There was no way out!

Ardonia pulled out the siege weapons as Heatherford launched the catapults. A few dozen of Ardonean men breached the walls, one of which was Kalac. Kalac was a tall middle-aged man with long black hair and a handsome tan. Everywhere he went he took his long broadsword with him of which he killed his crazy father. Dozens of men surrounded this beast-like man as he swung his mighty sword around slaughtering all of them.

In the far distance he saw his arch rival Derrog. Derrog was Kalac's twin brother who left Kalac for dead. Derrog was responsible for the massacre of many innocent knights including his brother Foren. Kalac charged down the steep stone steps killing those in his way. As he entered the courtyard Derrog was slashing many of the Ardonean soldiers. As one of the castle walls was hammered by a siege missile, the battered stone wall fell allowing the Ardonean troops to charge. Kalac lunged his sword at Derrog as he blocked it with his shield. Derrog swung his sword towards Kalac as Kalac ducked and slashed Derrog's arm. As Derrog heroically continued to fight Kalac eventually tripped him and lunged his sword into Derrog's lung. The battlefield got brighter and brighter as a burning comet aimed for them. Every single warrior gazed up as they looked helplessly. Finally the comet struck and wiped out mankind forever.

Liam Barnes (13)
St John's Catholic Comprehensive School, Gravesend

Say Cheese

Ruby stared intently at the bizarre mould which was sitting just centimetres from her nose. It was, in fact, an ancient lump of Cheddar cheese from several months ago. No one in the family had dared to retrieve the festering lump; each hoping that someone else would be bold enough to do the deed. Nobody was.

Ruby shuddered and gave the dastardly dairy product an apprehensive poke. A revolting green gunk encrusted her finger, causing Ruby to give a horrified shriek. Almost simultaneously, she slammed the fridge door and headed up to her room. Little did she know that the cheese was gradually growing bigger and bigger.

That night, Ruby was restless. Despite which way she tossed and turned, sleep did not come. Eventually, when she was able to drift off, she was awoken by a sudden squelch. 'Just my imagination,' she reassured herself. *Squelch!* She could hear it more loudly now. *Squelch, squelch.* Whatever it was, it was coming nearer!

She opened her eyes and stifled a scream. An indistinguishable figure was looming in front of her. Her eyes were now fully accustomed to the dark and what she saw made her gasp. Something nauseating was slithering towards her, something that was a rather unattractive shade of green ...

The next morning, Ruby's parents were perplexed to find their child missing.

'She's not anywhere!' exclaimed her mother, 'and you know the weirdest thing? When I went into her room this morning, I swear I could smell Cheddar ...'

Verity Theophanous (13)
St John's Catholic Comprehensive School, Gravesend

King Koban

This is the legend of King Koban and his followers, the Kobeards. It begins in the early hours of the morning before the treacherous and ransacking Odayos try to capture and invade the ceaseless kingdom Alldaz in which the king rules. The king and the Kobeards have been terrorised by them for decades. The king decides to pull up his armies and followers for one last try to rid themselves of the reckless Odayos. There is a secret weapon held in the Kobeard's stronghold. A beast so fierce and powerful no one can withstand it.

The great Kobeards line up on top of a hill overlooking a black mist. The Odayos were emerging from the smelly marshes below.

'My friends, this is the end, unless we stop them. Do not think of now, but the future, where all is good and evil is no more. *Ride with me!*'

A large wave of horses and men swept down the hill, heading straight for the ghastly beasts. The two sides clashed together with a great force. Arrows were whizzing through the air, swords were clashing and shields were smashing. Men were weeping.

Clank clank ... the enormous beast was let out and was throwing the Odayos about with its sharp claws. It was a dragon! The battle was over by dusk. The Odayos had been defeated and the Kobeards had won. So much joy, contentment and exuberance were with the victorious men.

Ashley McMaster (13)
St John's Catholic Comprehensive School, Gravesend

The Force

In an unknown city thousands of light years away from civilisation, there lived a pure evil human called Terranus. He went from planet to planet destroying every thing and being in sight, no one could stop him. Except for when a tiny baby was born who could change all the history that had ever happened. He had the power to save every living creature and thing. He grew up with powers that we can only dream of having. Powers so great that he could kill people.

One day Terranus finally reached Khan's planet and he caused chaos all over, murdering millions of people. He had a weapon so evil that the Devil himself would use it. A laseraber. A red glowing laser that could slice its way through any material.

Terranus threw his laseraber, and without Khan's mum knowing what was happening, the laseraber flew through his mum. Her body fell in two halves. When Khan heard this news, he fell to his knees with guilt that he hadn't protected her. He got off the floor and was powered up with fury and he wanted to dominate Terranus. He hunted Terranus down by sensing his evil. He found his lair, inside a volcano that he controlled. With all Khan's rage he bolted Terranus. Terranus was paralysed. With the force, Khan picked up Terranus and stared into his eyes. He saw nothing but darkness. Khan launched him into the lava.

From that day Khan ruled the universe. For his bravery and strength only good existed from then on.

Antonio Esposito (13)
St John's Catholic Comprehensive School, Gravesend

A Day In The Life Of An Ant!

'Left, right, left, right, come on troops, keep those legs working,' I screamed to my ant army troops. We were collecting rotten fruit to keep us going through winter! 'Storm a-brewing!' I passed my urgent message down the line of ant troops and they all passed it on.

'Storm a-brewing!'
'Storm a-brewing!'
'Storm a-brewing!'

Finally it got to the 5,000th soldier. They then passed back the answering message, 'What do we do?'

'What do we do?'
'What do we do?'
'Stay low to the ground,' I bellowed.
'Captain says, stay low to the ground.'
'Stay low to the ground!'
'Stay low to the ground!'

We carried on through horrific weather and stayed strong.

Finally the storm stopped and we came into the main street. Suddenly two giant horses galloped through the streets. 'Horse alert!'

'Horse alert!'
'Captain says, horse alert, horse alert, horse alert.'
'What to do?'
'Make a run for it,' I ordered.

We all dashed and scampered fearfully and frantically around the horses' horrific hooves.

'Soldier down,' was the message passed up.

I was horrified. We had practised horse alert many times. 'Who is it?' I asked.

'Captain said, who is it?'
'Who is it?'
'Who is it?'
'It's Declan!'
'It's Declan!'
'It's Declan!'

How did I guess? 'The hunt is off let's leave!'

'The hunt's off!'
'The hunt's off!'
'The hunt's off!'
'God bless you Declan!'

Beth Gwynne (12)
St John's Catholic Comprehensive School, Gravesend

A Fly's Day

Buzzing around all day, passing the beautiful scenery I found myself heading straight for a spider's web. Dodging out of the way I felt the stickiness on my body and realised I was doomed. I may have been a big fly but the spider was enormous. As I was caught, the spider was coming over to me and I quivered with fear. Suddenly I saw my evil twin brother and screamed for help. I bellowed to Jimmy as he walked away, 'Don't turn your back on me!'

He gave a sly glare and I shouted, 'Is that a challenge?'

'Temper, temper, Billy, I wouldn't dream of challenging you. I got the fly's share of the brains but when it comes to brutal strength I'm afraid I'm in the middle of the spider's web. Speaking of spiders!' he nodded.

I frantically turned and saw the spider. It turned out his name was Bob and he was very friendly. 'Don't eat me!' I pleaded.

'Oh no, I don't eat flies,' he whispered.

I thought he was being sarcastic. It turned out he was being very truthful.

'Us spiders don't eat flies! It's just a myth. It makes us look bad too!' he said.

'What's with the web then? Why do you make it?' I asked.

'We can't help it. It's like the slime on a snail, it follows us!'

'Well what do you know?' I said.

Then the spider helped me out and I flew off.

Elise Apps (12)
St John's Catholic Comprehensive School, Gravesend

Balamory Axed

Children and adults all over the country are in much distress over the most loved island being axed on the BBC children's show, CBeebies. Some of the most loved TV characters will be sadly missed. They lighten up little ones' lives in the morning.

We have to bid farewell to the most loved people in the children's lives, like the bubbly nursery carer, Miss Hoolie, the loved funky policeman PC Plum and the famous inventor Archie and many more precious island members.

For you people who don't know what Balamory is, shame on you, but I am willing to explain. Balamory is an island and has many lovely members, all looking after the Balamory Day Nursery for children. The children go on many adventures with the locals. They look at the wildlife and many of the children have fallen in love with the locals and their favourite adventures.

The reason that this famous show has stopped being made is because the makers have run out of money. So please donate as much as you can to Balamory on www.cbeebies.co.uk and pledge all you can. You will make so many children and adults happy once again.

Claire Comiskey (13)
St John's Catholic Comprehensive School, Gravesend

The Rogue Princess

'Once upon a time ...'
   'For goodness sake!'
   '... There was a beautiful princess ...'
   'Spare me the mushy stuff!'
   '... Who liked ...'
   'To listen to heavy metal.'

'Princess Nala, Princess Nala, let down your golden hair!'
   'Sure, give me a sec ...'

Nala ran over to her little cupboard and pulled open the door, she looked for the secret compartment at the back of the cupboard. She reached in and pulled out a few water bombs and rotten eggs, plus a bag of some kind of leftover dinner. 'A bit of music I think,' she said.

The prince was shocked to hear heavy metal roaring out of the tower. Nala threw her collection at him.

'Argh!' he screeched as he ran away.

'And don't come back!' Nala yelled.

A bell rang. Her father wanted her.

She entered the throne room. 'Nala, I have called you here to tell you that I have chosen a husband for you.'

'No!' Nala stormed out of the room and ran to her tower. She bolted the door. Time for action. 'I will not marry a prince,' she said, reaching into her cupboard. 'I will not.' She pulled out a pair of scissors. In one swipe she cut off all her long golden hair leaving a small bit on top. She grabbed her pink hair dye. One hour later she had done a punk rock hairstyle.

Nala moved out, to a small cottage right next to a racetrack and bought a dragon. She lived happily every after.

Zoe Burton (13)
St John's Catholic Comprehensive School, Gravesend

A Day In The Life Of A Tortoise!

I opened my eyes to the first rays of sunlight. The sky was as pink as candyfloss and the wind rustled gently through the luscious vegetation. I clambered out of my cosy bed of leaves; I stretched and let out a huge yawn. For me it was the start of a beautiful day. I munched on a scrumptious and utterly juicy pile of leaves and within minutes was full to the brim and off on my expedition. I poked my head out from the huge blades of grass. The coast was clear and I made my way out to the big wide world.

No sooner had I stepped out of my house, there was a huge wall blocking my path. I wondered should I go around it. I was interrupted from my thoughts, when something huge opened a gap in this enormous wall. I took advantage of this and crawled through. Standing right before me was an enormous heap of leaves. I decided that this was the perfect place to have a little doze. I soon awoke to a blazing fire all around me! My whole life flashed before my eyes, was I going to die? I saw a small opening in the leaves and slowly began to plod towards it. I made it but just between the scales of my shell. Maybe that was enough of an adventure for me. I then sat down in another pile of leaves, hoping there would be no fire!

Joseph Coates (13)
St John's Catholic Comprehensive School, Gravesend

Soben's Wars

It was the night before Monbeys invaded the forsaking forest of Hallibow, and tried to capture King Soben of the eternal land. This rancour had been going on for years and would end tomorrow. There would be no mercy. Judgement Day had arisen. There was no way out of this enormous jungle; it was Armageddon in a cage.

A dark cloud arose that morning. King Soben gathered his army and they marched to the pit of death in the centre of Hallibow. The trees started to shake, all creatures fled to their homes. End of the world is now.

The sweat dripped off the Sobenos as the Monbeys approached. The disturbance in the force was great. The Sobenos switched their laserfabers on. All of a sudden the screeches of the Monbeys surrounded them and the dark red colour of their laserfabers blinded them.

The voice of King Mogo echoed round the jungle, 'Charge!'

The ground shook and laserfabers collided. Bodies fell to the ground like rag dolls. Blood oozed out of the bodies as the two kings fought each other. Neither of them could find a weakness in each other except one thing, warriors. The Sobenos seemed to be wiping out the Monbeys. All of a sudden a Sobeno ran at King Mogo but it was like he had eyes in the back of his head. But then King Soben slashed his head off. Terminated. They may have won the battle but this war had just begun!

Nathan Cronin (12)
St John's Catholic Comprehensive School, Gravesend

A Day In The Life Of A Rat

The past few days have been a real trial for me. I never imagined the world to be quite like this. Every day at dawn the great shiny beast which shares our cave trundles slowly out into the open before speeding off. My mum has told me not to be afraid of this beast because it does not do anything while it is in the cave. Apart from that the cave is quite empty with only a few large black mounds which crackle when you touch them and the collecting of flower pots where my nest is. I haven't really had time to explore anywhere else properly.

It happened a few nights back. I had been out exploring for longer than usual so I got back late to the nest. Although there was no nest; and no flower pots either. I crawled into the shadows and waited for my mum to return. Eventually I grew so hungry that I forced myself to move.

I cautiously proceeded into the kitchen. Normally I would never have ventured in here alone, but my hunger had made me desperate. Luckily all was dark and I could sense no movement in the air. Then I smelt it. The tantalising smell of cheese melting in the warmth. I spotted it lying on a small block of wood by the wall. In my elation I ran over to it. I could not believe my luck. I reached forwards and took a bite …

Michael Sears (14)
Sir Joseph Williamson's Mathematical School

The Alien Landing

'Blee, blee, bloo, bloo,' went the alien as they prepared to land on Earth.

'Now we are on the Earth we must blend in with the normal people,' said the other.

'Prepare for landing,' said the voice of the ship, 'and fasten your seat belt.'

Bang! went the ship as it hit the ground. Luckily it was night so no one could see them.

'Let's move,' whispered the alien.

'OK,' said the other.

Little did they know that they were in for a very big surprise ...

Michael Jelley (14)
Sir Joseph Williamson's Mathematical School

The Day I Trapped My Thumb In The Car Door

It was a dark, dreary, misty day; it looked as if the heavens were going to open up. We had just come back from holiday and we were unpacking the car.

I took something heavy out of the car. Then it happened. A thing most terrible, so terrible, I never thought it would happen. I pushed the door shut with my foot. It shut with a clink. The next thing I knew, I was standing there with my thumb shut in the door. At first I felt no pain at all. I opened the door and felt this sharp, searing pain in my thumb.

As I walked back to the house, I bit my lip trying to hold the pain in. I got back to the house and shut the door behind me. I put down what I was carrying and I am ashamed to say I screamed. My dad came in and quickly ran me up to the bathroom where he put my thumb under freezing cold water. It felt as if it was causing me more pain, but it was actually soothing it.

The next day we went to the hospital where the nurse checked it and sprayed something on it, it stung. The nurse told my mum off for not bringing me in earlier.

After all that, the nurse put lots and lots of plaster on it and left it to heal.

Harry Brown (12)
Sir Joseph Williamson's Mathematical School

Diary Of A Prisoner

Chicago Town Jail - Diary of Steven Millovich, Cell 201

28th October 1998

I've got 2 weeks today until I'm out of jail, finally. I'll get to see my daughter and Charlotte. I am, however, slightly apprehensive, since there are rumours going around about a jailbreak. I can't risk destroying the only chance I have of getting out of this hellhole. Tony in cell 202 told me about the break and also told me not to get my hopes up.

1st November 1998

The jailbreak (it turned out to be an attempt at taking over the jail) happened last night, it's like a constant riot now. Why aren't the police coming?

3rd November 1998

I've just found out that the prison officers are now being held in some of the cells. The cops still ain't here. One of the guards was killed today, because he was struggling. I do not approve of this, I am not an animal, so I won't act like one.

4th November 1998

What I saw today will never leave my mind. I looked out of the window (something I haven't done in a while) and saw flames bursting up all around the city. People are rioting. I know why the cops haven't shown up. At least the food's better now.

6th November 1998

Some of the big Mafia types who have been doing time in here, declared the jail as locked down. Hundreds of people are trying to break in. Why?

7th November 1998

They are coming.

Matthew Woodcock (14)
Sir Joseph Williamson's Mathematical School

A Day In The Life Of A Dog Called Gizzie

17th May 2005

I wake up at six o'clock every morning. Next I have my stretch and my yawn. The alarm clock is blurting out some gobbledegook, then Liam gets up and turns the alarm clock off. I go downstairs and get let out by Mark. I do my business and sniff the air. I can smell the food being cooked in the restaurant down the road and it is starting to make me feel hungry. The dogs next door say hello and I say hello back before being called in to have my breakfast.

I eat my breakfast, which is always pasta and dog biscuits and Gunner has dog meat and biscuits but I don't mind. I prefer pasta. After my breakfast I go back out. Now it is time for me to lay back down and go to sleep. Today my sleep is only disturbed by me having an epileptic fit. I hate my fits because I always try to get to dad but I can't move much. If I do get to him he tells me to lie down and keeps me from moving.

After my fit eases off I have another tablet to stop the fits from happening again today. Then I go back to sleep.

At about four-thirty I welcome Liam and Mark home, then I have my dinner. It's bed at nine.

Liam Sammon (14)
Sir Joseph Williamson's Mathematical School

The Blue Dress Code

If you have ever visited Bluewater on a weekend you will know that there are usually groups of teenagers who hang about and act as if they have nothing to do. These teenagers are a big problem in places like Bluewater; these are the people who behave in an antisocial manner. In a lot of these instances punishments have been given out such as bans.

To prevent young teenagers from acting like this the Bluewater committee have invented a new dress code. You are not allowed to wear hoods and baseball caps and you must not go around in groups of five or more. These new rules have helped security in a big way; now security can see people who are committing these crimes.

Last week Tony Blair released a report about antisocial behaviour and how we can prevent these crimes. He has enforced dress codes all around the country, especially on high streets. Many people believe that this is a good idea and that they will feel more comfortable around these teenagers.

Do you think that there should be dress codes in places like Bluewater?

Alexander Fisher (14)
Sir Joseph Williamson's Mathematical School

Blood On His Hands

They stood, eye to eye, their weapons and clothes heavy and sagging from the rain that covered them. Kal's sword was red from the blood of his enemies and dented, the blows it took were just as bad as the ones it gave.

The monster advanced towards him, swinging his talons at Kal, trying to score a wounding hit. His head was covered in the sticky slime from an open wound created from Kal's sword.

Kal sidestepped, then charged into the monster's side, his sword stretched in front of him. The sword penetrated the monster's skin and the slime began to pour out, covering the sword like flies on food.

The monster screamed in agony as it tossed and turned, trying hard to shake off the pain of his wound. It stumbled to the floor, Kal stepped back. The monster was dying and Kal could see it. Without a second thought, he leapt onto the wounded creature, stabbing and slicing the monster's torso.

The monster lay covered in rain and its own blood. Kal drew his sword to the creature's back and started to slice. It sliced the monster's carcass open along the spine. The monster split apart and Kal reached inside and grabbed the monster's heart

The monster's heart was still beating, even without a body. Kal's eyes sharpened on the heart, his grip tightened on the heart. It began to pop. Suddenly the blood splashed onto Kal's mouth, he licked his lips, 'Revenge is sweet,' he muttered under a sick smile.

Matthew Salt (14)
Sir Joseph Williamson's Mathematical School

A Day In The Life Of An Ex-Footballer

My eyes slowly flickered open; I rolled around to check the time, 8am. Oh no! I was late for training, my mind started whizzing around, thinking of all the consequences of turning up late for a training session. Then I remembered I no longer had to be at training. I had retired from football a couple of months ago. Football had been such a huge part of my life for so long and I could not get out of the frame of mind of a football player.

Now I was faced with another day of wandering aimlessly around the house. Ever since I had retired from football I had no purpose in life, no reason to get out of bed. Every morning I woke up thinking *what shall I do today?* That was how it was going to be for the rest of my life. No more big games, no more challenging training sessions, no more of that extraordinary buzz of excitement you get from playing professional football, just a lifetime of boredom. Football had always been my childhood dream, now it was over. I was never going to find anything as good as football, which was all I had ever been good at. What I had lived for was over, now I was pointless.

Thomas Ward (14)
Sir Joseph Williamson's Mathematical School

The Legacy

Aröglæsia, land of dwarves, wood, dark and high elves, humans and dragons, in the valley of Falcor, a little village prospered through ages. This settlement was insignificant to the world (well, according to the people), until a boy discovered something far more vital than he thought. In this ancient hamlet lived a boy, a simple young man at the age of sixteen, his name was Feragon.

He only had his father and his best friend Graledor for company. Since he was six years of age he had always loved the story of the Dragon Riders.

Graledor was a very wise man and always imparted his knowledge upon Feragon, this helped him greatly in his life.

One day, he was hunting in the Ragothorn Mountains. He had been hiding in the undergrowth since the morning dew, bow strung and arrow knocked, when finally, a herd of stags came strutting past. Feragon prepared to fire, when suddenly a huge explosion of white flames and sapphire dust wrenched him from the ground, sending him into a tree. He crept up to the epicentre of the blast and spied a white crystal with azure veins. He picked up the small stone, examined it then thought, *this might buy me the food that I lost in the blast.* He placed it in his bag and sprinted to Graledor.

When he arrived at the old man's hut, he shut the door behind him and showed Graledor. Graledor said it was a dragon's egg and told stories of elves and dragons living in total unison and how one elf found an egg. He became the first of the Dragon Riders. The elf's name was Feragon …

Alexander Thring (14)
Sir Joseph Williamson's Mathematical School

We've Finally Won It

England bring World Cup home for the first time in forty years.

England yesterday completed their dream in winning World Cup 2006 in Germany by beating the hosts themselves.

Wayne Rooney went on to score a hat-trick in a match that ended 4-1 in England's favour.

The England boss, Erikkson yesterday claimed it to be the happiest day of his life. In-between gulps of champagne, he told the Mail that he owed it all to the players who rose to the challenge of playing at such a high level.

In particular he praised wonder-kid Wayne Rooney, who scored 22 goals in the competition, making him the highest World Cup scorer ever. He also reserved special praise for the England skipper himself, David Beckham, who guided the team to victory.

'David guided the team like a true captain, setting an example of true effort to younger players in the team. Recent press reports into his personal life were brushed away by his tremendous performances', Sven reported.

England heroes Frank Lampard and Steven Gerrard were in tremendous form as per usual, creating an unbreakable rock in the centre of midfield. However the player who shone out the most was 21-year-old cover player Dean Ashton, who in the light of Michael Owen's pathetic performances was called up from the under 21s' squad.

'Dean has been incredible,' said Sven, 'bringing him into the team proved to be a huge success and I feel that if he continues to play well, his place will be safe for many years to come.'

Robert Smith (14)
Sir Joseph Williamson's Mathematical School

Heir To Austrian Throne Assassinated

Yesterday, Archduke Franz Ferdinand, heir to the Austrian throne and his wife, Sophia were killed whilst on a visit to Sarajevo, Bosnia-Herzegovina. He was 35 years of age.

This happened just hours after an earlier assassination attempt at ten o'clock. A man, who cannot be named for legal reasons, threw a grenade at the archduke's car, but the driver sped up, leaving the bomb to explode under the following car, seriously injuring two of Ferdinand's ministers and many people from the crowds lining the street.

The would-be assassin drank cyanide and jumped into the nearby river, but survived against all odds and was arrested by police. He is currently being questioned.

The fatal shots occurred after the archduke had spoken in Sarajevo Town Hall. He decided to visit the ministers injured from the earlier bomb.

Whilst driving down the Appel Quay, to avoid the busy town centre, the driver took a fatally wrong turn. Whilst reversing, the car drew just three feet away from a terrorist thought to be in the same group as the bomber.

He saw his chance and stepped forward, drew out his gun and shot three bullets, one entering Sophia's abdomen and one piercing Franz's neck.

An onlooker told us, 'He had evil in his eyes, the eyes of a killer.'

The assassin, thought to be a Serbian, Gavrilo Princip, was arrested and interrogated.

The driver told us of the terror in the car. 'The archduke held his wife and cried, 'Don't die! Live for our children!' but when we got to the hospital it was too late'.

This is one of the worst murders in the country's history, but the consequences are as yet, unknown.

Matthew Hilton (14)
Sir Joseph Williamson's Mathematical School

Persephone And The Pomegranate

Persephone was the goddess of the sea in Greek mythology. Zeus was her father and Demeter, goddess of harvest, was her mother. She was a very beautiful woman loved by everyone, especially Hades, god of the Underworld.

One day when she was collecting flowers on the plain of Enna, the earth suddenly opened and Hades rose up from the gap and abducted her. Demeter realised something was not right and that Persephone had gone missing. Helios revealed the awful truth to Demeter.

When Demeter found out, she withdrew herself from being the goddess of the harvest so the land became infertile. Zeus could not put up with this and so sent Hermes down to Hades to find out what was going on. Hades agreed that before Persephone went she would have a bite of a pomegranate. When she later ate it she was bound to the Underworld forever and had to stay there for one half of the year. The other months she stayed with her mother. When Persephone was with Hades, Demeter refused to let anything grow and winter began. When they were both together, Demeter allowed things to grow and therefore summer began.

This Greek myth explains how the seasons were created.

Harry Stevens (13)
Sir Joseph Williamson's Mathematical School

A Day In The Life Of A Cat

I wake up. My eyes scan the darkness for light, I find none as the sun is still asleep, along with my humans upstairs. I stretch my legs, yawn and decide to wake up my pets. I get up and quickly move towards the stairs. It takes me five seconds to scale the stairs.

It's getting light now as I open my mouth and wail. Instantly the whole house is awake, but it takes five minutes for my pets to get downstairs and prepare my meal.

The sun is high in the sky now. I have just found a mouse and killed it. I am feeling happy with myself.

I see movement in the bushes, there is something moving, a squirrel. I pounce on the creature within seconds, but I am too slow and the squirrel dodges out of the way. With a growl I prepare to give chase, but I realise the squirrel has gone and in its place is a big fox. I run as fast as I can back to my home, not realising the fox isn't chasing me.

When I reach the back door it is opened by the female. I rush in. Naturally the humans comfort me and bring me more food.

The sun is now asleep and so are the humans. I feel myself getting tired as well and before I know it I am asleep waiting for the next day.

Benjamin Chandler (13)
Sir Joseph Williamson's Mathematical School

Running

The long trees swaying in the wind cast a shadow across the snow-covered road. I couldn't let them catch me; I had to keep on running. My hands were frozen from the coldness of the night and I had to keep the snow from getting in my eyes. Just ahead, in the distance, I could see the brown metal girders that made up a bridge. I hesitated at the edge of the bridge, breathing heavily in the bitter cold air. I heard a noise and looked up; two large headlights of what looked like some type of tracked vehicle were beaming brightly. I looked left and right and stumbled into the dark woods enveloping me on either side. I crashed through them, clawing down anything that got in my way. I had to stop to catch my breath; I looked around and saw a small cottage in a clearing.

Inside I could see some children and their parents sitting around a small fire. I wiped a tear from my eye and remembered how old times used to be before this terrible war started.

Suddenly there was a shout from the woods and two men ran out wearing dark, warm clothes and each one was brandishing a rifle; they ran over to the cottage and started to smash the door with the butts of their rifles. Eventually the door collapsed and one of the men ran in.

I could just see inside that the man was pointing a gun at the terrified child's head. I couldn't let this happen.

Without thinking I made a sudden noise and one of the men spun round and saw me. I couldn't move, my feet felt like lead weights glued to the floor. He raised his rifle and took a shot! The mother and child sprang back in horror.

Instantaneously my eyes were bloodshot and I felt my legs start to give way. I stared at my stomach, shocked to see a small wound. The man lowered his rifle and squinted over the top to see what damage he had inflicted. I fell to the white, snowy floor and gently closed my eyes.

Charles Creese (12)
Sir Joseph Williamson's Mathematical School

On The Run!

I turned the corner into the alleyway, watching my back on every turn. The alley spiralled round corners and led to a dead end with only rubbish bins in front of me. I heard a faint motor in the distance. I dived into the nearest bin, the motor got louder!

It is hard to believe, hiding in this bin with my heart thumping in my ears, that only yesterday I had been sitting on the bus minding my own business.

Travelling home on the bus, looking out of the window, an old man sat next to me. I turned around to face him and noticed that his eye had been gouged out, probably many years ago and that he must have been in fights as his face was smothered in scars and burns. I swiftly turned my head back round.

He muttered something like, 'It's ma face isn't it?' Then he turned and looked me straight in the eye and said, 'Do you know what I do to people like you?'

I shook my head, too overwhelmed to speak.

'I eat them!'

I quickly leapt up and tore off the bus and as I stepped off he shouted out menacingly, 'I know where you live!'

Now off the bus, I started to flee for home, shaken and frightened. I didn't go through the woods as I thought he could be in there and I was right because I could see a skulking figure. I turned the corner out of sight and then heard the rusty sound of a motorbike's engine. I looked back and saw the motorbike coming straight for me. I started to run down a slope with trees either side of me. I ran down round a bend and into an open road. I heard the motorbike getting closer so I looked around and I saw a few trees. I threw my school bag into the trees so it didn't weigh me down and started to climb. I reached a safe position just in time as the monster on the bike came around the bend. He stopped and gazed around, then carried on. I gave out a huge sigh of relief.

That night I stayed in the tree. I was certain he would be watching my house and my parents were away celebrating their anniversary. I didn't sleep at all in case that lunatic returned.

In the morning I went into town to get some food! I came out of McDonald's and there he was with that face of his. I threw my coffee at him and legged it.

I turned into the alleyway and here I am now with a maniac in front of me …

Nicholas Walding (13)
Sir Joseph Williamson's Mathematical School

Working Together Is Best

In a small forest there lived three little pigs. Ken was the oldest, then Jon and the youngest, Carl. Their mother couldn't afford to pay anymore so they had to live by themselves and make money. Their mother gave them one hundred pig pounds to help them start off.

Ken decided that he needed to get some goods and decided to buy electronics and goods. He spent all his money on that and decided to get the other things he needed later but Ken had nowhere to sleep or sell his goods.

Jon thought he needed to get a shop first and decided to use all his money on a shop in the centre of the city. Like Ken he decided to get his other important things later but had nowhere to sleep and nothing to sell.

Carl decided he first needed a good place to live and then would decide what to sell so he could get a good night's sleep. He used all his money on a house with a king-sized bed. The problem was that he had no money to buy any goods and nowhere to sell them.

The three siblings decided to walk around the city to found out what else they could do to get rich like other people. While walking around they all bumped into each other and they found out what they each did. They had a great idea to work together. They soon all became rich and found working together was best.

Thomas Mo (13)
Sir Joseph Williamson's Mathematical School

Fish Fingers

One morning Sam Blangy woke up to the shrill sound of a scream next door. Next door lived the Terrors who were always watching horror films, day and night. Sam banged on the wall and he heard a faint 'Sorry,' in the background. He turned on the voice-activated telescreen as a hover car sped past the window with booming rap music.

Sam sat down and watched GMTS because he liked to know the news of the day.

A post van threw a newspaper and several letters and bills through the window, hitting him on the head, making a clunk, before dropping to the floor. Sam rubbed his head and picked up the paper, noticing that Ocelat United had beaten Kaligua 3-0 at liveball. This meant that Ocelat had won the ZA Cup four times in a row since 4004. He was shocked.

Sam stepped outside and took in a breath of polluted air and coughed. He could smell fish fingers. Sam hated fish fingers. A hover car skimmed just above his hair. He waded his way through the dense crowd, striding past tall, shiny robots, pushing them out the way. Sam hated robots as he thought one day they would take over all the businesses in the world.

Sam walked into work and sat at his desk where his computer screen welcomed him and asked him if he wanted a coffee. He said he preferred tea and out popped a cup from the CD drive. The work robot was on third patrol; the robot was watching him intently; so Sam jumped up, twisted the robot's arm around and over its head before snapping the arm as it dropped to the floor and said, 'Fish fingers Sir?'

Liam Borner (12)
Sir Joseph Williamson's Mathematical School

The Golden Claw

And there it was. The golden claw, just sitting in the dark and gloomy cave, shimmering from the moon's light, awaiting an owner. After 12 years of loneliness it had found a companion. The more human eyes watched upon it, the more beautiful it became. Time stood still, but then silence.

As Joe approached the magnificent golden claw, he hesitated, then shuddered as he thought about the power he would possess if he owned the wonder. After all the golden claw could turn anything to gold when it touched an object.

Joe continued to approach the marvel, wondering more and more as he gradually moved further. Just a few more steps to go. Then another wave of silence swept across the whole forest. But this time it was different. It lasted double the time and continued. Suddenly a high-pitched screech was produced from the guardian of the cave. It was the sirens. Their voices lulled anyone or anything into a false sense of security, then they would proceed to destroy you while you slept.

Joe had a plan. If only he could reach the monument he could turn the evil creature into a statue. As the last few steps approached his legs felt like they had turned to lead. He couldn't move.

Just one more step was needed. As the left leg lifted, Joe slipped. The forefinger touched Joe's abdomen and he instantly turned into a statue. Never to be found.

Jack Conn (14)
Sir Joseph Williamson's Mathematical School

Slayers

In a dark age, where demons reigned, there were battles, death, fury and flame. However amongst this dread lived courageous heroes who fought for the greater good, their might would eventually prevail.

At the heart of the human empire lived a bold man, who knew no fear. His name was Gamma Ultimo the wielder of the magical sword, Rex.

When there is no hope left you are sure to see Gamma and his loyal followers, the last slayers. In war the empire needs its heroes more than ever and thus our story begins.

Amongst the clearing stood a tall figure fully dressed in battle armour, glittering in the evening sun. His sword hung by his side, the magnificently powerful Rex.

He turned and muttered breathlessly, 'Tonight we fight to the death for the slayers, our kin.'

The five hurtled into the open, slicing through the air, but saw nothing. They stood there bewildered, in silence.

Suddenly the ground trembled, a huge demon rose from the soil. His hands were as big as boulders and clasped a chain and hammer. The swoosh of swords, scythes and axes filled the air. For a split second there was silence.

With a single scream, 'Attack!' the five hurled themselves at the demon like flies to a carcass. The sound of battle filled the air, metal clashing and wood splintering. The demon swiped his hammer round, sending Gamma and his companions flying. Gamma, with pure fury in his eyes, threw his head back and charged.

Alexander Siamatas (14)
Sir Joseph Williamson's Mathematical School

The Buffalo Soldier

Throughout the last 150 years there has been the legend of the Buffalo Soldier. The legend speaks of a persecuted man and the experiences of the American Civil War.

As the Bob Marley song goes, 'He was taken from the island, he was a buffalo soldier'.

'I've seen many deaths in my life, but this is bad and I live in Dry Gulch,' exclaimed the sheriff.

'Who do you think would kill a man in this way?' questioned the bar owner.

'Man! There are six people lying dead, covered in blood which I'm going to need to sort out!'

Nobody dared come out of their house for fear of accusation and the town was deserted. All you could hear was the sand flowing through the air. There was suspicion as a black man walked towards them with what looked like blood covering his shirt.

He stepped into the bar.

'What are you doing out here Dark Skin?' the sheriff questioned.

'Nothing Master, I was wondering why the town was deserted,' said the mystery man.

'What's your name? Why is there blood?' the sheriff shouted.

'Bern, Bernard is the name that my master gave me, but my friends call me 'The Buffalo'.

'Why?' said the sheriff.

'That is my own business; it has nothing to do with y'all.' Buffalo reached into his pocket and the sheriff pulled his gun. Before he could pull the trigger the Buffalo had already shot him.

Skip six years and six bullets before …

Ashley Collins (14)
Sir Joseph Williamson's Mathematical School

The Zanar Plane

'So … here we are,' Geller broke the silence that fell around the three friends.

'We've made it … nothing, nothingness.' Sarah continued the conversation that stood as still as they did on top of the lifeless Zanar Plane. There was now apprehension; as Michelle felt she had to continue in breaking the overhanging silence.

'I expected this; the end of the world we know. Untouched silence; even the air seems undisturbed by a gust of wind or a bounding creature.' Michelle described the landscape Sarah had travelled all her life to reach. Sarah had so many words in approaching her final goal, now it seemed she was speechless.

The Zanar Plane, the end of the known world, was a desert of no movement; no sand, had become unsettled and no creature had laid a limb on this tranquil emptiness of apparent land. The horizon lay low, like a cheetah in the grass of its prey and the few scattered rocks were as indistinctive as the white of fallen snow.

This was the outcome of Sarah's life. Geller and Michelle had supported Sarah every step of the way, guarding her with their lives. A lifetime journey for a landscape of barrenness had become Sarah's story; now to wait for the horizon to disappear from sight, with Michelle and Geller by her side. Her friends could only comfort and wait anxiously with her. They had fulfilled their duty and were to go to the better place - believed to exist beyond the Zanar Plane.

Daniel Herbert (14)
Sir Joseph Williamson's Mathematical School

A Day In The Life Of A Lion!

'I'm bored!' I exclaimed to Dad. 'I fancy some nice juicy zebra!'
'Jamie …' said my dad.
I looked at him very curiously.
'Shut up!'
You see, I had been up since seven in the morning and it's now ten and still no food. Dad told me that we would be moving nearer the vast and astonishing Serengeti. Auntie Wilma told me that it's predator heaven! I can't do anything though, until Dad hurries up and teaches me how to *hunt!* Oh yeah and my exasperating sister too! Ever since I can remember, I always gone and wandered off and wherever I go I have her as my shadow. How aggravating. She is good fun sometimes, like right now I was hiding in a log, waiting for her to find me!
'I can roar louder than you,' she'd bellowed.
'You can't even roar,' I told her back.
'Can.'
'Not.'
Now this would usually go on for ages, until I roar so loud it hurts my voice, but this time Dad had broken it up. 'Look,' he'd whispered …
To my eyes came shock. It was a green field with buffalo everywhere. Dad had said it would be our new home. There were rocks, tunnels and even logs and as usual, my sister and me were playing hide-and-seek.
I ran over into a log and as soon as I looked up, all I could see was a big, wet, soggy nose, with these massive, bulging eyes.
'Buffalo!' I screamed.

Jamie Degiorgio (14)
Sir Joseph Williamson's Mathematical School

Artemis Fowl: The Diamond Earring
(In the style of Eoin Colfer)

Mulch was pleased: the LEP had dropped all charges on him, and he had a pigeon egg-sized diamond in his pocket. He had stolen it from the stealth shuttle Opal Koboi had used to hide from Holly and Artemis when she tried to send a giant ore body to the centre of the Earth.

Opal was a crazed pixie that was hungry for power, but like all people who wished to take over the world, she was stopped. Holly and Artemis, with of course the help of Mulch (a kleptomaniac dwarf), combined their talents to stop her. Mulch was instructed to steal nothing, but he couldn't help it, it was his nature. Five hundred years of going in and out of prison left a mark, not the handcuff marks on his wrists, but the mark on his soul.

Mulch was itching to take the diamond out of his pocket, but he knew a relaxed thief was destined for prison, so he held on for a little longer. He reached Holly's apartment.

'Mulch, you're late!' Holly shouted at him. Holly had set up her own private eye business. She used to be the top Recon officer for the LEP, but she had quit when Commander Julius Root was killed when Opal planted a bomb around his chest.

'I'm sorry, I had to go to the bathroom after breakfast, and I ate something I shouldn't have.'

Holly didn't ask what happened. It was going to be nasty, whatever it was …

James Hall (14)
Sir Joseph Williamson's Mathematical School

A Day In The Life Of A Bee!

Again the sun rises and heat is once more. The hive awakens and a buzz is sent around. The work begins. The bees fly away in search for the food of life, their treasure. The bee will fly from flower to flower wanting, needing the treasure. When the bee finds the food he longs for so much, he collects the golden pollen grains. He's as happy as a clown; he's on the top of the world; feeling great. He returns the prize to the queen and the hive. He is a hero with all the other hunters. He has won the day. His life is fulfilled. He knows his work should be enough to get a personal thank you from the leader, the *Queen!*

All his efforts on the day help towards the beekeeper's profit and the hive's satisfaction of completeness. This effort will continue to mount up for the rest of this bee's short, but complete life.

Benjamin Lee (14)
Sir Joseph Williamson's Mathematical School

The Battle Of Okehazama

The huge Imagawa forces rushed towards Kyoto. If he could seize control of the capital, he would be shogun of all Japan.

'Lord Imagawa, the locals have vanished,' Yoshimoto, Imagawa's top general, said.

'Tell the peons to set up camp, and send out some scouts,' Yoshimoto ordered, as his horse slowed down.

'Yes Sir!'

It's all planned, we will not lose, and I am in Heaven's favour. I am Nobunaga Olda and I will rule Japan, a man thought to himself. He could hear his sister arguing in the next room.

'Whaddya saying? Of course we're gonna win!' Nobunaga's sister Oichi screeched.

'Please m'lady, don't get angry but we are greatly outnumbered. Our chances of victory are very slim,' a general whispered to her, looking scared.

'That means … erm … they have lots of people and we don't?'

Nobunaga walked out of his room and looked at his little sister.

'Hey brother, I'm coming too! You're gonna need all the help you can get!' Oichi laughed.

'What!' the general exclaimed. 'Promise me you will stay close though, Oichi,' Nobunaga said.

'Yeah! I will!' she replied, beaming.

Nobunaga's strategist walked into the room. 'It's all planned. Let's go,' Hideyoshi, the strategist, said.

The Oda forces reached the top of a steep cliff; heavy rain hid them from the enemy. But they could see the enemy perfectly.

'The outcome of this battle will determine the fate of Japan,' Hideyoshi said.

'This storm proves I am in Heaven's favour.'

'It proves nothing, brother!'

Andrew Turbine (13)
Sir Joseph Williamson's Mathematical School

The Dream Police

As Gabe turned, he saw a bullet whizz past his face. He dropped to the floor and pulled out two guns, returning fire to the Dream Police. The first of his bullets hit the officer in the stomach throwing him back. The second ricocheted off the wall. Gabe leapt over a wall into an abyss. He hit the floor with a clatter and stood in pain. He spun and aimed his gun at the temple of the officer who had followed him. Just as he went to pull the trigger he noticed it was Patrick, his accomplice. He pointed to the open door and Patrick took the hint. Staying in the shadows he slid to the door and silently shut it. When he turned, Gabe had gone. He saw a flash-bang grenade drop from the sky. The police were tailing them.

As Patrick ran towards the armoury of justice, he noticed that a bomb had been planted. He didn't have time to run. Gabe heard the last words of his companion. *'Run!'* Gabe did as his friend had insisted. He entered an empty room to hide from the force. He sat there eyeing up the door, a gun in each hand. What happened next was a surprise. From behind the bar came two grappling hooks and took from him his guns. He would be fighting by hand. As he fought the many police bravely, he was hit in the face. All he saw was black, nothing but black.

Jack Baker (14)
Sir Joseph Williamson's Mathematical School

PlayStation And Gumballs

Once there was a young boy named Dan who was obsessed with his PlayStation. He played it most of the day and most parts of the night. If his parents turned it off, he turned it back on. His parents even tried hypnotism, even that didn't work.

After a while his parents got fed up and told him if he wanted to play it, he had to play it all of the time, no breaks. He had to spend all night playing it, skip school playing it, miss shopping playing it, but he had to play the PlayStation, not go and play with his friends, not eat dinner, not do anything else!

So Dan agreed. He thought, *great, I get to miss school just to play PlayStation!*

That is where the fun ended. About two hours after this discussion, he was feeling peckish. He wandered downstairs and asked his mum for tea.

'Oh, don't you remember, you're not allowed to do anything except PlayStation,' said his mum.

'Oh yeah,' replied Dan, 'it doesn't matter anyway, I have a gumball dispenser in my room,' he muttered under his breath.

After his tea of six gumballs he began to play his computer game.

After a couple of days of constant PlayStation and eating gumballs for breakfast, lunch and tea, he went downstairs and said, 'I never want to eat a gumball or touch a PlayStation controller again!'

His mum replied, 'You had to learn it the hard way, didn't you!'

Simon Howton (14)
Sir Joseph Williamson's Mathematical School

The Doll's House

Nancy was nine years old. She lived with her grandma and grandad. The reason for this was that a few weeks ago, her mum and dad were in a terrible train accident and were killed instantly.

After the accident, Nancy kept to herself, not talking or playing with anyone like a normal nine-year-old would; but she did not know that all this would change.

'Nancy!' shouted Gran.

Nancy slowly walked to her Gran's voice.

'I wonder if you could help me, up in the loft. I need to get my old clothes down; it's for the charity shop.'

'Yes Nanny,' Nancy said, in a dull voice.

So her gran pulled down the ladder and sent her granddaughter up. She searched for the clothes and once she found them, she picked some up and uncovered a beautiful doll's house. 'Nan?' Nancy said.

'Yes!' Gran exclaimed.

'Can you help me to bring down this doll's house?'

'OK,' Gran said. 'But I don't remember any doll's house,' she whispered to herself.

When all of the clothes and the doll's house had been brought down to the foot of the loft, Nancy quickly grabbed the doll's house and ran into her room. Nancy studied the doll's house to find where it opened; she looked in one of the windows and saw the most beautiful doll, just staring out of the window.

Nancy wanted so much to play with this unique doll, and continued her search for an opening and found that the only opening was in the front door. She bent down to see what was inside and suddenly, the doll was there. She picked up the doll.

'Got you!' exclaimed the doll.

Nancy now found herself inside the doll's house, with the doll now a human; she had to wait for the next person to get her out.

Thomas Foreman (14)
Sir Joseph Williamson's Mathematical School

Busted!

'Gotcha!' said Detective Montgomery Peters. 'We've been after you since 6am this morning.'

'Good for you,' said Tom sarcastically.

'Take him through,' said Montgomery.

Tom was taken through to a dark, dull room containing nothing but a chair, table and a tape recorder.

'For the benefit of the tape, state your name,' said Montgomery.

'Tom Davis,' said the prisoner.

'Now,' said Montgomery, 'you have been detained for withholding evidence, and grand theft auto.'

'I think I know,' said Tom.

'Witty comments won't get you anywhere,' said Montgomery.

Montgomery's eyelids started to twitch as he became more and more stressed with the stupid comments from Tom.

'Now we have reason to believe that you, or one of your partners, has a stolen vehicle in their possession, would this be true?' asked Montgomery suavely.

'No comment,' replied Tom.

Looking exhausted, Montgomery sat down. 'I'm getting sick and tired of these silly games,' said Montgomery. 'Anything, please just tell me anything, no matter how big or how small.'

'Why should I tell you who stole the car?' Tom asked. 'What's in it for me?'

'If you tell me who stole the car, I will give you police immunity and you will not be liable for any punishment in this case,' said Montgomery. 'So, do we have a deal?'

'OK,' said Tom.

'So,' said Montgomery, 'who stole the car?'

Tom looked up, and with a gentle smile said, *'I did!'*

Lloyd Horslen (14)
Sir Joseph Williamson's Mathematical School

Government Gone Crazy!

Twisted Tony declares war on the rest of the world!

Tony Blair, the first president of Europe, has destroyed his reputation as a bad leader; today he has established himself as the worst leader in the history of the world. Our great leader, Mr Blair, has decided to declare war on the rest of the world.

Mr Blair has threatened to take action against the rest of the world before, but has been advised not to by every member of the Cabinet. Mr Blair has also tried to put forward this idea to the House of Lords and the House of Commons and failed; Mr Blair received three votes.

I hear you asking, how then did he get this idea to be approved? He did it by, you can tell that only Tony Blair could think of this great idea, starting a new party! He managed somehow to branch off from Labour, making a new political group called 'Against The World'.

Mr Blair made this statement today, 'I've decided that America and all the other countries, you know, the ones that aren't America, have gone too far!'

Turn to page 6 for more information.

David Beckham's right foot has starred in its first major Hollywood film. Mr Right Foot stars in the blockbuster 'A Foot for a Foot'. This is the sequel to the smash hit 'A Foot is Always Watching'.

Jacob Roberts (13)
Sir Joseph Williamson's Mathematical School

A Day In The Life Of Al Kaholic

Friday, 13th March 2000

Hello. My name's Al Kaholic, and before you think about it, I'm not an alcoholic. I'm 12 years old and today is my birthday. As a birthday present my parents are finally sending me to school after constantly asking them for eight years. My mum and dad are a bit strange, because my mum just cannot stop talking and my dad is scared of grass. I also have a stepsister called Eve Hill, and she ... tries to kill me. Anyway, it's time to go to school now!

Six hours later ...

School was so fun today! ... I wish. I was bullied by this weird boy called Dane Geruss. Apparently, he has this 'problem' of flushing people's heads down the toilet. Guess who he did it to today? *Me!* There wasn't really anything else going on at school, so there's nothing else to say. Anyway, I have to go downstairs now because I have to blow my candles out.

Two hours later ...

Oh great! As I was about to cut the cake, Eve snatched the knife out of my hands and tried to slice my leg off. I tried to 'retaliate' by calling her a 'Barbarian', but unfortunately she threw me into a well. I don't know how she does it, since she's only six years old, however she sure is strong. Well, now that I'm trapped, I'll probably never escape, so my last words are, 'Shoot! I'm running out of ink! Someone help me!'

Haroon Latiff (12)
Sir Joseph Williamson's Mathematical School

The Task Of Fericles

Fericles wasn't the strongest, nor was he the smartest, but like Hercules, he was invincible. He couldn't be killed by bullets, but he could be killed by a falling boulder. This didn't worry him until his mother sent him to school …

When Fericles arrived at school, his tutor was the weedy weakling, Durystheus. Durystheus was a cruel tutor and set judgmental homework. One of Fericles' tasks was to kill the Nemean lion. This lion was said to be invincible, but Fericles didn't fret.

When he arrived at the mouth of the lion's cave, he called to it. 'Come out you stupid lion or I'll shoot.'

A great roar from inside the cave bellowed out and Fericles cowered at its intensity. As the lion emerged from within, Fericles took out his AK47 and fired a couple of rounds at it. The bullets ricocheted off and fell to the floor; undeterred, Fericles then took out his machete and slashed at the lion. It was unscathed and advanced ever further. Fericles then decided to use his lunch his mum had packed him. He took out his cheese sandwich and nibbled on it. He then threw his Granny Smith apple down the throat of the lion. It had a perplexed look as it swallowed it down, but then it abruptly fell down dead at his feet.

After defeating the lion, Fericles returned home with pride at achieving such a prestigious award. His mother asked him what he'd done to get it.

'The usual!' he replied.

Tom Brookes (13)
Sir Joseph Williamson's Mathematical School

Beast Book

I was going into market one day with my parents. Then I spotted a book stall with the most magnificent book, bound with leather and 'Beast Book' written in gold on the front.

I then went into an alleyway with my new book. I opened it at the first page, which had a painting of a butterfly. Its name was underneath, 'Sapphire Princess'. Suddenly the book shuddered, then the butterfly fluttered out of the book. I then turned to the next page which had a red dragon under a palm tree. I tried to shut the book but it wouldn't while the dragon roared out of the book.

I then thought that there might be something else in the book that could fight the dragon. I opened the book in the middle. Out came a white horse with swan wings; a hippogriff.

I jumped onto the hippogriff and shouted, 'Fly your fastest to the pebbly waste!'

It soared away with extreme speed. The dragon saw us and chased us. The dragon could not keep up though.

There were no trees to be seen for miles. The dragon was getting very hot because of the heat so needed to rest in the shade, but there weren't any trees. I landed and opened the book. It roared and glided into the book. I then shut the book. I then went back to the alleyway and let the hippogriff go to its page. I then went home with my parents.

Alexander Mold (13)
Sir Joseph Williamson's Mathematical School

Nesfaratus' Doom

In a city, over sixty millennia ago, a young teenager lived completely unaware of his destiny about to take an unexpected turn. In the city of Nesfaratus, Ori, a boy with brown hair, a red shirt and a pair of brown trousers, lived.

'C'mon Riu! We haven't got all day!' Ori yelled up to the window of a sandstone house.

'Coming!' replied the girl, as she jumped down from her window. 'So, we going?'

'Yeah,' he said as he gazed up into the morning sky. 'Huh, yes! They're here, the guardian dragons are back!'

As he said this, four dragons flew over the semi-desert city. The lead dragon was a red, the second a blue, the third a yellow and the last was a green. Both teenagers gazed into the sky at the city's guardians, unaware of the figure behind them shrouded in a black cloak. Ori heard something, pushed Riu out of the way and jumped back as a dark ball whizzed past them. As the dark warrior turned to run, the four dragons swooped down firing fire, water, lightning and gusts, binding him. As they did this, a sword was produced. Ori grabbed it.

He yelled, 'Elemental blade!' As he said this, a light came out of the sword and hit the shadow warrior.

In this second the dragons, the shadow warrior, Ori, everyone and all of Nesfaratus were sucked into the sword. All that was left was the sword, until the day when Nesfaratus will be resurrected.

Grant Field (13)
Sir Joseph Williamson's Mathematical School

A Day In The Life Of A Parliamentarian

What a horrible day; well, another horrible day actually. They all are. It's just march, march, march, trudge, trudge, trudge. It's all a waste of time, this civil war.

We had to get up way too early today. Six o'clock! And what reward do we get? More stupid marching! We haven't even had to do any fighting yet, and I've been here for five months. But we still have to 'stay on our guard' and 'always be alert'. What rubbish!

I suppose I'm benefitting from this quite nicely though; good money to be had, being in Cromwell's New Model Army.

I'm not even sure what the fuss is about; this war. I just got swept up into it all when a Parliamentary Scout came to our village looking for 'fighting men'.

Food's a bit boring. We had bread and cheese for lunch; again! Not much variety in the army kitchens! But the thing is, they give us the food, force us to eat it to regain our energy, and just forget to slip in the fact that the cost is coming out of our wages! It's the same with our uniforms. What a rip-off!

Maybe the lack of action isn't so bad though. Have you seen the weapons? They can do as much damage to you as they can to the enemy! There's as much chance of the thing killing the opposition as there is of it backfiring and killing you!

This army lark's silly; too much like hard work!

Richard Stockwell (12)
Sir Joseph Williamson's Mathematical School

A Day In The Life Of A Worm!

6.30, it's a bit early for me, but you know what they say, the early worm beats the bird.

I slithered out of the ground poking my head out of the flower bed that I called home, and took a long hard look around the garden. No one was around; for once there was no danger of birds or the cold, sharp blade of death. I decided to go visit my brother, who was towards the east side of the garden. It was quite a long trek, but I hadn't seen him for ages.

I started my journey, always cautious of any unseen birds across the garden. I heard a large cry overhead and started to hurry, unaware of the large, pink, dirt-infested chewing gum that I slithered into. I tried to free myself from this pink prison, but I couldn't. Then my worst dream came true, out of nowhere a sparrow landed right next to me. I suddenly panicked and uncontrollably tried to free myself. This only excited the bird even more and it started to advance. I decided to give up and let the bird win. As the bird went for the kill, I heard the best noise I will ever hear: the deep, rough bark of a dog. In a split second it was barking the bird away. I was safe, but for how long?

Callum Bowie (13)
Sir Joseph Williamson's Mathematical School

A Day In The Life Of A Bird

I usually wake up about 7am, but today was different. The worm family at the bottom of the old oak tree were celebrating a new birth, and everyone was going to be there, so I had to make it my duty to get up and greet the new one in a friendly way. I went to the bird bath in the garden to have an early splash to freshen myself up before the big greeting. After, I went to the usual breakfast bar behind the house for a worm sandwich, and off I went …

Down to the bottom of the old oak tree where the celebrations began. Not everyone had arrived yet, so I decided to perch on the low-hanging branch above and wait for the cavalry to arrive. I could see banners and micro balloons below me where the family grouped.

Before I had expected them to exit, they walked out. I thought to myself that this was the time to go. I flew down from the old oak tree to greet my unexpected prey. The first try I missed, but the second try I got him and flew up to the top of the old oak tree to have my well-earned treat.

Before long, it was getting dark and it was nearly time for my night bath, but I couldn't be bothered to because of all the action today, so I went straight to bed, where I wait for my next adventure to appear.

Jonathan Prenczek (13)
Sir Joseph Williamson's Mathematical School

Mother Nature Has Her Say

When the Earth was created, God put Adam and Eve in the garden of Eden and mankind began. Things became complicated, people began to exist and God found his time being very stretched. He began to feel he was neglecting the Earth for the people in it. So he created a very special woman to take charge of the Earth so he could concentrate on the people. Her name was Mother Nature.

Things went well for a while, but then Mother Nature got cross with the people and how busy and neglectful they were of the Earth. She gave them many weathers to help grow their crops, but Mother Nature noticed that in the hot sun, people were lazy and sat in it and did not look after the land. She told God of her worries, but he said that people needed time to rest, so Mother Nature said that she would sort it for herself.

Mother Nature gave people sun and time to rest, but after a while she would get very cross and send lightning down to make people scared and would make it rain so plants were watered and people could not lay in the sun.

God did not like this and grumbled at Mother Nature every time that she did this. This can be heard as thunder. Mother Nature said that she would only send this lightning after long spells of warmth and rest but still, after she sends lightning, God can be heard grumbling.

Kierran Boden (12)
Sir Joseph Williamson's Mathematical School

The Parents' Evening

Tonight it is parents' evening, but I'm not going, so it won't be as embarrassing as last year. *What!* You want to know what happened? Alright, it's a long story and it started when my mum came down the stairs in a crop top that showed all of her fat; all her blubber was bulging out from her middle. She had her tight, cropped leather trousers on, which she had worn as a costume at a 'Grease' party. The seams were ripping on those. Her vibrant coloured platforms were hideous. I told her to get changed, but her huge earrings blocked the way to her eardrums.

When we got there, we went to see my English teacher. My mum started picking her nose, and it's not normal for anyone to pick their nose. My English teacher said how well I was getting on, and suddenly my mum shouted, 'Ooh, my little honey bunny. He's such a good boy.'

The head teacher was just about to make a speech and everyone went silent, but my mum just shouted, 'Look, Babykins, it's the head teacher, *cool!*'

Halfway through the speech my mum got thrown out because the members of staff were not very happy about her behaviour. I followed her out with a red face because she'd embarrassed me.

That is what happened last year and now my biggest fear is that she is going to embarrass me again. Please don't tell anyone else. Never say a word of it.

Iain Hopkins (11)
Sir Joseph Williamson's Mathematical School

The Barn

Something big and hairy dashed across the cornfield like a rocket; it headed for the barn. I walked slowly across the field towards the barn. I could feel the corn scraping and tickling my hand as I crossed further and further over the field.

As I got close enough to see inside the barn, I saw lots of old farming equipment scattered over the place, odd-shaped tools and even a rusty old tractor. As I looked around the barn, my eyes adjusted to the light and I could see piles of boxes, it smelt as if animals had been using it as a public toilet.

I walked in and said, 'Hello, anybody there?' There was no reply, apart from a quiet grumbling coming from the corner of the barn. I could feel the hairs on the back of my neck stick up as I saw a big, grey, hairy creature picking away at something in the corner of the barn.

As I tiptoed quietly towards the creature I was trembling with fear and nervousness. When I got closer to the creature I could make out the shape, it looked familiar to me, but I couldn't remember what animal it was. At last I got so close that it turned and growled loudly, *'Go away'*. I didn't move, I didn't know what to do. Just as I was about to turn, *'Raaaa,'* it leapt at me and that's when I saw him …

Samuel Dixon (11)
Sir Joseph Williamson's Mathematical School

Mr Jeffery Atkins

Jeffery Atkins is a rapper for 'Murder Inc', an American record company. He is on the way to do a concert at The Elephant and Castle for the release of his new album.

He is a man in his mid-thirties who glides smoothly into the train, blue jeans, New York vest and a black bandana. Passenger 54 moves his feet so he can sit down. As he is about to sit, he nods at a very pretty lady his own age and then sits down, pressing his index finger against the line of his mouth.

Jeffery is an American pondering Britain and he thinks to himself, *a honey like that back home would have been all over me if I looked at her like that, here all the honeys are very shy and quiet. This country is nice, but not many people talk about rap, but like to talk about security, jobs and CCTV.* Jeffery isn't really bothered, as long as they keep buying his albums *I wonder how many of the passengers that are on this train are going to go to the concert? Is it going to be packed out, or will I barely have anyone there?*

Jeffery is very nervous and is going over the songs that he is going to sing from his new album in his head. *First I am going to start with 'Livin It Up' and then I will do 'Smoking and Riding' and then 'Between Me and You', I will finish it with 'Always on Time'. I wonder if Christina and Ashanti are there yet?*

Jeffery's phone rings, it is Ashanti, she asks where he is and he says that he will be there in three minutes.

Jatinder Singh Dosanjh (15)
Sir Joseph Williamson's Mathematical School

How The Cockerel Got Its Crow

One morning as the sun was rising, the cockerel sat on top of its barn overlooking the fields of barley, which surrounded the farm where he lived. It was a beautiful morning, the sun rising over the hill slowly, the barley swaying gently in the breeze. There was only one cloud in the clear blue sky, which seemed to be hovering over the cockerel.

Suddenly a dragon appeared from the cloud. The cockerel noticed the dragon was crying. 'What's the matter?' asked the cockerel to the dragon.

'Everyone in the clouds is laughing at me because I have nothing to make me look courageous and brave like the lions do.'

The cockerel thought for a few second and had an idea. 'You can borrow my horns from my head for the day to show the other creatures you are courageous, though you must return them to me by sunrise tomorrow morning.' The cockerel was a very kind creature and liked to help the other creatures.

The dragon replied to the cockerel, 'I promise I will return your horns by sunrise tomorrow,' and off he went to the clouds with the cockerel's horns to show the other creatures.

The next morning the cockerel sat on its barn watching the sunrise, as it did every morning, waiting for the dragon to return. However the dragon never returned to give the cockerel back his horns. The cockerel was angry, as his kindness had been abused. The cockerel bellowed out a crow to call the dragon, but he still did not return.

That is why every morning the cockerel crows when the sun rises, in hope that the dragon will return with his horns.

Harry Jennings (15)
Sir Joseph Williamson's Mathematical School

Korea Crisis 2009

Sergeant James Langley held his SA-80 close. He was ducked down behind a burnt-out North Korean Jeep, the heat of the flames only made him feel worse, had all his men died? Had he led them to their deaths? A dead Korean lay next to him, hideously burned. He was in the Jeep when the Allied troops opened fire. At the time, in the battle, you don't feel like the enemy are humans, until you realise you've killed another human being.

'Sergeant?'
'What the hell?'
'Sorry Sir, if I startled you.'
'That's OK soldier, are you the only one?'
'Yes Sir, I'm afraid no one else made it through, Sir.'
'How many enemy are there?' Sergeant Langley asked.
'Four Sir, and one jeep with a driver and gunner.'
'OK, here's the plan …' Langley went on to explain their almost suicidal tactics.

Later, Langley looked over the side of the Jeep. He edged forward, reached for a frag grenade and threw it over the burnt wreck. It landed in front of the Jeep and exploded. The front of the Jeep raised high into the air and crashed back down with a thunderous thud. Both the driver and gunner died. The driver's smashed-in face rested on the horn and the constant noise echoed all around. The other four Korean soldiers instinctively took cover. Langley shot around the side of the Jeep he was hiding behind. He shot a round of bullets at two of the soldiers, killing one of them. The other shot back, hitting Langley just above the heart …

Daniel Barrett (14)
Sir Joseph Williamson's Mathematical School

Diary Of Tony Robinson

Chicago Town Jail: Cell 202
October 27th 1998

Told Steve about the so-called jailbreak everyone's been talking about. I'm sure he won't go along with it because he actually *wants* to get his parole. I don't trust anyone, so I'll stick with him.

Wild rumours about riots have been flying around, but I don't want to worry Steve, since his wife and daughter are in town.

Chicago Town Jail: Cell 202
November 2nd 1998

9am: The jailbreak happened yesterday in the dining hall. Three people got killed but we have control of the jail. The Mafia types who are running the jail have put me in charge of guarding the entrance in case the cops come. I 'can be trusted' apparently.

5pm: I'm still guarding the doors. No cops yet, surprisingly. The riots must be horrific. Better not tell Steve.

7pm: I've been guarding the doors for ages now, but a while ago Frank shot a screw saying, 'He'll thank me later on …'

Chicago Town Jail: Cell 202
November 6th 1998

6pm: We can really see the riots now and Steve is getting really worried. I can see the flames and smoke from my window. Lost at poker today which is always a bad sign. The cops *still* haven't shown. Must be busy.

9pm: An hour ago the 'bosses' told us to lock down the jail and barricade the doors. When we asked why, they told us to look out of the window. It looked like hundreds of people are trying to break in! why though? Maybe the cops are doing a good job …

Chicago Town Jail: Cell 202
November 7th 1998

People broke in, lots of fighting. I'll write … if I live.

Max Cambridge (14)
Sir Joseph Williamson's Mathematical School

A Day In The Life Of David Beckham

Today I woke to a typical Spanish day, the sun shining and my sea view from my bedroom as beautiful as ever. I rushed downstairs, realising the time, to a huge uproar from my three boys. I gave my wife, Victoria, a kiss and clambered into my BMW. I realised the paparazzi were lurking just outside my driveway. I carried on as ever to training in the suburbs of Madrid.

When I arrived, I found the press as usual were following me, but there were more today for some reason. The smell of paella slightly sickened me so early in the morning. I carried on training as usual, although my left knee gave me a bit of trouble. I saw the team doctor who showed me some English newspapers, the headline in one, 'Becks and Sven Dressing Room Fallout!' I couldn't believe it, and the reports were not true at all.

I had to hurry to my promotion with Adidas to model some new gear and the boots I would wear in next week's clash with FC Barcelona.

About one hour later I left and hurried home to see if I could catch Victoria and the boys before they left for their monthly visit to the UK. I didn't, so I made myself a salad and grabbed a bucket of 'Ben & Jerry's' and a had a night in with 'Kill Bill Vol II'.

Sam Huggett (13)
Sir Joseph Williamson's Mathematical School

Soulless

Eliza and Sarah were walking home from school after a late night swim. They were hurrying to get home because they wanted to watch an episode of Buffy. Eliza suggested they take a short cut through the cemetery.

They were walking through the cemetery when Eliza heard a noise in the trees. 'What's that?' Eliza asked.

'Probably just a squirrel or something,' Sarah replied.

Eliza and Sarah continued walking through the graveyard. However, they didn't get far before a mysterious man appeared from the darkness.

'Hello, my lovelies,' said the tall, dark-haired stranger, 'what are you doing out this late?'

'Go away. We're late,' said Sarah.

'That won't be possible.'

As he said this, he pounced on the helpless girls and bared his fangs. He was a vampire! He was about to sink his teeth into Eliza's neck, when suddenly a large creature jumped from the shadows and attacked the man. He pulled a stake out of his pocket and pushed it through the vampire's heart. The vampire immediately turned to dust.

'Who are you?' Eliza asked.

'I know. He's Dave,' Sarah replied.

'As in … ?' Eliza asked.

'Buffy? Yes.'

'Why are you here?'

'I'm here to find a new Slayer.'

'Good luck!' said Eliza.

'Thanks. You should be more careful walking through a graveyard at night. The world is full of vampires looking for an easy snack like you. I hope I won't have to save you again. Goodbye.' With that, he disappeared back into the shadows.

Michael Davies (14)
Sir Joseph Williamson's Mathematical School

A Day In The Life Of An Alien Intent On Taking Over The World

Message: Vonen to base. Day 24 of invasion.

It is an unknown hour of the morning, or maybe night - I can't see the sundial properly. Cheapest clock I can afford, I think it's solar powered.

I have discovered much about these humanoids involving their interests and pastimes. At the 'school' they serve one meal a day of what is widely known as 'cafeteria food'. Apparently, they are able to consume *and* digest it! I am being forced to eat more of my precious quamba supply every day; if I do not obtain non-toxic, edible material, I will surely not survive the month.

Message: Vonen to base. Day 25 of invasion.

It is the time of lunch at school. I am writing this hurriedly as I cannot hide the message device for long. The children of this race now pay less attention to me than before. I used to be the 'new kid' but now they have a new 'new kid'. In a way I feel neglected, but they are now oblivious to my actions.

Message: Vonen to base. Day 25 of invasion.

This school building seems to be an area of punishment. The children are forced to behave infinitely. Today we redeemed ourselves after yesterday's 'glue incident'. I am now convinced that the school is a building of military endurance to protect the planet. I shall return to the base and investigate further. Invader Vonen signing off.

Greg Ceely (14)
Sir Joseph Williamson's Mathematical School

A Prisoner's Diary Entry

Ten years I got. Sent down to save my brother's skin. He's a footballer, you see, high paid and all. He got caught smuggling drugs and I took the rap, so he's giving half his weekly wages to me. I'll be rich when I get out, but I deserve it for what I did.

It's hell in here. I was led to my room by a guard with a bald head, and he looked at me like a piece of chewing gum stuck to his shoe. I just wanted to hit him, but I knew I couldn't cos I'd just get longer.

My cell is so boring, with its plain white walls and rusty bunk beds. There's a toilet in the corner, complete with urine stains, and the whole cell stinks of it. You'd think they would've cleaned the cell since the last person, but it looks like it's never seen a mop. I tried to sleep last night but I couldn't cos of the constant sound of cell doors slamming, and prisoners hurling abuse at each other.

I can't take this, always being slated in the news; I've only been in here for three days, and I'm already counting down. I'm seriously thinking about grassing on my brother, but that would lose me money and ruin his career. Anyway I've only got another three thousand, six hundred and forty-nine days left in this hellhole.

Kurt Robinson (14)
Sir Joseph Williamson's Mathematical School

Mount Ice Murder

'What kind of haunted house is this?' exclaimed Helen.

'Okay, let's calm down, Helen,' said Oliver quietly, his eyes never turned away from his desktop screen.

'How can you be so calm when five people in our class turned up dead? This is all Jan's fault. She's the one that convinced us to come on this ski holiday,' shouted Helen.

When she finally cooled down, after a whole bottle of orange juice, she murmured, 'Oliver, I am scared. What if we are next on the list?'

'We won't be,' said Oliver firmly. 'Besides, I have a pocket knife with me and the door is electronically …' Then, he looked around. As he focused back onto the screen, his face became very serious. Helen did not dare disturb him. When he got into deep thoughts such as this, no one could move him, even if a gun was pointing at his head, he wouldn't notice. Helen could not stand the silent tension. She opened her mouth to speak, and a deafening gunshot sounded.

Helen only got her senses back when she realised that Oliver was standing up to leave the room.

'Let's go!' said Oliver.

Helen continued to stare into his sea-blue eyes, thunderstruck that his expressions could remain unchanged, despite knowing that they might lose their lives.

He saw her blank face and laughed softly, 'We need to hurry or they might think we are the murderers.'

Helen's face stayed unsatisfied.

Christopher Lee (14)
Sir Joseph Williamson's Mathematical School

Bandicoot The Majyker

'So you're a magician then?' asked Tamis timidly.

'A what now?'

'That is to say, you do magic, do you?'

'Magic? Magic? Suggest I do magic, eh? Trying to undermine my reputation in front of all these people are we?' Sweeping his arm in a wild arc around the empty room. 'That is the *meanest,* most *spiteful* thing anyone has ever said to me!' he bellowed, showering Tamis with spittle.

'So you don't do magic then?'

'No! I do majyk; it's very different. Magic is all trickery and mirrors and disappearing elephants. Majyk is … w … it's majyk!'

'So you're, what, a majyker?'

'Exactly, now if you don't mind I need to run away.'

'From?'

Bandicoot looked up from packing his seemingly bottomless case, bemused at the naïvety of Tamis, 'A loan sharke, who else?'

'A … what was that?'

'A loan sharke.'

'Yeah, that one. You mean a loan shark?'

'Principally yes.'

'Right, so why the weird pronunciation, or spelling or whatever the hell it is?'

'For starters, it's entirely a mental thing that changes it; secondly it makes it sound more mystic. By the way, you don't happen to have vast sums of money about your person I could borrow and never return do you?'

'Well yes, as it happens. But you have to come with me to help me find the holy grail.'

'That's easy, turn left at the glassblowers, and it's in the alley before the bakery. Money?'

'Thanks, here you go. See you around sometime,' she said over her shoulder, as she dipped through the tent's arch, departing.

Harry Clarke (14)
Sir Joseph Williamson's Mathematical School

Insanity

'They're coming, all coming here now. There were dark shapes flashing around haunting me, hounding me. They wouldn't leave. I screamed, twisting, flailing. Someone sprinted in; I tried to hit them, they retreated. More returned with them, but I couldn't take them all. I ran into the corner and cowered. One of them whispered to me, this calmed me. I knew that voice from a distant memory. I blacked out.

I awoke. I was not scared this time; lighter colours were swirling around. I knew I had something to look forward to, but I could not remember what. I stayed like this for several units (at this point in my life I had forgotten the measurements that are hours, and measured time in units). Then as always after a 'happy' session, memories began to invade my brain. A screaming child. A tribunal hearing. Death, corpses everywhere. Dark hooded faces. Pain filling every sense. I smelt pain, heard pain, saw pain. All my senses during these flashbacks were distorted as I confused reality with imagination; heard what I saw and tasted what I felt. Soon, havoc ruled in my brain and I descended somewhere, sometime, and I screamed for everything to leave to black out again. Nothing happened, so I sat and rocked back and forth with fear.

Freddie Morgan (13)
Sir Joseph Williamson's Mathematical School

The Penny Trail

After an hour, Jack finally admitted that he was lost. He was a stubborn, money-loving schoolboy, who had wandered into the woods alone. Now and then he would listen for any sound, but all he would hear was his pounding heartbeat and the nearby trees swaying in the mid-autumn breeze. Every step he took, the leaves around him became deeper and soggy leaves brushed his legs. He felt a chill up his spine. There was a great darkness which surrounded him, but suddenly the sparkling moon shimmered through the trees and he saw a line of pennies. So he followed the shining penny trail. He walked through brambles and climbed over boulders. He never thought to look up at what was above him; he was far too interested in the money. As he grabbed the final pennies, he realised that he couldn't feel the forest floor anymore, but he could feel a rough concrete below his feet. In the distance, he could see flaming torches that he followed, and it was there that he discovered that this place didn't look like a palace. It looked like a tomb. As he followed the torches, he saw an ancient scroll on the slimy wall. It read, 'You come to obtain the jewels of Aradereous, but no one leaves this place alive. You cannot escape.'

Just then, he heard the door slam shut and arrows fired at him. He then realised this place was booby-trapped, but it appeared too late.

Joel Calder (12)
Sir Joseph Williamson's Mathematical School

Alien Attack

The complex smelt of their rank breath. Dobus jumped as the nearest tannoy sounded over the dull thudding of the security forces as they ran to cover all the exits. 'Delta squads 1 and 4 to main entrance. Repeat, Delta squads 1 and 4 to main entrance.'

The men around squad Commander Dobus moved out of whatever cover they were hiding behind. They followed their commander along the main corridor of the subterranean military base, home of the 41st platoon of the Black Shadows, the mysterious elite of the US planetary army.

'OK people, let's lock and load, live ammo only, we don't know what's out there. Visors down, only communicate on secure channels. 2 and 7, get those missile launchers ready,' barked Dobus as his squad positioned themselves around the blast door that, for the moment, was holding back the alien horde.

Outside the blast doors, the surrounding area had been blasted to dust. The aliens swarming around the doors looked on the scopes to Commander Dobus like a huge, pulsing, green being, but in the middle of all this an arcane, wide-muzzled, cannon-related weapon was being set up. 'They're coming.'

Andrew Brown (12)
Sir Joseph Williamson's Mathematical School

A Day In The Life Of A Goldfish

Hello. I'm Blinky, a goldfish. I, like most fish, have around a three-second memory. Why am I talking about memory? Never mind. My day normally starts with me 'waking up', and this morning I found a castle in my bowl! Amazing! I'd never seen it before!

Hello. I'm Blinky, a goldfish. I, like most … wait - I've already done that bit, haven't I? Where was I? Oh yeah - my day. After 'waking' it starts raining food pellets from the surface of my bowl out of a box. Then this *huge* creature comes in and stares at me with his mouth half open, watching me. Huh? Who watches me? What am I talking about? Um, hello. Who're you? I'm Blinky. Hold on - I did it again, didn't I? I have a very small memory you see, so I tend to wander off mid-sentence.

After it rains, I do my exercises. I swim around my bowl 50 times and then I practise going up and down. Then for the rest of the day, I watch the house. I am a very effective guard-fish, you know. In all the time I have been here, the house hasn't been broken into once.

Hey! This morning I found a castle sitting in my bowl! Amazing, eh? Sometimes you just don't notice these things. Don't know how it could have gotten there, seeing as I never close my eyes.

Sometimes my owner leaves the TV on and I can watch cartoons all day. Human TV is very interesting. I can't quite remember what was on this morning - can't think why.

At the end of the day it rains again and I go to 'sleep'. That's about it, my life. Wow - look at that castle! How did that get there? I could have sworn it wasn't there a minute ago …

Matthew Thomson (12)
Sir Joseph Williamson's Mathematical School

He's A Fire Starter

Last night Jonathon Smith, a 15-year-old student from the York High School, was arrested on suspicion of attempted murder, vandalism and breaking and entering.

Jonathon Smith broke into number 25 Hitchliffe Court, home of the Daniels, Alex, Chelsea and Ben. Jonathon broke in through the downstairs living room window and sprayed his initials on the TV, mirror and on all four walls. Then he moved on to the kitchen and turned on the gas oven, grill and microwave. This added up to make a fire in the kitchen. Jon then ran out of the house and back to where his gang hung around, Littlebrook Lane, outside Mr Singh's grocery shop.

Meanwhile back at the Daniels' house, the blaze had spread to the dining room and by 3 o'clock on Saturday morning, the hall. The fire detectors went off and woke up Alex Daniel, who then woke up his wife, Chelsea. Chelsea ran to her son's bedroom and whisked him downstairs, but the way was blocked, so they waited upstairs for the fire brigade.

We talked to their neighbours, Mr and Mrs Dixon, who said, 'We don't know who'd do this to them, we've never seen so much terror in our lives'.

Jonathon Smith has already received an ASBO and is said to face a prison sentence.

Gavin Hyder (13)
Sir Joseph Williamson's Mathematical School

The Arena

I stood close to my opponent. Corpses lay around, the wounded being dragged away. The sandy floor beneath my leaden feet seemed a million miles away. My opponent looked like a giant and he held the largest axe I'd ever seen, enough to cut me in half in one slash. His face was large and beads of sweat clung to his forehead.

He clenched his hands around the handle of his axe and lifted it to chest height. I raised my sword … my heart was in my throat. Suddenly he swung his axe, I ducked underneath jabbing my sword towards his legs. He stumbled backwards. I raised my sword and stabbed into his thigh. He cried out. He pushed forwards and knocked me to the ground; he raised his axe high over his head and brought it down upon my arm. I watched the blood spurt out: it oozed across the floor. Tears came to my eyes. I saw my arm laying limp next to my body, the pain coursing through me. My enemy brought his axe to my neck. I raised my sword once again, fighting the pain, trying to defend myself.

He finally brought his axe down, penetrating my chest. The pain grew and blood poured out over my hand. I dropped my sword, there was nothing I could do. I cried out, but in place of sound, only blood came out. I lay on the ground as one of the corpses, waiting to meet my brothers that had fallen before me.

Edward Brookes (13)
Sir Joseph Williamson's Mathematical School

Life As It Is

We live in a world with hate, fear, pain and disbelief. Have you ever wondered why we were brought here? For which purpose and why?

We are gluttonous and deceiving, We speak evil words to each other and are evil in our actions. We kill like wild beasts and tear each other apart; bone by bone, heart from heart. Every man is a sinner and since the moment sin entered 'our world' we forgot God. It showed us wrong and inhumane ways.

There are two sides to everything: the good road and the bad road to life. And even with a choice of picking, we always seem to choose the bad road. The human race is not what we are … but humanity's disgrace. Even animals treat each other with more care and love for each other than we ever do. We are talented and gifted and God gave us powers beyond anything else. So why are we the ones who use it so irresponsibly? Are we really the intelligent ones? Who knows? All I do know is that we shouldn't be blinded by the dark side and we should stop our cruel pitiless ways before there is nothing left of us. We should live every day to the extreme, because you never know what will become of you tomorrow.

Karl D'Souza (13)
Sir Joseph Williamson's Mathematical School

A Day In The Life Of A Ping-Pong Ball

'I am so awfully bored,' said Ping.

'So am I,' said Pong.

'Who the hell are you?' asked Ping.

'An illusion,' replied Pong. With a puff of smoke, Pong was gone.

'Oh no, not those boys again, they hit me ever so hard. Ping watched the two boys set up the table. When they had finished, one boy got Ping out of his box.

'Argh!' screamed Ping.

He was served backwards and forwards, and backwards and forwards, and backwards and forwards. Then he fell on the floor. 'Ouch!' He was picked up and hit backwards and forwards, and backwards and forwards. He fell on the floor again. 'Ouch!'

A boy came running over to him, but he slipped and fell on Ping. 'Ouch!' said Ping. The boy got up. To his surprise he had squashed Ping. The boys started to kick him. Backwards and forwards, and backwards and forwards. Ping flew up into the air and landed in a bin. 'Ouch!' said Ping.

Through a hole in the bin, Ping could see a rubbish truck. *Oh no,* he thought, *I must get out!* He jumped up and down, and up and down, and up and down, but however hard he tried, he couldn't get out of the bin.

Ping found himself being rattled around. He looked up and he saw a big hairy chin. 'Ugh!' said Ping. He flew through the air into the back of the truck, where he was shaken; backwards and forwards, and backwards and forwards. 'Ouch!' said Ping.

Ping saw a sign that read, *Recycling Plant.* Ping was thrown through the air and landed in a hot oven. 'Ouch!' said Ping. He was melted and melted and melted and melted. 'Ouch!' said Ping.

The remains of Ping were made into Pong.

Lee Maingard (14)
Sir Joseph Williamson's Mathematical School

The Wearbeasts

The wearbeasts broke into a run, saliva dripping from their mouths. The beasts leapt over the walls, they needed no ladders or rope. Micholas drew his axe, slamming it into the back of the wearbeast's head. The beast collapsed on the walls, his large talons lashing out. The next beast leapt at Micholas, howling a blood-curdling cry. Micholas, his axe still wedged in the last wearbeast's skull, jumped at the wearbeast chanting the Rainan war cry. Micholas punched the beast in the gut; the beast, injured and humiliated, retreated.

On the other wall we were not faring so well. The wearbeasts had gained a foothold and were slowly forcing us back. Our men fled. The wearbeasts turned on them, ripping them limb from limb. The huge beasts charged at the hospital, but standing in the way were the white-caped priests. They charged at the huge beasts, tulwars in hand they pushed the wearbeasts back. Adam dived under the huge talons and drove his blade through the beast's stomach. The huge beast collapsed on top of Adam. He screamed and kicked, but the carcass didn't move off him.

I ran to his aid. My mind raced. I was stopped by the last three wearbeasts. The first one bounded towards me. Its teeth gripped my arm; I struggled to keep consciousness. I beat the top of the creature's head. I fell to the ground. The crows were circling above and the three creatures leaned closer. The one who had bit me, lifted up his taloned hand …

Ryan Badham (12)
Sir Joseph Williamson's Mathematical School

Deep Space

Down in the deepest parts of space, something was dormant; it had been for years. Many pilots spoke of this legendary creature, and claimed to have seen it. But today it awoke. After sleeping for millennia, the monster was finally awake, and stared at a small ship speeding towards it.

The alarm sounded loudly and a helium-enriched voice exclaimed, 'Incoming, impact.'

Captain Tortilla jumped up, already dressed in marine combats. He ran swiftly to the control room, his long black hair swaying from side to side. As he looked out at the depths of space he saw nothing, yet the impact timer was zero, but as he looked closer he could see a large black creature. The creature's enormous head turned; its huge eyes were staring right at him. Suddenly it dove, smashed through the control window and Captain Tortilla was knocked off his feet.

As he woke, he realised he was lying in a wet pool. As he sat up, he realised it was his own blood. He looked up to see the monster licking it up. He looked and saw that he was missing a leg. He had to kill it. The captain threw his arm back, reaching for something to use as a weapon. His hand reached a sharp rod. He reluctantly embedded it in a gas canister which was about to explode. The ship flashed into a mass of colourful explosions, and Tortilla and the monster flew away. They died.

Alex Jarvis (13)
Sir Joseph Williamson's Mathematical School

Japanese Soldier Found In Remote Jungle - He's Still Fighting The War!

On the remote island of Ocacia in the Pacific Ocean, Japanese Second World War soldier, Huka Chi, is still fighting for his country. A research team for oil company Texaco came across the 82-year-old private still defending his island. It seems hard to believe that this poor man was still fighting his own private war.

In 1944, Huka was one of 30 Japanese soldiers sent to Ocacia to defend this island against the western enemies. They were told that it was an important lookout post, watching for American ships on their route to Japan. Unfortunately this band of loyal soldiers lost radio contact with their base in October 1944. They continued to watch over the Pacific Ocean for any signs of enemy attack. They were unaware of Japan's surrender in 1945.

In the years that followed they became self-sufficient by growing their own crops, breeding livestock and using drinking water from the fresh water springs. They were still unaware that the war was over, and as they guarded their island, one by one they passed away due to old age and illness. The sole survivor, Huka, has now been moved to mainland Japan, where he is receiving medical attention. He is also to receive the Tushca medal of honour, for his courage above and beyond the call of duty.

Stephen Rowe (13)
Sir Joseph Williamson's Mathematical School

The Hogworm Troll

Once upon a time in the middle of Hogworm Swamp lived the ugliest, most vile troll ever seen. He had a large green and purple body, was about seven feet tall and 15 stone in weight, but as nimble as a mouse. The people of Hogworm were terrified of the grotesque troll and would not go near the stinking swamp.

Jim, who was a curious 11-year-old that liked adventuring, had just heard about the troll from overhearing his friends talking. As he was so curious, he wanted to see if it was true. He collected his stuff and headed for Hogworm Swamp.

An hour into his journey, he came across a cave with a *No Entry* sign outside. Being curious, Jim entered the cave with nothing but a lantern and some chocolate buttons.

'Who goes there?' roared the troll.

'A curious young boy,' replied Jim.

'I can tell you're scared. I can smell it in your scent,' claimed the troll.

'I'm not scared, I just needed the toilet!' said Jim. 'Are you scared of me?'

'How can I be scared of a measly little boy?' snapped the troll. 'But what I would like is a juicy, crisp little … ?'

'Argh!' screeched Jim, as he ran out of the cave.

'All I wanted was those chocolate buttons!' shouted the troll to the boy.

Nicholas Simpson (14)
Sir Joseph Williamson's Mathematical School

Ambush

Harpies. Two of them. As tall as Magnus, with leathery bat wings. With the hard light of the sun behind them. The mercenary could see their muscular, brown-black bodies covered with thick shaggy hair, the breastbones that pulsed with the beat of their wings and the filth-encrusted claws that stabbed from their hands and feet. Their tiny yellow eyes scrutinised Magnus. He could see the sharp teeth behind their snarling lips and smell the carrion on their breath. He could almost taste the blood that matted their fur.

He was supposed to hide, hoping selfishly that they took somebody else from the caravan he was guarding instead. He was supposed to die here, amongst the blood and futility and the never-ending cold. But he had always been arrogant enough never to do what he was told.

Magnus forced down the first harpy, and stamped on its throat, grinning wildly as the creature issued a gurgling howl. The second was shrieking for its comrade, and rounded on him.

'Come on!' he screamed. It dived, slashing with marauding talons. Magnus took a gash to the shoulder, but swallowed the pain down and kicked it in the shin. It squawked and dropped a metre. Kneeling in the small of the creature's back, he slammed his fist over and over the creature's blasted skull until it gave way and his arm was slick with blood to the elbow.

'What have I done?' he whispered, and as he succumbed to unconsciousness, he began to cry.

Sam Day (14)
Sir Joseph Williamson's Mathematical School

The Death Of Charlotte, Daughter Of Gemini

Gemini, the rain god, watered the plants and crops for mankind. He had a daughter called Charlotte. She was the most beautiful girl you'd ever seen, and Gemini cherished her with his life.

One day, Charlotte asked her father whether she could go to Athens to visit her friends. Gemini was unsure whether to let Charlotte go to Athens because of the dangers of the journey. Eventually he decided to let her go.

The following week she said farewell to her father and left on her journey. On the way, Charlotte had to pass through a forest. Some hunters were looking in the forest for deer and bears. They had not made a kill in over three days and were desperate to find something. One of the hunters spotted Charlotte through the trees. Mistaking her for a wild animal, they blindly took aim with their bows and arrows and fired. Charlotte felt a sharp pain go up her arm and in her chest. She cried out in pain. Her legs crumpled beneath her. She fell to the ground, dead.

A week had passed and Gemini started to worry. Charlotte was due back two days ago. Gemini sent people out to look for Charlotte. He waited two days for a report. When the report came, it was devastating news. Charlotte had been found dead in the forest, with an arrow in her shoulder and chest. Gemini was distraught. His daughter was dead. To avenge her death, he sent a flood through Athens.

He did this every year, on the anniversary of the day she was found dead in the forest.

Alex Cochrane (11)
Sir Joseph Williamson's Mathematical School

Derelict

Smash! The ball had bounced and shattered the glass of the derelict building behind me. I groaned. *Not again,* I thought to myself. It was the third time today and it was my turn to fetch the ball. 'Can't one of you get it?' I asked.

They shook their heads and teased me about being a 'believer'.

I ran up and carefully crawled through the broken window, avoiding the jagged shards of glass still standing on the window ledge. My face cringed when I entered the building, at the stench of the desks and furniture infested with woodworm and other insects. I was in a large room filled with desks and old, bulky computers. Paper and smashed beer bottles were strewn across the floor. I gazed around the room, but my ball was nowhere to be seen. There were two doors leading off from this large room; one was labelled *Managing Director*, the other had no sign and was swinging on its hinges. I chose the door labelled *Managing Director*. When I entered the room there was a mass scurrying of tiny feet. I shuddered. I *detest* mice; small, creepy, sneaky little things. When I had calmed down, I saw my ball lying in the corner of the room. It had landed on a pile of cans and cigarette butts. I quickly picked up the ball using the tips of my fingers, so not to get any germs on them. I then quickly picked my way through the mess to the broken window and that's when I saw it … !

Douglas Ebanks (12)
Sir Joseph Williamson's Mathematical School

Zeus, Record Breaker?

On the 23rd August, Mount Olympus, King of the gods, Zeus, broke a world record for the biggest number of children produced by a god. Zeus managed to produce 13 children, but not by the same woman.

First came Herakles - the hero of heroes. Then Perseus - rescuer of Andromeda. Persephone was next - the wife of Hades. Aphrodite - the goddess of love. Then it was Epaphos - son of Lo and Zeus. Sarpedon - the King of Lycia. Hermes was next - Herald of the Immortals. Athene - goddess of wisdom. Dionysus - god of wine was next. Next came Rhadamanthys - one of three judges of the dead. Then came Apollo - the god of prophecy, music and healing. Helen - the fairest woman in the world. And last, but not least, was Aries - the god of war.

The last record was broken by Odysseus, who managed to produce 10 children. Again, not all by the same woman.

Our special reporter, Jason, along with his crew of Argonauts, managed to get an interview with Zeus and ask him why he wanted to break such a record. He said, 'I always wanted such a big family because my father ate all of my brothers and sisters. I would never do that to my own. I was brought up secretly, with nobody to play with, and it was such a lonely time. I never want my children to feel like that. This is why I have had many children, so that they will never be lonely'.

Joseph Dodson (12)
Sir Joseph Williamson's Mathematical School

Glitch

Atrus' vision blurred as he touched the surface of the book, and he felt his body jerk upwards as he transported to Spire. Go in, check all the nuts and bolts are tight and make sure there's absolutely no way he can escape. Atrus had designed this whole place so that Sirius, his craftiest son, couldn't escape and destroy any more of his handcrafted worlds. Atrus picked up his linking book, his key out of this world and back to his home, and locked the linking chamber door.

Atrus inspected his handiwork as he descended the staircase into Spire. The thin, cavern-filled mountain towered high above the barren, empty planet. Ever-dark, rolling clouds and spectacular electrical storms filled the sky. He shivered as the haunting voice of the singing rocks of Spire echoed up from below him. Everything seemed to be correct as he had written.

As he turned to begin the arduous climb to the linking chamber, he noticed something out of the corner of his eye. A glitch. Something he hadn't written had found itself into *his* world. How could he have been so careless? He started up the stairs, but it was too late. It was growing. There was only one thing for it. If Sirius got his linking book there would be no hope for his peaceful home and his loving family.

Atrus hurled himself off the edge of the desolate mountain and into the dark abyss.

Joshua Heyes (14)
Sir Joseph Williamson's Mathematical School

The Trooper

I levelled my gun and then squeezed the trigger. The surprised man turned to look at me, his eyes meeting mine that split second before the bullet hit home. When the bullet penetrated him the shell exploded, causing his ribs to fly everywhere, blood to splatter out against the ground and wall, followed by a giant thud as his body hit the floor; his expressionless face distorted by the shockwave, his torso destroyed.

Being trained to fight doesn't make it easy. The fact that if I had not shot him, he would have shot me, comforted me little, but nothing mattered now the terrible deed was done and now he was dead.

'Tim! What happened? I heard a shot,' the voice in my ear said.

'I'm OK,' I voxed back. 'Just a Mirk. Perimeter search complete.' I then switched my com-bead off. Reloading my Bolter, I started to trace my squad.

Only Shaftesbury Street stood between my squad and me, and that was one hell of an obstacle. The street had been under the Mirk's control since the invasion, and in that time God knows what they'd done. Quite easily gun emplacement galore.

As I approached the street, the ominous silence was only broken by the sound of explosions and gun fights all over London. Checking my gun and setting it to burst, accuracy would not be needed in my flight, just enough to keep their heads down. I plunged into Hell itself, not expecting to exit.

Timothy Hampton (14)
Sir Joseph Williamson's Mathematical School

The Thing

Suddenly out of the darkness it came hurtling towards Tommy, a dark green figure, screaming and slurping. It came closer and closer until it was within touching distance. It grabbed him by the neck with both hands; it came so close, Tommy could read his dog tags. They read, 'The Tiger'. Tommy was frozen on the spot as it breathed deeply in his face. Tommy was petrified, looking around for something, anything, that may be in the slightest help to him.

The thing shifted him around and released his neck, expecting Tommy to fight back. The stench of its breath was becoming unbearable. It raised its arms high above his head and hit Tommy hard on the shoulders. Tommy fell and lay there in fear. That's when he saw it. There was a long pole staring Tommy straight in the eye. Tommy grasped it with one hand, as he couldn't feel the other one. The thing picked him up with both hands and fully rotated his head, psyching himself up for a strike, but Tommy struck first, right at its left arm. The thing fell, plunging Tommy down with him …

They both lay there, motionless!

John Kallend (14)
Sir Joseph Williamson's Mathematical School

Alone

When Billy woke up on the 22nd April 2007 in his house in Scotland, he had no idea of what was going on in the world outside his bedroom window. He spent a few moments absent-mindedly gazing at his posters and calendar before struggling to his knees and climbing out of bed.

As was routine in the mornings, he took his dressing gown and went to brush his teeth. Feeling now slightly more awake, he returned to his room to get dressed. As he was rummaging through his drawers in search of underwear, he glanced at the mirror on the wall. Staring back at him was a boy of thirteen, wearing a mop of dark brown hair, and two large, brown eyes.

After getting dressed and furiously trying to get his hair looking at least half decent, he wandered lazily over to his window to see what the day's weather was like. As he pulled open his long maroon curtains he stared out, well he didn't actually stare out at anything because there was nothing there, just an open, barren plane.

'What the … ?' were the only words that he could say, he was bewildered. What was he to do? *Mum and Dad,* he thought, and with that ran out of his room and into his parents' bedroom, but there was a small problem. His parents were gone.

His face dropped as he realised the true horror of the situation. He was alone …

Lee Bell (12)
Sir Joseph Williamson's Mathematical School

Alone

A swirling mass of soft mist slithered along the wet earth which I was traversing. Chills flowed through my aching body as I cautiously moved towards the ancient forest. All was terribly silent; no companions, no voices, no footsteps, this was all I could think of when suddenly, the call of an owl put me on the edge. I stared into the gloom of the black forest, expecting to view an owl. Instead I saw a large, humanoid creature materialise from the shadows; a troll shaman.

The huge creature came into my view; a ghastly thing with thick, grey, rough skin, standing some eight feet tall with malicious spiked teeth gnashing together, with blood and spittle falling from its venomous fangs. The troll shaman leapt towards me with an enormous mace weighing more than myself. I, however, was fast and nimble in those days, and I dived to the left of the troll, drew my ruby sword and slashed the side of its torso, breaking the thick grey skin. This blow caused the evil troll to draw its last breath, and with this, he screamed a fierce howl. This troll howl could be heard along the forest and soon, many other troll shamans were materialising from the shadows to avenge their kin.

More than twenty more troll shamans rapidly advanced to where I was standing, their huge bodies convulsing with rage. All the red, hypnotic eyes were focused on me, one task they were all obliged to fulfil …

Michael Lewis (14)
Sir Joseph Williamson's Mathematical School

A Day In The Life Of A Pupil

If you ask any pupil what their day was like at school, there's a ninety percent chance that they would say it was terrible. Most pupils say it was terrible, when actually it wasn't. But this is far from the truth in Damon's case.

His day started out like any normal day because he got up, ate, brushed his teeth and got into a car to go to school. A short while later, he arrived at school and played a little football until the pips went. He walked in with a smile on his face, but this soon changed.

The day's lessons were fine and he had just eaten lunch when the pips went again for the last two periods. The last lesson was Latin and as he walked in, he realised he hadn't done his homework for the third time in a row. He knew he was in trouble, but he didn't know how terrible it was.

The teacher started to come round the class checking everyone's books, marking a tick or a cross by their names in the register. As the teacher came to Damon, he could feel something was wrong. To Damon's surprise the teacher said, 'See me after lesson, boy.'

The end of the lesson came slowly and as everyone left, he stayed seated. From the front of the room the teacher said, 'Come here.'

Damon got up and walked to the front of the room, dreading what was about to happen next …

Tom Brown (14)
Sir Joseph Williamson's Mathematical School

Angry Aliens Attack America

People in America had the shock of their lives yesterday when a UFO landed.

The spaceship touched down at midday yesterday in the deserts of California. Locals were alarmed at the sight that faced them and informed the police immediately. After approximately two hours, a sliding door opened on the side of the ship, emitting a bright white light, illuminating the surrounding landscape.

Robert Staple, an eyewitness, told us, 'I couldn't believe my eyes at first. It just appeared out of nowhere and landed next to the road. I hopped out of my car to investigate, but when I discovered what it was, I soon leapt back in'.

Police were on the scene in minutes and soon called for back up. A special team of extraordinary investigators came and rapidly cordoned off the area around the spaceship. They forbade any photographers from getting any images. However, we were able to get an exclusive interview with the director of the investigating team: 'We are not sure where the Unidentified Flying Object has come from, but are looking into it. Nothing has come out of the ship up until now, but we are always ready for something to happen'.

Paramedics were called to the scene to deal with shocked and stressed members of the public. One person was hospitalised after they collapsed, but we are told that they are in a stable condition.

We will inform you as soon as we get any new information.

James Dance (14)
Sir Joseph Williamson's Mathematical School

Aliens Land In Maidstone!

In a shocking incident yesterday, a large metal box fell out of the sky to land in the town of Maidstone, in Kent.

The metal container, measuring roughly 3m long, fell into playing fields at Mote Park, to the amazement of local people, and left a crater 200m wide. When people rushed over to see what it was, a hatch in the side opened and four extraterrestrial life forms of the green kind sprawled out onto our planet.

'I couldn't believe my eyes!' said Harry Sidebottom, 64. 'I was walking my dog, Flopsy, when it came hurtling from nowhere. I only just managed to dodge out of the way'.

Aliens

The aliens are said to be about seven feet tall with a number of tentacles. As yet, they have not said anything in Earth language, but have made frequent high-pitched warbling noises. They have no eyes but appear to have very large nostrils in the back of their heads. Just what kind of planet could spawn life forms like this?

Tentacles

A platoon of Ghurkas who were rushed to the scene from Maidstone barracks was disarmed by the aliens' tentacles, but no one was hurt.

Does this mean that the aliens come in peace or do they have ulterior motives? Only time will tell. Catch all the action as it happens in this space!

Jonathon Very (14)
Sir Joseph Williamson's Mathematical School

A Mysterious Discovery

The tyres skidded to a halt along the Egyptian sand as Will and his dad climbed over the doors of the truck. Will's father was an architect, who was taking his son to see Tutankhamen's tomb.

Will wasn't as excited as his dad hoped; he hated these adventures, and always had, but reluctantly followed his father.

The tomb would have been pitch-black apart from the small torches in the room. The stone floor was dirty and had insects running across it. Will stared down at them watching one's progress, before his dad pulled him towards the centre of the room.

He handed Will an architectural brush; Will sighed and stepped away from his father to a wall filled with hieroglyphics. He was drawn to a small gap in the wall; he touched it and it opened. Will stepped inside.

Inside was a small room, no more than the average size of a bathroom, dimly lit only by Will's torch. In the centre was a chest, neither open nor closed. It was gold plated; extremely valuable, but strangely enough this wasn't what drew him to it most. He felt a huge urge to open it, a voice inside his head egging him on. He stepped towards the chest and touched its surface.

Will jumped back, the surface was white-hot, searing his hands. But this did not stop him. He returned to the box, not paying any attention to the pain. He opened it and looked inside.

The box was empty …

Matthew Ainsworth (14)
Sir Joseph Williamson's Mathematical School

Benvenuti A Valvori

The red-orange sun penetrates the South Italian horizon. 'Il cucù' hollers its awakening call, just like it has done since the first Volscian tribesmen ascended this green and pleasant mountain to retreat from the predators hiding below. The window shutters swing open with a heavy din. The day has begun …

These simple, generous and jolly people are colloquially known as 'Valvorese'. There is no point in separating these 'Valvorese' into families, The Rossi, Notarianni, di Mascio, Fella and Gallone, due to the fact that their descendants were all from the same Family anyway. Officially they are not Family, but physically they are. A clever way to live life maybe. They all know each other, trust each other and enjoy the simple South Italian life together. Everyone's lives are intertwined with each other's, being so close together at the summit of an Apennine mountain.

This rustic South Italian village is not like the bold, crowded and malevolent metropolises where your life is ruled by society, neither is it like the remote Sicilian villages where your life is in other people's hands. Why complain about life when you can glance out at Valvori Mountain and see paradise? Rolling hills, rustic houses and the U-turning road twisting and turning down the mountain.

This hilltop village is calm, traditional and most importantly, a secure home for the Family. That is, of course, if the local 'Mafiosi' aren't lurking in the village square, waiting for their prey to emerge. The day has begun …

Christopher Rossi (14)
Sir Joseph Williamson's Mathematical School

A Day In The Life Of An Eagle

I prepare, once again, to ascend on the adventures of flight, my great wings arched like the sun rising on the horizon. My talons perched to perfection, my eyes planning out my route for this morning's hunt. The moment I have been preparing for has come, and my feet leave the canyon's edge. I take off with my right wing bent differently to my left and I feel my body plummeting to the ground, at a speed which will surely kill me. I am merely three metres above the ground and I suddenly recuperate from the shock of almost meeting the end of my destiny. I flap my wings, blood still racing from the fright, and I am able to stay on course.

I am in the air, although I have been made to make a correction in my planned route. I am flying, doing this and becoming the definition of perfection. My eyes dart around the landscape scouting for food.

Suddenly, a careless rodent - a mouse - appears from a burrow. I swiftly dive and execute a great catch of the stupid rodent. As I gloat over my innings, I get obstructed by another eagle, superior to me. I drop my reward for the day, and I go home with nothing.

Jason Cornish (14)
Sir Joseph Williamson's Mathematical School

The Royal Mint Break In!

Ryan, Mike and Adam were three courageous triplets on an adventure, a big adventure. Ryan was a computer genius and could hack into anything, anywhere. Mike, however, was a rock-climbing expert, climbing 64 feet in 30 seconds. Adam was a fantastic mechanic and had won the world go-kart racing competition. They were only 14. Their mission was to hack into the Royal Mint in order to borrow £4,500,000 to pay for their grandma's heart operation.

'This is it, no time to back out now!' exclaimed Mike nervously, as they were standing outside the Mint.

Mike and Adam walked into the reception area, and while Adam started asking the receptionist questions, Ryan was in their hi-tech van changing all the cameras to off. Mike ran towards the brick wall in which the ventilation grille was above him leading to the main printing room. As he did this, Adam flicked a button on his watch and six bullets flew out, towards the receptionist and the five guards. Ryan was able to see Mike at all times, as he had control over all the cameras, but he changed the guards' view to a fake. Mike climbed up the wall into the ventilation grille, watching every step carefully.

When Mike reached the printing room, he got to work. Climbing over the supports wasn't easy, he had to lift £1,000,000 of the money at a time, off the machines that raised the money high into the air.

'And who might you be, young boy … ?'

Michael Hutchings (13)
Sir Joseph Williamson's Mathematical School

The Last Stand Of Arthur

The Saxons numbered two thousand; we, the British, were one thousand. The battlefield was a tight valley with impassable rocky hills on either side.

The Saxon scum arrayed a shield wall. I ordered Gwydre, my second in command, to form ours. I thought how the Saxons might eventually pierce it, opening a great wound. Would the Saxons then exploit this hole, and would the killing begin?

I donned my splendid scale armour, and leather boots with iron plates in their fronts to stop the nasty sword strike under my shield whilst fighting in the wall. I then put my magnificent helmet on.

I left my tent to take my place in the middle of the shield wall. It was a cold day and the wind swept the battlefield like a shrieking ghoul. The cold bit deep into our skin.

The Saxons started their advance, their wizards hurling spells at us. My druids and Merlin countered these spells. My men spat to ward off evil.

Crash! The shield walls clashed and the fighting began. I embedded my spear deep in my attacker's belly. Death quickly spread. Somehow my men made a hole in the otherwise solid Saxon war machine. We exploited this; the battle was ours. I thought it was Merlin's magic and screamed in triumph as we destroyed the Saxon army. At the last moment a spear was rammed into my back and I fell. My army panicked and fled.

This is how the last British kingdom fell.

Remy Holmes (13)
Sir Joseph Williamson's Mathematical School

The Infamous Samurai

Midnight. The usual time for a nightly hunt. As the strong wind brushed my hair, I felt as if I was one with the elements: fire, earth, air, water. Still running like the wind, I saw a flash out of the edge of my eye. My tiger instincts paid off well. Drawing both of my new katanas, I managed to deflect the sword of my enemy and counter attack. The sudden swipe of my sword caught my unlucky enemy off guard, leaving him wounded.

All was now silent, although I could sense someone within these forsaken woods. The first rule of samurai; to be the hunter, not the hunted. As I harnessed the air's energy, I allowed it to sweep me off my feet. This was lucky, due to the fact that where I had been, was now a large amount of poison darts and arrowheads. I caught sight of a misled glint of hope in someone's eye as he fired an arrow. Once again, one katana met the arrowhead, while I fell from the sky producing a critical kick to the stomach.

Suddenly, a look of panic swept across my face. The sun was coming up. I ran for dear life, but even that could not help me. It left me a prime target for the bounty hunters that, I think, were following me.

As I reached the brink of the woods, a sudden pain flowed through my body, leaving me weak and defenceless …

Nicholas Hanchet (13)
Sir Joseph Williamson's Mathematical School

The Mystery Painting

The painter had been painting all day. The people sat outside the café had been watching him as they ate their pasta dishes and drank wine. It was warm and the painter got restless.

The painter, who was not very smartly dressed in his T-shirt and shorts, was painting the statues in the square and people who had stopped to admire them.

Just as the painter began to pack up, an unusually-dressed woman walked over to the painter. She rubbed one of the paintings and walked off without making a sound. This was mysterious to the painter and he shouted, 'Hey come back, you could have ruined my painting.' The painter started to pack and he went home for the night.

He parked up his car and it started to thunder. He quickly opened the door, took his paintings out of the car and ran inside his house. When he got in, all was quiet. He stacked his paintings in the corner and shouted, 'Anyone in?' There was no response.

He switched on the television; the unusually-dressed lady was on the TV and she said, 'I am coming for you.'

As soon as she said that, one of the paintings flashed and the lady was in it. It showed when the lady came and touched the painting. He was amazed at what was happening to him, it showed that the lady came out of the back of the picture …

Chris Shaw (13)
Sir Joseph Williamson's Mathematical School

Dangerous Beauty

Muazzez Tahir was a beautiful Turkish woman with long, flowing black hair. But look into her large blue eyes, you'll see that her beauty is only skin deep.

Tahir was a dancing bear handler, a very ferocious one. Any person who disagreed with her was known to be found in a dumpster, if they were found at all.

She was giving one of her performances, the nose of the bear bleeding badly, when she heard sirens in the distance, getting louder. She moved fast. At a run she bounded over boxes and ducked under pipes. She looked to her left and seeing an old storehouse door, she ran at it. Thankfully, decades of rust had almost destroyed the lock and it fell through.

She heard the police searching the warehouse; she knew she only had a few seconds left to run. She ran for the exit, bullets whistling past her. When she reached the door, she continued to run through the alleyway. It was a dead end. She spun round and saw no less than a dozen police officers coming up the alley. Suddenly an ambulance screeched round the corner and stopped near to her. Three men in black overalls jumped out and she felt someone grab her from behind and throw her into the ambulance. It sped off past the officers and out onto the road.

One of the men spoke, 'You messed with the wrong people, Tahir.'

A single gunshot echoed around the alleyway; there was a long silence …

Andrew Bowdery (13)
Sir Joseph Williamson's Mathematical School

Eztur The Warrior

Eztur jumped on the saddle of his horse and ordered it to gallop. He was on another mission for the gods. He hated these so-called favours for them, but yet he had to do them if he ever wanted to get rid of the dreams and memories.

These memories were from when he was under the influence of Aires, the god of war. Aires promised him immortality if he fought for him. Of course, Eztur accepted almost instantly due to his greed, but what he did not realise was that he would have to kill women and children, so he went to the other gods for help. They said if he carried out some tasks for them, they would take away his horrible memories and this would be his final mission: to kill Aires.

He burst into Aries' fort and began his rampage of slaughtering any of Aires' evil minions and demons. He sliced off heads, dismembered limbs, tore out organs and caused utter mayhem. He now went for Aires.

Both creatures skilled in the way of the sword, this would be an epic battle. They battled for hours giving everything they had, using any means possible to try and discourage the opponent. Finally Eztur went on an all out attack. He overwhelmed him and buried his sword within Aires' gullet. Aires laid motionless. Suddenly, the clouds opened and down came the gods, and as promised, the gods took Eztur and cleared his memory of his awful deeds.

Ryan Evans (13)
Sir Joseph Williamson's Mathematical School

Pete The African Elephant

Pete the African elephant hated his life in the circus performing stunts and walking along the hard and cold concrete floors with his aching feet.

It was Sunday and the circus had just come into town. People were cheering, laughing and clapping as the marching band marched down the street, closely followed by the animals: tigers, parrots, horses and the main attraction, the elephants.

Pete the baby elephant was bored and hungry from the long walk and being in the train. Out of the corner of his eye, he saw a grocery shop with all his favourite foods: cabbages, carrots and his most favourite, peanuts. He slowly walked over to the shop, just missing a car, and waved his long trunk and accidentally knocked the potatoes all over, and the manager got angry. He didn't want to hurt Pete, so he started hitting him with rhubarb. It didn't bother Pete, so he just carried on eating all the peanuts. His trainer, the almighty Bob, ran over and started pushing the elephant away. Pete moved, filled up with peanuts, but now he was thirsty …

Ryan Dowsett (12)
Sir Joseph Williamson's Mathematical School

The King's Murder

November 19th 1356

The king slept after an angry exchange with Jerryl. He never awoke.

The squire walked into the room to comfort the king. He saw the sword of Cyprus, gripped firmly in the murder's hand, dripping with the king's blood. Mortified, the squire grabbed the other sword in the room and demanded a duel. The murderer, now recognised as the king's trusted older brother Jerryl, declined. The squire, surprised at this, lashed out at Jerryl, landing a fatal blow to his shoulder. The squire then realising the trouble he was in, knowing his account would not be believed, panicked and cleaned the swords thoroughly and hid in a wardrobe silently. He knew he would be seen exiting the house.

The king's servant came in at dawn and saw Jerryl and the king motionless next to each other. He knew the culprit was still in the room as there were four sets of footprints entering, yet none leaving. He retrieved the sword of Cyprus and searched. After an hour of searching, there was only one place left to look: the king's wardrobe. Anxiously holding the blade in his hand, the king's servant opened the wardrobe to find the squire cowering in the corner. Despite the squire's screams of innocence, the servant ended his life.

Running out onto the street, the servant announced the death of the king, but people took it the wrong way and hung him.

James Black (12)
Sir Joseph Williamson's Mathematical School

The Shadow Man

I stood at one end of the alley. At the other end was a tall, broad figure. The figure started to walk towards me. I turned away cautiously, not aware that the figure was getting close to me. I started to walk away; I walked over the road to the alley opposite me. I tripped over a bag of rubbish that someone had left out. Turning around as I lay on the floor, I saw the figure's face, with cold, piercing eyes and he had long brown hair and a brown beard. He pulled out a knife. With a shining steel blade pointing towards me, I closed my eyes.

My life went before me. The next thing I remember is seeing the man running away into the shadows. Looking down to the floor, I was laying in a puddle … of my own blood. The pain in my shoulder was immense. I tried to call for help, but I just did not have the energy. I thought I was dead. My eyes closed.

When I woke up, I was laying in the safety of the hospital. I closed my eyes in relief. As time passed, I opened my eyes, and there in the shadows lurked a figure …

Ryan Smyth (12)
Sir Joseph Williamson's Mathematical School

The Job

It happened. I had done it. Done what others thought was impossible. I galloped out of the room, brushing past a doorframe and clattering my elbow on the handle. Down a flight of stairs I jumped, the assailants tracing my steps. I had killed 'Major'.

We use codenames in this business, just so they don't know who I'm going to assassinate.

I paused around the corner, gasping to catch my breath. This job hadn't gone well as I had lost two men, but it was all for money anyway. I glanced at my watch; the time was 8.30. I sprinted again to escape, following signs which led to an exit. I could hear commands and shouts from Commander; he was Major's right hand man. He carried a 50.0 calibre sub-machine gun, a new addition to Special Forces' arsenal, and he knew how to use it. I jumped from the fire escape to the floor. I was three storeys up, but I escaped uninjured. Suddenly, someone cried out, 'I've got him!' I heard gunfire and felt a shower of lead penetrate my left thigh, it was Commander. I span round and fired my own firearm, killing him instantly. He didn't need to die.

Ahead of me I saw a car, a Jaguar X type. I smashed open the window and got in. After hotwiring the car, I drove as fast as it let me. I escaped, but at what cost?

Cai Jarvis (12)
Sir Joseph Williamson's Mathematical School

Dark Forest

One dark night in the hills of Westwood, just on the borders of Mirkwood, a very strange and evil creature spied on his unaware prey. He was waiting in the darkness of Mirkwood Forest, his eyes gleaming with evilness and anticipation, waiting, just waiting for her to slip over the wet lush grass, or to trip over one of the ancient rotting tree trunks that had fallen down years ago.

She almost fell over one of the tree trunks and he came streaming towards her and suddenly stopped when he found that she had regained her balance and started to walk towards him. He started panicking, trying not to be seen, but then he found that she was just drunk and was walking in all directions, falling over almost all of the time. When he realised this, he waited for her to walk in front of him, then he pounced. He went straight for her legs, piercing her skin, taking huge chunks of flesh from her right leg whilst he was being kicked by the girl trying to get him off. She was screaming as loudly as her lungs would let her.

A few people from the same party as the girl, heard the commotion and rushed to the scene to see what all the noise was about. He heard them coming. He wasn't sure what to do and he started to panic, he ran back into the forest and waited for them to come …

Jamie Aldred (13)
Sir Joseph Williamson's Mathematical School

A Day In The Life Of Jurgen Kohler

On 29th day, the fighting stopped. It came to a bloody end as we were defeated by the ruthless Germans. We were the cowards, hiding in holes, ditches and drainpipes. The real men had died making an attempt of freedom from the dreadful ghettos we were forced to live in. it was useless since we were without food or much arms, and the Germans took us down like flies.

The Germans fiercely yelled at us to get out of our hiding holes, waving their bayonets at us. After a painful 18-mile death march, we were thrown into a green muddy van, with the words 'Austez hoffnung'. This means 'abandoned hope'.

In the van with me were two friends of mine that had fought with me in the ghetto, Karl and Stefan. Also in the van was a tired, old-looking woman, holding a baby with a small girl beside them. None of these people spoke German, they all spoke what I thought was French, but I did not know. Stefan tried to talk to the old lady, but she just hid in the corner crying, squeezing a cross, saying, 'Dieve progér novs.'

The German guard who was presently asleep, earlier told us that we were going away to a Jew colony to work. I knew there was no such place. We were told to get out and stand at the top of a hill, alongside other innocent Jews. They set up their machine guns.

Their search of me had been brief; they had not noticed a small hand gun in my sock, loaded with a single bullet. I shot up into the air, the distraction this caused gave us enough time to escape down the other side of the hill, along with Stefan and Karl. Some other Jews managed to escape, but unfortunately, most of them were shot.

We made it through the war by working at a nearby farm. There were regular searches of the barn where we were staying, but the Germans never found anything.

Nicholas Harlow (13)
Sir Joseph Williamson's Mathematical School

Da Ching

The Ching went into a room where the four leaders of his order sat, and his competitor for the place in the Ssanghing Board, the most powerful martial arts assassins ever. Ching took off his cloak and threw it out of the dojo, as did his opponent. He was one of the most skilful men known to the Ching; his opponent had no name.

They unsheathed their chosen weapons: his opponent, the sword of the samurai and for the Ching, the telescopic, double-ended spear, made of metal and perfectly balanced. A silent signal began their battle, they leapt and thrust in with their weapons. Metal rang on metal and both were deflected away from their targets. They thrust, cut and blocked, and yet the Sshanghing remained absolutely motionless.

Suddenly, the Ching and the opponent were thrown back from each other. They both looked at the leader of the Ssanghing, his hand was held up. Although both opponents clearly wanted to continue, the leader chillingly whispered, 'Fight well, or you will not be able to fight at all.' Both players nodded, resumed their stances and fought again. Chops, punches and kicks were blocked every time. The Ching and his opponent were so evenly matched that neither could make any headway.

However, the Ching was becoming tired, and as he collapsed, his opponent gave him his peace. The opponent went to the Ssanghing, and the leader shot him.

Alastair Cole (14)
Sir Joseph Williamson's Mathematical School

The Scratch

It was just before midnight. All was still inside as Harry lay in bed. He could just see the outline of a tree through his dark curtains being blown about by the howling wind. Harry lay still, freezing cold and scared. It was the night of Friday 13th May, the one night he'd been dreading all year. He was never a lucky boy, even in the safety of his own home.

Gong! The clock downstairs struck twelve. Harry jumped out of his skin. Then it started. He could hear a tiny scratching sound, as if mice were scratching against the wall, or a monster was scratching its way from underneath Harry's bed. He tried to scream with fright, but no sound came out. He shouted for help, but no one came. He was alone, all alone.

Harry knew he had only one choice. He pushed away his duvet, got up and reached for his dressing gown. Finally, something good. He clutched onto it tight and put it on - at least he wasn't cold anymore. He walked over to the wall and reached for his slippers. They weren't there. He couldn't look for them; it was pitch-black except for the small ray of light coming from the street lamp outside his window. Forgetting his slippers, he walked up to his cupboard. It was then, and only then, that he discovered his fear. It was his birthday tomorrow, and on his list was a hamster, and there one was, scratching away.

Josh Hoskins (13)
Sir Joseph Williamson's Mathematical School

The Thief

Paddy O'Brien was an Irish medical student by day, but a diamond thief by night. He was the best in Ireland, probably the best in the United Kingdom, but tonight was going to be the worst night of his life.

It started off all right, his job was to go to the top floor of Guinness' headquarters to steal the secret of why Guinness is so smooth, but rough at the same time … it was the Irish Diamond.

Getting in was easy and so was the stealing part, but the bit that Paddy always messed up on was the escaping part of the job. He sweated and fumbled. This time was the worst. He tripped over every vase and chair in his way and after five minutes, the whole building's security force was chasing after him. No one in a million years could have guessed what was going to happen, but it did. About seven yards down the hallway was a broom handle on the soaking wet floor. Paddy tripped over the handle and slid on the water all the way to the end of the hallway and shot straight into the laundry chute, landed in an unoccupied deliver van and made his getaway.

The next day, Paddy went to see his partner in Irish crime, Seamus O'Reilly, to check out the value of his diamond. Seamus worked out that in fact the diamond was a fake, it was a decoy. All Paddy could say was, 'Oops.'

Ryan Bryson-Payne (13)
Sir Joseph Williamson's Mathematical School

The Kingdom Of Courage

Galvador lifted the great sabre and violently slashed down several enemy warriors. Galvador knew time was running out for he needed to lead a small rebellion to save the ancient wizard.

Vlanador had raised an army to crush Galvador. Galvador and his small rebellion would not give up as they were from the kingdom of Courage. Vlanador rode through his hordes. He engaged battle with the rebel fighters. He knocked several down with his mighty mace; yet Galvador's men still fought courageously. Vlanador pulled his arm back to swing his mace to crush Galvador's first captain, Cheeveseby. But within seconds, Galvador rose and stabbed his nemesis in the back. Vlanador was dead.

With no leader, Vlanador's army was defeated, so his men fled; through this act, Galvador's men were lifted and a new level of courage was given to Galvador's men. Galvador and his men regrouped and went onwards towards the tower of Senitoth. They ran up several twirling stairs to get to the top of the tower, where they found the wizard dead with his cut throat. He had been slaughtered by Vlanador's right hand man, Besivon.

The new battle was to begin. Besivon stood tall, holding his fierce throwing stars. Galvador charged, crying. Besivon threw several stars, one of which severed Galvador's left arm, but Galvador kept running in spite of his wound; his courage allowed him to run on. With one almighty blow from Galvador, Besivon was only to be remembered as a thought.

Daniel Routledge (12)
Sir Joseph Williamson's Mathematical School

The Thing

'There it was, what I'd spent 25 years of archaeological research looking for, and it was here all time,' gasped Arthermedies Powel, standing in front of 'it'. He fell on his knees, covering them in a nauseating stench of snake and contaminated rat droppings. It was dark and the menacing sounds gradually faded away as the professor seemed to fall under a spell, staring ... staring at 'it'. This trance was crudely interrupted by the most revolting odour that he had ever smelt before. It brought back the sounds of the snakes hissing and the rats squeaking, and then he heard it.

It was a terrifying moaning noise coming from behind the wall in front of him, behind 'it'. He froze, again just staring ... (Author's note: OK, I'll tell you what 'it' is. It's an old slab that, hypothetically, ancient Egyptians left in the hope that in the future someone would discover locked up in the tomb, and unlock their little secret.) The groaning got louder and louder, and the professor turned ghostly white. Then it stopped. He was relieved and got back up slowly to start to make observations. As he arose, he mysteriously smelt the revolting odour again and a warm breath of air on the back of his neck. He shivered, took a big gulp and turned to look. He then saw, standing in front of him, a giant, sordid, blood-tainted creature! It reached out for him, and the professor screamed ...

James Spencer (13)
Sir Joseph Williamson's Mathematical School

Jimmy Blunt, MI6 Agent

The day started like any other for MI6 agent Jimmy Blunt. A pile of paperwork was waiting for him in his office. But that didn't really bother him, he was on the trail of a Mexican drugs gang and once again they had evaded him. As he pulled into the MI6 building, he could tell something was wrong, very wrong. There was no security and as he advanced to his office, he saw something that shocked him. The secretary was laying dead with a hole in his chest. Jimmy looked at the phone and saw a message. 'If you want to see your boy alive, come alone to Heathrow Airport, Terminal 4'.

He raced downstairs and jumped into his Aston Martin Vanquish. His only weapons were a pistol and a knife, but he couldn't worry about that. As he tore down the motorway, he radioed for help. He saw the terminal and some armed guards. He smashed through the fence and ran over the two guards. He saw another guard rush towards him, so Jimmy shot him. He stole his machine gun and rushed onto the Lear jet that was parked there. Jimmy shot another two guards, but the Jimmy saw him, the legendary gang leader, Vincenzo Del Boco. He had a gun pointed at Jimmy's head. Jimmy dropped his eyes and heard a shot. He opened his eyes to see a hole through Vincenzo's head. He turned around to see his partner, Danny Dingle, and his boss, Charlie Pease.

Aaron Dimmick (13)
Sir Joseph Williamson's Mathematical School

Parents, Girls, Friends!

Slowly they swept up the hill in pursuit of the girl, her mother in tears as she reported to the police that her daughter was last seen sitting under a tamarind tree.

The girl had been missing for an hour; her mother was progressively weakening.

'You were meant to stay together!' said Yasmin's mum.

'I know, we're sorry, we never meant to go anywhere, we just lost her. We were playing hide-and-seek and it was Yasmin's turn to seek, so we all went together and went up the big tree. It got boring, so we got down and we couldn't see Yasmin anywhere. We looked for ten minutes and thought we ought to get help.'

'There's no time to waste, start looking and stay together.'

They went to search for Yasmin; they started at the village and the entrance to the open trees. They searched for fifteen minutes before one helper saw a tree moving and shouted for everyone to come. They found nothing; it was an animal scurrying through the bush. The mother's hopes were fading quickly.

They were tired and decided to go back. The mother wasn't happy, but she was assured that everyone in the village would help find her darling daughter. They turned back into their huts. The mother lay down and suddenly she heard a familiar voice.

'What is all the fuss about?'

Michael Puddy (13)
Sir Joseph Williamson's Mathematical School

The Amulet

Many years ago in ancient India, in a small, busy town called Bilga, many unexplained mishaps occurred. Lightning struck every night, but the village has not had any clouds lingering above for over thirty centuries. The village was between two great mountains, which the people of Bilga called Gog and Magog. The people believed that behind these mountains were holy armies, one led by the evil god called Seluda, who possessed a ruby-red amulet which could summon evil beasts from Hell. The other army was led by the heroic god, Munzil, who the people believed was missing the blue diamond amulet, which could summon holy beasts from another world. The amulet was lost during the battle of these two gods in the Sharakh Sea, where the blue amulet was washed up in a nearby cave; the Cave of Roti. Only the chosen one would be allowed to enter the caves.

Prince Ikhlas, was the chosen one, prepared for his guest. His sharparrows were in a long pouch that went on his back, with his bow around his body, and then his sharp broadsword, which was cherished and blessed by Munzil, slid perfectly into a covering on his back. The silky sound of the sword sliding into its covering made the prince sound dangerous. He let his long hair down, but wrapped a red bandana round his forehead. He wore no top, white baggy trousers which were tight at his ankles. Ikhlas confidently jumped onto his phoenix and rode to the caves with pride to retrieve the ancient amulet.

As he arrived at the caves, after some delay with gargoyles and wolves, he found that the amulet was locked away in a chest. With one giant swing of his sword, the iron chest cracked open …

Mihaz Bokth (15)
Sir Joseph Williamson's Mathematical School

The Accident

I constitutionally made my way down to school, when I felt a sharp stabbing pain in my stomach. It caught me out and I had to sit down. I thought to myself, *I never get stomach aches,* and I thought about what I had for breakfast. I'd had two sausages, two slices of bacon and a fried egg. I had that every morning and I have never had a stomach ache.

As I was sitting down, my mates passed and I joined them in a deep conversation about the cup final. When we finally got to school about half an hour later, we saw two older pupils having a fight across the road. My mates ran over to join the big crowd which surrounded the spectacle. I was just about to join, when another stabbing feeling passed over me. I was short of breath and I knew I had to sit down again, but I knew I just had to see the fight. So I stepped out into the road. I turned my head and saw a car braking. It was strange. I could not hear it, but I noticed out of the corner of my eye the crowd of people looked in my direction. The next thing I knew, I was in the air having just rolled over the bonnet and up the windscreen. I remember having the same pain in my stomach as I landed. The crowd ran over to see what had happened, and that's the last thing I saw … permanently.

Robert Tear (15)
Sir Joseph Williamson's Mathematical School

Out Of Orbit

It's the year 3010. A new satellite, LOJ (Life on Jupiter) is sent into orbit around the planet Jupiter, because scientists at NASA have discovered enough evidence to believe there could be life there. The satellite is designed to give pictures and information of what it observes while orbiting around the planet. Two months later there are problems with the satellite and the scientists lose contact with it. They discover that the satellite is no longer in the same orbit. Three astronauts are sent up to find the satellite and bring it back to Earth.

'This is Jenna Thompson of Delta 419, reporting that we have discovered that LOJ is not where it should be. There are, however, indications to where it could possibly be on the planet. We need to check it out. Permission to land, Sir?'

'This is base control, you are authorised to land.'

After seven hours of searching, the three tired astronauts, Jenna Thompson, Matt Bryn and James Johnston, find the satellite, but it is nearly completely destroyed.

'It must have been hit by a meteor or something and crash-landed,' said Matt.

'Yup, and now we get to take it all the way back to the shuttle,' replied James.

After taking the long journey back to the landing site of the Delta, they find their space shuttle has also been completely destroyed. Jenna finds the radio and reports to base control, 'Base control, we have a problem …'

Daniel Sams (15)
Sir Joseph Williamson's Mathematical School

Strange Happenings

There he was, in the study, shaking like a leaf, trembling with fear, skin as white as a ghost and yet Mike could still sense something far worse was still to happen. The stranger had trespassed before with his Great Dane by his side, and there was definitely something not right about this man. The air surrounding him seemed to turn cold, as a white mist gathered, constantly orbiting him. Then there was the dog; ferocious in looks, disturbing in size and looked willing to swallow a whole human without chewing.

As they stood there in the centre of the three-acre garden, next to the statue of Sir George himself, something was clearly being orchestrated as they stared directly into the eyes of Sir George's son, Michael.

'Lock all the doors and windows now!' bellowed Michael as he instructed his maid. Julie did as she was told and all went well. This was the case until the last window, at least, when she was jolted to a halt. There in the foreground, flashed the fiery image of her master, cast in flames, although her master was really up in the study, peering out of the window. It was as if she had foreseen his demise. *Bang!* was the sound as she hit the floor with a huge thud, echoing around the whole mansion. As the sound travelled through the ears of Mike, a sudden expression sprawled across his face, an expression of pure fear. He then picked up his baseball bat, and edged his way down the stairs …

Ben White (14)
Sir Joseph Williamson's Mathematical School

Re-Awakened

An hour from now, all the planets within the universe will do the unthinkable, the greatest myth throughout all the stars, a complete planetary alignment. According to legend, when the planets align, the power from each of the Greek gods that departed from Mount Olympus and resided in each of the planets will be bestowed on one mortal being, who will, for whatever circumstance, behold the greatest gift in all time, the power to control it and all matter in the universe. The fate of the gods decides who it will be bestowed on, as their immortal nature cannot control from the heavens for another eternity. However, there are other powers at work here that cannot be controlled and with the last of the remaining guardians gone, the universe is unbalanced.

The night was young and the air fresh, the moon was full and rain began to fall from the heavens.

'Jeez, watch where you're going next time.' Curator of the modern art museum in Los Angeles, Mr Ivory Kauniere's eyes dropped from the tobacco-rich, darkly dressed man to his broken suitcase which had been knocked out of his firm grasp. As he knelt down to pick it up, light began to glow and grow from the darkest ends of the universe … When suddenly light began to pierce through the night sky and he felt a surge of adrenaline and power, to which he replied with painful screaming. As the screaming grew louder, everything else went quieter. Kauniere dropped to his knees, his irises disappearing, eyes white as ghosts, his clothes dematerialising and a blue, god-like aura surrounded his entire body. Speechless, he lay still, the gods had chosen.

He was now God.

Simon Yau (15)
Sir Joseph Williamson's Mathematical School

A Day In The Life Of a Homeless Man

He wakes to the sound of the rubbish men clearing up the street. No thought or feeling for those who were in a peaceful state.

The city seems quiet and dream-like, as he wanders to his 'pitch' for the day. Some drunks view him in the distance and shout abuse, before attempting to chase him from the area he knows.

With no money, or friends, he positions himself outside Waterloo, admiring the food opposite in the bakery, trying to distract himself from the scent of the freshly baked bread and the smell of the freshly brewed coffee. The routine begins once again.

8 o'clock. The world begins; working class fills the streets, entering from every direction.

He sits and stares, questioning *why?* Why do they have to rush? They get up late and rush. If they slowed down, would they stop, and finally accept the creation of the world?

Ignored. They never stop. No one answers his plea of, 'Spare change, please?' No thought for the hunger he feels, or the want for the taste of the creamy coffee making his mouth water as the smell hits his nose. Every day he has done this exact routine for two years. His feeling of loneliness has built up and created an internal scar on his mind. Today he has decided to end his life of being unloved and lonely, and become happy.

He strolls to the job centre, admiring how his new life will be. He ascends the stairs and sees a window. He is on the fifth floor, can view London perfectly. He inhales the air, it smells fresh, but polluted. He is happy.

He is there. In reality. No love, no friends, all about to change.

And he jumps …

Lloyd Sceats (15)
Sir Joseph Williamson's Mathematical School

A Day In The Life Of Me

Waking up at 6 o'clock in the morning is never a teenager's first choice. I am no exception. Parents screaming at me to get up just irritates me and eventually I fall back to sleep. 20 minutes later, five minutes before I should be leaving for school, my dad grabs me and tosses me out of bed. The rush is on to get ready, washed, pack my bag, and of course, do my hair. Running to the car, my dad already revving the engine and constantly reminding me how he is going to be late for work and how he will lose his job, and me just nodding, half asleep. Getting to school already knowing I have done none of my homework and face a constant rollicking all day. First lesson, detention, second lesson, detention, third lesson, detention, knowing the rest of my week is now booked.

The relief when lunchtime occurs, somehow still getting in trouble with the teacher for having a tie too short - moody or what! Last lesson, one hour then I'll be homeward-bound, until I find out the teacher wants to keep me behind and remind me about my 'behaviour', in the end having to run to catch my bus. Getting on the bus and finding all the seats are taken, all thanks to my last crappy teacher.

Getting home and finally the relief that the teacher can't get to me sinks in. Having dinner, going on the computer and realising tomorrow I'll be doing it all again.

Edward Jarvis (14)
Sir Joseph Williamson's Mathematical School

Dragonlands River

The sun began to rise once more, light was licking the trees on the edge of the forest. The wet leaves glistened as a calm breeze blew among them, rustling of the leaves was clearly audible as the rest of the forest was deadly silent. The sound of the waves in the swash came as the water touched the beach. A crash came from the forest and a flock of birds flew through the tops of the trees.

The noise came from a traveller, he was on his back struggling to get up, then finally released himself from his bulging rucksack. He breathed heavily as he tried to pick it up once again. He was a middle-aged man and had a rough look about him. His face clearly wasn't shaven and his muscles were prominently seen from his clothes. The traveller could hear the trickling water coming from the forest clearing, he once again picked up his rucksack and walked at a slow pace towards the clearing. He was walking through the vines and small creatures that innocently scattered about.

He came close to the clearing and heard a roar; he came out of the clearing and sat his pack down, then took his water canister and drank the remaining liquid. The noise then led him to the small cliff which towered over the flowing river. He heard the roaring again and looked down the cliff. He gazed in wonder at the sight; he had found the sacred dragon.

Alexander Souter (14)
Sir Joseph Williamson's Mathematical School

Välkommen Till Ekedalen

In-between the two largest lakes in Sweden lies a large, beautiful area of dense natural woodland and small secluded villages. In one of these villages lives my Swedish family. The village they live in is called Ekedalen. Here there is no need to lock your doors as everyone knows everyone. There is no crime, no gangs, no fighting, just the nature and your closest friends and family by your side.

The seasons in Sweden are all unique and still all as important as each other. In the summer there is no rain and the plants and trees are at their peak in life. In the autumn there is lots of rain and you can always hear the quiet thud of the leaves falling off the trees. In the winter there is plenty of white, silk-like snow everywhere and the air is so quiet all you can hear is the snow falling. But the most beautiful season is spring, here the forests are alive with excitement and the sight of nature can be seen everywhere.

But all in all, it is not the nature that makes this place so special, it is the people who respect the nature and who do not fret over idiotic matters that lead to violence, for it is this that ruins our modern day society. And so this is why I think Ekedalen and all the other little villages and towns in Sweden, make the world a little more happier.

Halvard Green (14)
Sir Joseph Williamson's Mathematical School

War Of Survival

Seth surveyed the battlefield in front of him. With his battleaxe in one arm and a wooden shield in another, he was ready for combat. He charged forward with his battleaxe, signalling to his army to advance onto the battlefield. This started the battle. Seth started to engage the enemy with his elite bodyguards. They attacked a small group of light infantry that was armed with light armour and short swords.

His army was attacking the bulk of the enemy army that included spearmen and horsemen and more light infantry. Many were slain quickly by the almighty surge of the main group of heavy infantry armed with large wooden shields and two-handled long swords, which could almost completely destroy the enemies' shields with one swift strike.

After Seth disposed of the small group of light infantry, he and his bodyguards quickly moved on to the spearmen that were causing them much difficulty and some death to the main army. He rushed at the spearmen, thrusting at them with his battleaxe, raising it over his head, swiping at them as they fought furiously back. Seth broke off from combat with the spearmen and headed for the general at the back of the battlefield. He had a ferocious battle with Thelos, the general. After much fighting, he succeeded by chopping Thelo's head off. With no commander, the enemy army fled the battlefield and Seth claimed his victory.

Lewis Moran (13)
Sir Joseph Williamson's Mathematical School

Strange Places

The sea rumbled onto the beach, then rushed back out. The rain beat down onto Danny's scratched and hairy face. Then *crash!* A thunderbolt of lightning lit up the sky for a few seconds, then faded away. All three boys woke up in a rubber raft, which had been washed up onto a small island.

'Where are we?' Jake questioned.

'Pardon?' replied Joe at the top of his voice so Jake could hear over the howling wind and pelting rain.

'I said, where are we?' shouted Jake.

'I don't know,' replied Danny.

All the boys ran to get shelter from the wet.

That night the boys discussed how they got to the island.

'I wonder why the plane went flying into the sea?' Joe wondered.

'Probably an engine failure, I suppose,' Danny replied.

Jake walked back carrying a pile of logs for a fire. They made a shelter out of leaves and trees. They were eating coconuts and drinking the rainwater.

A few days later, the boys had eaten all the coconuts on the island and it had stopped raining. They decided to have a look around the island. They found nothing. The island was completely deserted.

'I am so hungry, Danny groaned.

'Yes, well we are all in the same boat,' Jake answered.

The next morning, Joe and Jake made a big fire on the beach to seek attention from passing planes. Then a plane flew over. The plane came back later to rescue the boys, their nightmare was over.

Ben Dance (12)
Sir Joseph Williamson's Mathematical School

Heaven

A perfumed smell thickened the air, and fluffy white clouds with angels drifted quietly through the sky. Matthew opened his eyes.

'Next please,' said an idle voice.

'Hello,' said Matthew uncertainly, getting up from where he had been lying on the ground. 'Where am I?'

'Heaven. People go there when they die,' said the voice in bored tones.

'I'm dead! And I'm on a cloud!' exclaimed Matthew disbelievingly.

'Yes,' replied the voice. 'You were run over twelve minutes ago.'

Matthew looked around nervously. 'Where are you? I can't see you.'

'No,' the voice remarked. 'You can't. Name?'

'Matthew Charmer.'

'Passport?'

'I don't think I have it.'

'Tut tut,' mocked the voice. 'Peter!'

An angel appeared from thin air, but his glittering gown had been replaced by a thick leather jacket. His hair was purple, and he was chewing gum.

'What chu lookin' at, punk?' spat the angel.

'St Peter?' said Matthew dazedly.

'That's me,' he replied to Matthew. Then to no one in particular, 'What's up, God?'

'Peter!' said the voice which was apparently God. 'This lad here's forgotten his ID.'

'Oh dear,' said St Peter, grinning nastily. 'Have fun in Hell, dude!'

There was a whoosh, and he was back in his maths lesson with Mrs Crossbun. Phew! It had all been a dream! Or had it? He didn't remember Mrs Crossbun having a pitchfork and tail before.

She stopped scribbling on the board and smiled. 'Welcome to Hell!' she said, before continuing to write up her equation ...

William Friend (12)
Sir Joseph Williamson's Mathematical School

The Marriage Of Matheus And Perseus

There was once a god called Marcus and he had a son called Matheus. Marcus was god of lightning. There was another god called Lucas, who had a daughter called Perseus. Lucas was god of thunder. Marcus and Lucas were best friends and had never had a disagreement with one another.

Matheus and Perseus were in love, but didn't want to tell their fathers yet because Lucas had a promise that when he had a daughter, they wouldn't marry each other. He didn't want them to get married because Lucas had promised that she would marry the son of storms. This promise had been made before she was born. The god of storms' name was Jason.

After two weeks, Matheus asked Perseus to marry him and she said yes. They secretly got married to each other. A week later, they finally told their fathers. Marcus was really happy, but Lucas was furious with Marcus. Marcus was furious because Lucas blamed him. As they became enemies, they fought with their thunder and lightning. The lightning ripped through the trees and pulled out their roots, and houses were burnt and blown away. The thunder shook the whole world with its power and anger.

As years went by, Matheus and Perseus produced four children, and as each child was born, Marcus and Lucas became calmer. They both agreed that there would only be thunder and lightning on each child's birthday, but not as powerful and destructive as they had been in the past.

Jaspreet Sangha (11)
Sir Joseph Williamson's Mathematical School

Things Start to Hot Up For Icarus

Triremes arrived outside King Minos' palace today as Icarus, son of the great builder and architect Daedalus, was found floating in the sea. Could it be that King Minos murdered him? Could Icarus have committed suicide? Was it Daedalus' fault himself? Most of the evidence points to the last suggestion.

We interviewed Daedalus at Cumae, who told us that they had planned to escape from Crete and King Minos, who had turned against them. After building the labyrinth for the Minotaur to live in, mad King Minos imprisoned them. Daedalus and Icarus constructed huge wings from wood, wax and feathers, and had succeeded in flying out from Minos' palace.

In an exclusive interview with 'The Cronos', Daedalus described what happened. Poor Icarus flew too close to the sun and the wax holding the feathers together melted in the intense heat of the sun. 'I told him not to fly too close to the sun, but he didn't listen. Next thing, I turned round and he wasn't there. When I looked down, I could see the feathers floating on the surface of the sea', said Icarus' distraught father.

We understand that Daedalus is planning to build a temple at Cumae in memory of his son. Also King Minos has been placed under palace-arrest and is being questioned. And for the Minotaur? Brave-hearted men are being sent to find out how the Minotaur was created.

George Anderson (12)
Sir Joseph Williamson's Mathematical School

The Barrels

I stumbled through the long, unkept grass towards the huge row of abandoned warehouses. The grass was scratchy and kept pricking my bare legs. It felt like the sun was burning through my neck on this day during the heatwave. I found a small clearing in the grass and sat to have a drink. The water tasted cool and soothing on my dry, parched throat.

When I reached the warehouses, it was as if the sun had disappeared. I was in the dark, gloomy shadow of one of the old crumbling buildings.

All I could hear was the buzzing and humming of the insects and the chirping of the birds. As I walked round the old brick walls, I noticed the windows on the end of the buildings had bars screwed across them. For a minute this made me think it was a prison.

A few minutes later I came across an old rusty door hanging off its one remaining hinge. I pushed the door open and it fell off the wall with an almighty *crash!*

The odour from inside the warehouse nearly choked me; it was so damp and musty. Along the passageway was a row of old, smelly oil barrels. I glanced inside one of the barrels and that's when I saw him … !

Jack Paulley (12)
Sir Joseph Williamson's Mathematical School

The Ghost

It was a dark and stormy night and no one was moving, apart from the ghosts. One particular ghost, Joe Macinton, was out haunting when suddenly another ghost appeared out of nowhere and started to kill all the animals on the farm and Joe, who when alive owned the farm, thought to himself, *'e can't ruin me farm.* So he held a ghost meeting and everybody agreed for the new person to leave the farm.

They decided to get rid of him by starting a huge thunderstorm, which as all ghosts know, is the only thing to get rid of a ghost. However, he just stood there getting electrocuted and didn't vanish, so after that, everybody feared and respected him. They later found out that he had already been hit by lightning and vanished and was mad, and it had taken him 500 years to come back to Earth.

Joe was unhappy about this and became the only ghost who would stand up to 'Mad Flash'. He transported all the people and the animals away from the farm and made it appear to be a ghost town. Mad Flash got very bored with just ghosts to frighten and before long decided to move on to a place his terrifying antics would be truly feared. Joe then brought all the living beings back and was the hero of all the ghosts who remained there.

David Gay (12)
Sir Joseph Williamson's Mathematical School

Thunder And Lightning

Once there was a god called Zeus. He was the ruler of all gods in Heaven. But there was another god called Hades, Zeus' brother. Hades was the ruler of the Underworld (Hell). He despised his brother Zeus, so he had been planning an invasion of Heaven.

He wanted this so he could be the ruler of both worlds, Heaven and Hell. He had been planning for centuries and he had devised a plan to send spirits to Heaven to surprise-attack them. He had millions of spirits in Hell: murderers, thieves and cannibals, really they were bad people who had sinned.

On the 18th January the army fled Hell and headed for Heaven. The angels in Heaven fought strong and after days on end of fighting, Heaven prevailed.

Now, every nine months, Hades sends spirits to fight again but as Zeus knows they come, he throws thunder and lightning bolts to stop them. Sometimes he hits Earth, and that is the cause of thunder and lightning.

Cameron Bishop (11)
Sir Joseph Williamson's Mathematical School

The Dreaded Parents' Evening

Parents' evening just happened to be the day after my mum dyed her hair. I had told her to be careful, but something terrible happened. The dye turned Mum's hair bright orange and she said there was nothing she could do about it at such short notice. I really didn't want to take her to parents' evening, but my dad was away on business.

The walk to school was just as bad as I had thought it would be. People looked twice as we walked down the long road and up the hill to my school.

'I don't know what you're embarrassed about,' my mum said. 'I think it looks pretty cool.'

'I'm sure the teachers will get the wrong impression, Mum,' I moaned.

At last we entered the school and I'm sure I could see my friends sniggering in a group. I could feel myself going as red as my mum's hair and I tried to look as though she didn't belong to me. My first appointment was with my English teacher, Mrs Batwell. I was dreading it. To make matters worse, I knew that my mum's voice was very loud and she doesn't stop chatting. As we headed for Mrs Batwell's table, I was wishing the floor would swallow me up. My mum turned on her very best posh and jolly voice, which everyone in the hall could hear. I don't know how I survived the next few minutes next to my most embarrassing mum.

Eventually we walked home (not together). I stayed a few steps behind, but it was too late, I was dreading school in the morning. All I could hear from my mum was, 'I think that went really well, don't you?'

George Wright (12)
Sir Joseph Williamson's Mathematical School

The Night From Hell

I was dreading this day for weeks. It was parents' evening. I hate it so much for the reason my mum has to come. She shows me up at every opportunity.

A few weeks later and it was the day before parents' evening. My mum was sorting through some old photos of me when I was a baby and said, 'I wonder what your teacher would think if I showed her these photos?'

I was flabbergasted, but dare I say a word, or she would do worse.

The evening was drawing closer and I walked into Mum's bedroom to see a vivid, bright green chequered jacket and a skirt to match. I was horror-struck. My heart sank as my mates would all be there.

We were all just leaving for parents' evening and my mum looked like a dog's dinner (absolutely dire), but I knew it would be over soon.

When we arrived in school, I was mortified. I excused myself and said I had to help the teachers. I could hear tales around the school about a lady in a Scottish-type checked outfit, and how terrible she looked, (I would have defended my mum, but I had to agree). Then my worst nightmare happened, Mrs Atwal walked towards me with a grin and said, 'Daniel, I just met your mother, she is very proud of you. She has just shown me some elegant pictures of you as a baby!' And with that, she walked off with a smirk.

Daniel Forster (12)
Sir Joseph Williamson's Mathematical School

Spirits

Rondo climbed into bed that night, blowing out the candle that was beside him. It had been a perfect day, and Rondo lay there thinking about how lovely it was. But it suddenly went cold, gusts of frosty air swooping around the house. It was as if a fan were in his house, only colder, and a lot harsher. He looked up cautiously for a moment, then almost like nothing had ever happened, dropped down onto his hay pillow into a deep sleep. The strange gust of wind came closer as he was in his sleep, and closer, and closer still, until it was hovering above him. As fast as a bird, the hovering hair formed into a ragged cloth, with eyes as fierce as a bull. It screeched in an eerie voice, 'Get *out!*'

Rondo shot up from his pillow, a sweat and very high pulse about him. Thinking it was only a dream, he laid his heavy head back on the pillow, until he felt the gust of wind again. It wasn't a dream. Could Rondo get rid of it?

Rondo got out of bed, picked up his lamp and went searching, searching around the dark caverns and caves of his underground home. There was a scream around every corner, a whisper in his ear. He was getting closer; he could feel the cool, damp air masses around his face, freezing his facial expression. Suddenly, the same phrase met his ears again, this time from behind him.

'Get out!'

He span around, shining the torch at the bull-eyed cloth, which made it run and screech. Maybe they don't like light. That's why they are trying to claim the dark, dingy environment of their home. He chased it, further and further into the darkness until … no way out. The light from the torch was a gun to the spirit; it killed him.

Jamie Taylor (12)
Sir Joseph Williamson's Mathematical School

Sole Purpose

The six men tenaciously trudged through the dense jungle, ignoring the irritating drone of the mosquitoes. They had one objective: to receive the documents that would prevent the oncoming war. Sam knew how important the mission was. At 23, Sam had been in the SAS for two years but, nonetheless, he was still a vital member of the squad.

'Okay, guys, we're there,' the lieutenant whispered. Signalling to Sam and the others to follow him, he cautiously crept towards the entrance. Seeing a guard posted there, he turned to Sam. 'Take him out!'

Equipping a silencer to his pistol, Sam crept silently forward and pulled the trigger. *Thud!* The guard's limp body slid to the floor.

'Good job ...' the lieutenant began.

'Damn! Man down, I repeat, *man down!*' yelled a soldier, opening fire on the exposed group.

As Sam dived for cover, men exploded out of the camp, AKs chattering away.

Using the chaos to his advantage, Sam slipped into the camp, and made towards the main building. Seeing two soldiers, he quickly substituted his pistol for a pump-action shotgun and shredded the two mercenaries. Sam cautiously opened the door. *'SAS, don't move!'* yelled Sam, aiming at a soldier. 'Hand over the documents and no one will get hurt,' he said steadily.

The frightened soldier shoved the documents into Sam's hand. Sam made towards the entrance and gasped. His entire squad lay on the floor, dead. Something slammed into his chest. A crimson stain spread across his shirt. Then, blackness.

Tom Warway (12)
Sir Joseph Williamson's Mathematical School

The Last Thing The Human Race Will Ever Do …

Many people didn't believe me when I said that the world was going to end, but when it happened, they fell at my knees in deepest apology.

I'd known for centuries, probably because I was one of the oldest entities in the universe. There were others that were older than me, but on Earth, I was the oldest.

I lived my life scarcely, not letting on to people I wasn't actually human, and was made up of the force those pitiful humans called magic. OK, so I'll admit it, I was much more powerful than them, and could have been their king. But they didn't deserve it. They'd ruined my master's finest work and had disrespected and forgotten his name.

There was another reason: if I had have done this, another entity would rise and track me down and kill me. I didn't want to die, so I obeyed the rules.

I told those post-evolutionary apes that if they wanted to live, they should take sanctuary in the isle of Britain, a place wrought with residuary power of my master. At least there, I could sacrifice myself to save the minority of the human race.

It was what my master wanted, to save his most perfect creation. But the Earth had been placed in the orbit of a dying sun. This is the only time I shall say my master was incompetent.

The second time I called my master incompetent was when the human race did not even give thanks to me for saving them.

Jake Baker (15)
Temple School

The Red Sky

It was a lovely day at the beach. A young girl named Katie was on the way to the sea with her best friend, David. Both David and Katie were 11 years old.

'God, it's cold,' said David, whilst stepping into the sea.

'Blimey! Yes!'

Everything was going just fine, until the clouds turned red …

'Oh no! Thunder and lightning!' screamed David and Katie.

Suddenly the waves started to grow bigger and stronger. Everything went black!

'Argh!'

Everything started to flash red again.

'David, where are you?' Katie started to drift further into the sea. Then all of a sudden, out of nowhere, a massive splash! 'Oh my God!' screamed Katie … it was silent.

'Ouch.' Her foot had just been cut by something strange … it turned the sea the same colour as the sky, *red*. 'Oh David, where are you?' Another splash, and another, until she saw three sharks circling under her! And then David's body, floating above the shore. 'Oh David! And I said everything was going to be fine, but you left me David! I'm on my own with three sharks circling me, and the sea is the same colour as my foot!' At the last pant, she could just figure out a face in the sky. 'Why did you do this to me? What did I do?'

Just then, a shark opened its mouth ready to take off her head … 'Argh!' Katie woke up in her bed! 'What's going on?' she whispered to herself. 'Hhsst!' She looked at her foot; it was still bleeding. But how did she end up in her bed? 'I'm laying safe in my bed and David's dead! I invited him to die. Was I dreaming or not? I can't remember, but I've still got the cut on my foot …'

Tanya Waghorn (12)
The Bradbourne School

Just A Dream!

One dark, cold, misty morning, it was as cold as a freezer. A young girl called Kerry Jones was walking to her bus stop. She was humming, except she couldn't hum properly because her jaw was shuddering so much. Kerry was cold to the bone. She was walking through a dark park and she could just see the sun peeping through the mist. A young man came out of nowhere and grabbed her. Kerry was screaming, but it was no use, it was too early; no one was awake.

The man whispered in her ear and said, 'If you don't shut up, I'm going to shoot you.' The man was pointing a gun into her head.

Kerry was crying hysterically and she was trying to talk, but every time she opened her mouth, no words came out. She was terrified.

He took her to an old barn and covered Kerry in hay. There was a big bang. Kerry looked around and all she could see was the roof falling down on her. She tried screaming, but she couldn't. She fainted!

She felt something cold touch her face. Suddenly, she was tied to a chair with tape over her face. The man ripped the tape off her face. He said, 'What's your name?'

Kerry tried to speak, but still no words came out, so the man beat her …

Georgia Donovan (12)
The Bradbourne School

Maybe Mars, Maybe Life

Friday the 13th, unlucky for some, but not for American scientists. As more photos are taken of Mars, scientists' predictions are coming true. But what prediction?

Professor Andrew McHowen told us, 'I am not willing to say! We're not certain yet. What we have found is not harmful to humans. We will inform you with more details'.

This sounds serious. What could it be? We will follow this up with another report in a week's time.

It has been seven days since we spoke to Professor McHowen.

'Professor, have you any more information following last week's silence?'

'Yes, we have flown spacecraft up to …'

'It's to do with space then?'

'Ah, well, yes.'

'Why can't you tell us after this much?'

'I've said too much already. I will not continue with this interview!'

Don't panic folks, in next week's edition we will be speaking to a different professor.

It has now been fourteen days since the first interview. Last week we managed to find out that all this fuss is over outer space. Have they found a new planet? Who knows? Now we are going to speak to Professor Michael Newhall.

'Professor, we are now on the third week since this all started. What's it about?'

'It has now been confirmed, so I can say: we have found a possible life form on Mars.'

'What kind of life form?'

'We have found water and possibly amphibians.'

'Wow. How amazing for you. Thank you for talking to us.'

'Pleasure.'

So folks, a life form on Mars. Let us know what you think about it.

Rachael Fletcher (11)
The Bradbourne School

A Day In The Life Of Me!

I woke up one morning and fell out of bed. As I looked up, bleary eyed, from my position on the floor, I noticed the calendar and my heart sank. It was Friday the 13th. Everything bad happens to me on this day. Last year on Friday the 13th I broke my arm and the year before I cracked a tooth.

My uniform usually hangs on my cupboard door - but it wasn't there! I then heard a commotion outside my room; I got up and ran to open the door. There I discovered my dog and my little brother playing tug-of-war with my uniform! *'Stop it!'* I screamed at them. I pulled my uniform out of their reach and stomped back into my room to get dressed.

I went downstairs, grabbed my bag, and glanced at the clock to realise I'd overslept! I ran down the lane from my house, turned the corner and saw my bus pulling in at my bus stop; luckily I just managed to catch it.

As soon as I got to school it started to rain. 'Just my luck,' I grumbled to myself, 'netball will be cancelled.'

When it was time for netball, however, the rain stopped and the sun popped out from behind a cloud, and a glorious rainbow appeared! I played netball - my team won!

That afternoon I was first in the bus queue (*never* happened before) so I got the best seat! When I got home, Mum had cooked my favourite meal, and my homework seemed easier that evening too. As I fell asleep that night, I thought that maybe Friday the 13th wasn't such an unlucky day for me after all!

Rebecca Moore (11)
The Bradbourne School

Bullying

It was early in the morning. Everyone was at school sitting at their desks, but the teacher, Miss Pettigrew, got held up with the head teacher, Mr Sharp, because two new girls had arrived. The teacher took the two new girls to the classroom and introduced them to all the children. They were called Lisa and Hannah, they were twins. Miss Pettigrew sat them next to each other. She took the register and then asked everyone to paint a picture of the objects in front of them. Soon, the bell went for lunch.

When everyone had had their lunch, they went into the playground for a while. Lisa and Hannah went up to two other girls in their class called Stacey and Lauren, who were playing catch. Lisa and Hannah started being horrible to Stacey and Lauren by pushing them around and calling them names, and taking their ball and throwing it over the fence. When Lisa and Hannah pushed the other girls over, they really got hurt.

After lunch had finished, Stacey and Lauren went to Miss Pettigrew and explained to her what had happened at lunchtime. Miss Pettigrew was just about to go back into the classroom when she saw Lisa and Hannah pour paint onto another girl. Miss Pettigrew told them off and then took them to Mr Sharp to report them for bullying Lauren and Stacey, and pouring paint on another girl.

Mr Sharp talked to them severely and asked why they had behaved in this way.

They said, 'It was just a joke, Sir, we were being silly.'

He wasn't amused and sent them back to the classroom to apologise to the three girls and Miss Pettigrew in front of the class.

Chandni Patel (13)
The Bradbourne School

My Dad

It all started in the Second World War. My dad came down after tea, all dressed up in his uniform. He gave my mum a hug and said, 'I have to go, but I'll be back.' As he wiped a tear that was rolling down Mum's cheek, he re-hugged my mum, that's when he caught me looking.

He came over to me and said, 'Now you be a good boy for your mum now, won't you, and look after her.' He gave me a big grin, but I knew deep down he was nervous. I gave him a hug, trying not to cry myself. I had to be strong. Dad never cried in front of me or Mum, he was brave. You see, my dad's a soldier and he is going to fight in the war. When I get older, I want to be just like him. I took hold of Dad's hand and walked him to the front door. I watched as he walked down the pathway. I never took my eyes off him until I couldn't see him anymore. I knew deep down this could be the last time I'd ever see him.

That's when Mum let go of my hand. 'Now come on, go upstairs and put on your pyjamas, like a good boy,' her voice breaking as if she were just about to cry.

I did what she said, I could tell she was already upset, so I did as I was told. I got to the top of the stairs; I looked back and I could see my mum wiping her eyes.

Sarah Barden (15)
The Bradbourne School

He Takes Gold, Not Silver

My Grand National Champion will retire next year, after he's run his last Grand National.

He has just turned 15 years old this month, and in his lifetime, won 25 races. This summer he will be put into our 20 acre field for a month, and then be brought back into training for his last couple of races. At the moment, he is in his 20 x 18 wooden stable amongst the other racehorses.

Every week, he goes into his solarium for at least two hours. We then take him down to the gallops for an hour's sprint twice a week, and then he goes into the horse-pool every other day for 20 minutes. We also ride him to his local pub every Friday to meet his fans and supporters.

He is also racing at Ascot, Lingfield, Newmarket, and then the Grand National. At Ascot he will be racing against his table mate, Harry Hill.

At last week's grand National, I bet on Silver Spurs, £100. he was 20-1, which I still can't believe he won and I won £2,000, but I also won a champion cup, Moet et Chandon champagne and a £350,000 cheque. With our winnings, we are going to extend the stables and buy an Oakley Supreme horsebox. We are hoping that Silver Spurs will win next year's Grand National, and I want to thank all the fans and supporters of Silver Spurs.

Hannah Boyden (15)
The Bradbourne School

A Day In The Life Of Jordan (Katie Price)

Looking in the mirror, I think I need another boob job. I turn sideways, my belly is *sooo* big. Peter walks in. He says that I am beautiful. I just hope that my baby is as beautiful as he says I am. Not saying that my Harvey isn't beautiful, but he isn't very well. I hope my baby is well.

Right, I've got to do six photo shoots, three interviews and one radio show; busy day, plus I've got a scan at six o'clock today. Peter's got a rehearsal for 'Footballers' Wives' today, because he's making a one-off appearance. What to wear? What to wear? I know, I'll wear my designer poncho and my Luvaton joggers. I've already had a wash, so I don't need to do that. I don't fancy any breakfast and Harvey's with the nanny, so I jump in the car with Peter and we speed off.

Back at home, and the scan went quite well. Unfortunately, my photo shoot photographer said that I couldn't have any more shots until I had given birth, so that isn't very lucky. Peter's rehearsal went well and he's shooting in a couple of days. Oh my God, I just felt a kick.

'Katie, phone for you!' shouts Peter up the stairs.

I waddle downstairs and take the phone. Oh, we have just been offered to present a category in the British Soap Awards. I said yes!

That really was a day in my life.

Allanda Byrom (12)
The Bradbourne School

A Day In The Life Of A Prisoner Of War

It will not wash off. I supposed it wouldn't, not without soap. Spit, German spit. It has gone from my face, and yet it still stains me. It could have been worse, I could have been taken. They say that they are moving some of us, we all know they are lying. In some ways it is a relief not to have been taken. But my face has another stain; soon there will be nowhere for them to stain my face. Then it will be my turn, to do what they call moving to a bigger camp. But it is not true. They are really taking us to our death: extermination camps.

I knew one of the five they took today. He was young, with a wife and a child on the way. If he hadn't have looked up, he would have been all right. God didn't choose his death, he did.

Every three days we are made to kneel down and hopefully be spat at, or if not, you're taken to your death. I have lost track of the days now, they have all merged into one. How long have I been here? I don't know. Weeks, months, years even. I have given up hope. No one will rescue me, not before it's too late. They beat us too. We fight not just to stay alive, but to keep the little sanity we have left in us. I eat nothing, I drink nothing and feel nothing, not now I know the truth!

Helen Trim (13)
The Bradbourne School

Strange Things Happen

I was running as fast as my legs would carry me, my heart pounding. Where will I go? I kept going, following my nose. 'Come back, it's not your fault, I think'. 'I think', I was repeating those words over and over again in my head. As much as I tried, they wouldn't go away. I turned round the corner and froze. This was it, this is what I saw: an abandoned field, lying there for the taking. As I walked to the middle of the field, I was suddenly full of happiness again. All my worries gone, vanished into thin air. I entered a small forest-like place, then I saw it.

I climbed through a bush and there stood an empty cottage. I crept inside. It was so quiet, you could have heard a pin drop. The cupboards were so dusty they had turned white. There was a kitchen in the corner. It had a small stove for cooking, a sink which had so many dirty dishes in I lost count, and a clear surface to prepare food. Then as I turned, to my great delight was a bed. As I rested my head on the pillow, I felt as if I was floating away.

Suddenly, a loud gunshot made me jump out of my skin. I leapt out of bed and shot home. I was running so fast, I was barely touching the ground.

I was home. I walked through my mum. I'm dead …

Natasha Williams (13)
The Bradbourne School

Headache!

Mr and Mrs Jack Smith were driving along in their car through Darkbell Woods. As you can probably tell, they were very dark, dense, spooky, horrible woods.

Suddenly, the car came to a halt, and Mr Smith realised that they had run out of petrol. 'Sorry, Molly dear, we seem to have run out of petrol!'

Then they saw a spooky, yellow glowing light up ahead of them.

'Look, Jack,' Molly said, 'at that light. Up ahead, look. It might be a petrol station! Go on, get a can.'

'Fine, Molly.'

So off Jack went, heading towards the glowing, spooky light.

Bang! Bang! Bang!

What was that? A woodpecker maybe? thought Molly. She decided to ignore it.

Bang! Bang! Bang!

It was that noise again! Molly slowly got out of the car and looked out. *Bang!*

She looked on top of the car and she saw a woodcutter! But she could tell, it was no human. She could see right through him. He was holding an axe with blood on the blade, and worse still, he was holding her husband's head by the hair! She screamed.

Whoosh! Chop! Her head fell to the floor.

The next day, the police arrived at the scene of the crime, but there was no sign of a murder. They had sniffer dogs, detectives, police and members of the public on the case and they found … nothing. All they found was some blood on the floor. No car, no bodies, no nothing.

More deaths were reported, but when the police arrived, all they found was a message in blood saying, *'I am the phantom head-chopper, will you be next?'*

Amy Critcher (12)
The Bradbourne School

Help!

Dear Agony Aunt,

I am having a terrible time at school lately. I used to have quite a few friends, but when I broke up with my best friend, Natalie, she made everyone in the class hate me! I haven't got any friends to eat with, so I eat on my own on a table right at the back of the canteen! I am so upset that I start to cry all the time at home, and I take all my frustration out on my family.

Please help,
> Temelle (13)

Dear Temelle,

Whatever has happened between you and your friends seems to be having a bad effect on them and you. I think that you should make the first step toward being friend again by apologising, even If they laugh. You need to look like the bigger person in during this argument. You should also take up a club during lunchtimes and after school, this way you will make more friend and you may even pick up new skills! If Natalie continues this bullying, you should tell a teacher or your mum, because they could help it stop.

I hope my advice works, and do write back to tell me what has happened!
> Agony Aunt.

Dear Agony Aunt,

Thank you for your advice! I used it and made more friends by going to the clubs, which include art, technology and music.

Natalie continued to bully me, so I told my mum, who helped it stop. We are still not friends, but at least some of my form and teaching group like me again. I have also stopped crying and getting angry at my family, I have even started to help my little brother with his homework! The one good thing that has come out of our row is that it has brought me closer to my family, so that is the one thing I would like to thank her for!

But I am thanking you the most for putting my life back on track!
> Temelle (13)

Dear Temelle,

I am glad my advice helped you make more friends and gain new skills!

Good luck for the future,
    Agony Aunt.

Sophie Williams (13)
The Bradbourne School

The Walk Never To Forget

One day in November a lady, who doesn't want to be named, had taken her 12-month-old child to a park for the day to feed the swans. On her way home, she saw a lady who was looking at them weirdly, but she thought nothing of it.

Suddenly, the old lady took off her wig and ripped off her clothes, and she turned out to be a male.

He started to chase the lady, and when he got close to her, he pulled out of his pocket a microphone and said, 'Hi, we're here from the game show 'Money! Money!'' As he was speaking, a cameraman came out from a bush.

The lady said, 'I though I was going to die, I was so relieved when I found out I was going on a brand new game show'.

Phillippa Rowland (11)
The Bradbourne School

A Day In The Life Of A Five Pound Note

Hi, I'm a five pound note and I'm going to tell you about my day. Here goes …

I started off in a young man's pocket. I was very uncomfortable in there as he kept putting his hand in the pocket and rustling me around. He went into a shop and bought something. As he reached the till, he lifted me out of the pocket. Phew, I had air. He handed me to a lady, she pulled me, looking at me and plonked me in a till.

It wasn't long before I was handed to someone else. This girl folded me very neatly and put me in her purse. I was in there with two twenty pound notes and one ten, I had a chat with them and they told me they had been in that purse for twelve days. I thought that I would have a long time to wait until I saw light again. Anyway, I'd rather be in there than that man's pocket. The girl kept opening and closing her purse; each time I got my hopes up, but it wasn't me.

I finally got taken out, but where was I going? Argh, through a slot, round and round I went, until plop, I fell into a pile of coins.

Well, it may have been boring, but that was my day.

Kate Rivers (11)
The Bradbourne School

A Day In The Life Of A Stray Dog

Hi, I am Jess. I am a stray dog. It is only because my owners moved and didn't tell me. I was asleep and they moved, and when I woke up, they were gone.

Anyway, I've got over that. I normally sleep under the local bridge in Swanley. In the mornings, on Monday, I go to the Pizza Hut place and flutter my eyelids and they give me half a pizza. On Tuesdays, it's the butchers, I do a flip and they give me seven sausages. On Wednesday I go to the local bakery and I fetch the Daily Mail for them, and they give me a crusty roll, maybe with a bit of bacon in. On Thursdays, I go to the old lady at the end of the road and get some scraps from her. On Fridays, which is today, I go to Tescos where there is some lovely burnt toast for me to eat. (Yum-yum.)

I think that now I have had my lovely toast, I will go and have a short nap where I sleep. You know, under the bridge. I told you earlier. Oh look, I am here. Well I suppose I am going to have to say goodbye for now, seeing as I am having my nap. I hope you enjoyed hearing about my life. See you soon. Bye!

Laura Seare (12)
The Bradbourne School

It's A Catastrophe!

This tragic story took place on Friday 13th at around 8.30 at night. Suzanne Dale, aged 32, was walking home from her job at the local Sainsbury's supermarket. As she walked past the corner shop on Wilby Road, she heard a miaowing noise coming from a plastic bag beside the wall of the shop. It was not moving. Suzanne was intrigued, she untied the knot on the bag and looked inside, where there lay four black and white kittens!

Suzanne was amazed! She looked around to see if any one was there, and quickly rang the RSPCA to tell them what had happened. Unfortunately they had closed for the day. Suzanne took the kittens home, looked after them for the night and waited until morning to take them to the centre. The kittens were diagnosed with breathing problems and were rushed into theatre immediately. After a long and difficult operation only three kittens survived. Suzanne was allowed to take them home two days later, she had become so attached to them the night she took them in. They are all doing fine at the moment and are in good care.

The person who left the kittens outside the shop still hasn't been found, but the RSPCA are still looking. If the person is caught, they could face fines of up to £2,000, or be put in jail.

Nicole Young (12)
The Bradbourne School

A Day In The Life Of Molly!

I don't live with my family! I was taken away when I was only small, to a boarding house. It's very clean and the food's good, plus I've made loads of new friends.

When I woke up this morning the sky was blue and the sun lit up my bedroom. I couldn't wait to go and play in the long wavy grass with my mates. But first, I had to eat my breakfast. I fancied an apple today, don't know if I'll get one. At last I've finished, I can go out now! The door is open, here I go.

We played for hours until we came across a hole in the fence that we'd never seen before. Peter crawled through and ran straight towards the main road. We all called him back, but he didn't listen and he just kept running. I went running after him, still shouting out for him to come back, but he couldn't hear me over the sound of the traffic.

I followed him over the road and into the bushes. It was then that Peter realised I was behind, when a huge Great Dane came bounding towards us. We both turned round and ran as fast as we could, over the road, down the grass field and through the hole.

It was getting dark now. We played one more game called 'tag in the dark', it was really fun. Then I got tired, so I went back to my hutch for the night.

Alice Jamieson (11)
The Bradbourne School

A Day In The Life Of Amber

Hi, my name is Amber. I live on a farm, not a very big one, it just has ducks, chickens, cows, sheep, goats and some horses. I'm going to take you around a day on the farm and what we do.

The day starts off at 7am when I have breakfast, then I wash and get dressed. After I'm dressed, I go out and milk the cows. I do about four buckets, then I feed the goats. I like to feed Betty, she never bites and has a patch over her eye.

After that, I get the eggs from the chicken houses, but Dad always says to stay away from Sparky, he's the boss and doesn't like people. I take 20 eggs from each house. I have lunch now, which is soup with ice cream, then I fetch Nana, our sheepdog and round up the sheep.

Finally, I ride my horse, Starfire. She's black with a lovely personality, and we go in the field with Nana. Starfire is a three-time champion at racing and jumping.

I hope you enjoyed the tour of my day. Bye.

Helen Hayes (11)
The Bradbourne School

A Day In The Life Of Brooklyn Beckham

'Brooklyn, Brooklyn, breakfast is ready! Come and get it.'

I wake up at … I dunno what time and then go and see what Daddy has cooked me. Yes! My favourite, egg with soldiers. Mum stays in bed. Daddy calls her 'Sleeping Beauty'. Romeo eats his sausages while Dad feeds Cruz and takes breakfast in to Mummy. Baby Cruz is so cute, I love him.

After breakfast, I go and watch 'Tweenies'. I like Jake the best, I like his hair. When 'Tweenies' finish, me and Romeo go in the pool with Mummy. We love playing in the pool, especially when Mummy puts the bubbles on. Then I get dressed into my Real Madrid kit. Today I am allowed to go to training with Daddy.

When we get there, Daddy has a little kick around with me, then he has to start training. I like watching my dad. He is the best in the world. Daddy is playing a match tonight against … I don't know, but I know he is going to score and the team is going to win. After training, me and Romeo play for a bit while Daddy gets ready for the match, and Mummy gets Cruz ready. Me and Romeo like playing together. Sometimes we fight, but not all the time. We love Cruz, he is so cute! Daddy said he is going to be a footballer because he kicks his legs a lot!

After, we all go to the match. Mummy talks to these people while me and Romeo play football. When we watch Daddy play, we shout and jump up and down. When the match is over, because Daddy's team won, we all go to the party after, where we have our dinner and dance. I love days out with Mummy and Daddy. When I get older, I am going to be a footballer like my dad. You wait and see.

Georgia Satterly (13)
The Bradbourne School

A Day In The Life Of A Cart Donkey

My day starts at the break of dawn. My master will saddle and bridle my sore back and lice-eaten face. I then troop on down the rickety old road where rocks cut into my lame feet, and if I fall, my master will whip and beat me with a sharp stick. He does not seem to know the pain I go through just for him, and that pulling a heavy cart in the hot sun all day, every day, is making me suffer and I am very unhappy.

But one day, I did not get up at dawn, but when I felt like it. As my eyes adjusted to the light in my leaky shelter, I saw a well-dressed English man. He was patting me, but I moved quickly away into a corner, thinking he was going to hit me. I closed my eyes for I thought that he was coming towards me, but there was nothing, so I opened my eyes and he was gone.

Plucking up the courage to leave my shelter, I heard English voices as well as others, I then came across my donkey companions tied up, having their wounds and sores bathed, and their hooves trimmed. I was confused. Were they helping us or hurting us? Then a kind-looking lady came up to me and gave me a deep, cool bucket of water and filling oats, and she steadied my nerves. I now knew I was loved!

Emma Cooper (13)
The Bradbourne School

A Scuba-Diving Experience

It's a hot sunny day here in Greece and I am on the boat preparing for my dive. I have got all my equipment on and I'm ready to go in the sea, which is 25°/28°.

I've now got on the seat and have my back to the water, ready to roll in. I'm holding my mask and regulator in place and am now rolling back into the sea. I have now entered the inner space, a totally different place and experience. I'm now descending and going down to 18 metres, equalising on the way down. I've reached my depth and I am now finning along with all the different species of underwater life.

I've now come across a sea urchin and am breaking open the top, and as I am doing this, all of the fish around me are coming to feed. It is fantastic because I am feeding the fish myself, by hand. The fish are now going, after feeding on the urchin. On the rocks there is a jet-black, slimy ball, which I have now just touched, which happened to be a living sponge. It is all soft and smooth, better than the ones we have in our bathrooms.

I have just looked at my computer and my air time is coming to an end, so I am now ascending slowly on my way up. I've now returned to the surface and I'm climbing back on board.

It was a fantastic experience. I thoroughly enjoyed it.

Rhonda Trevillion (14)
The Bradbourne School

The Wizardry Spell That Turned Ugly

On one cold winter's evening, deep in the darkest woods upon the tallest mountain, lived a wizard. The wizard had a tall blue hat and an extensive cloak, which reached the floor; he also had a white bushy beard like a ball of fluff. This wizard wasn't your ordinary wizard, or have a normal name, he was Calim Zugiefz, who was a very disorganised man. There were bits and bobs everywhere, you couldn't walk through the house without falling over.

One day, Mr Zugiefz was mixing a spell together to make him beautiful, until it went terribly wrong and got mixed with some dog face potion. Calim didn't know that this had happened and drank some. Nothing happened straight away, but something was sure to go wrong.

The next day when Mr Zugiefz woke up, he felt some sharp teeth and floppy ears. He jumped out of his bed and looked in the mirror and saw this dog. Calim hated dogs. So he went back to his potion room and tried to mix together a cure, but it was no use. Everything he tried didn't work and he became so angry, he threw his dog face potion into the local town's spring water supply, but he didn't realise this till the next day …

Abigail Allfrey (13)
The Bradbourne School

House For The Entities

Kamoto was a young girl who worked at a place called The Spirit House. The Spirit House was an inn for the spirits. Magical creatures stayed there when they were travelling. Kamoto was a human servant girl who worked there. She was about 15 years old and her best friend, a lady called Rosieka, was around 24 years old. She had been Kamoto's friend and guide since Kamoto was only 9.

Kamoto was always running errands for the landlady, Raven. This time she had to travel to a place called the Rainy Basin to deliver a package. The package belonged to Raven's sister, Shanty. But on the way to the dark and mysterious Rainy Basin, she came across a dojong. Dojongs were dark and mysterious creatures that were once good, but had turned to the dark side. Even Kamoto was afraid of them. She had no choice but to face it …

The Spirit House remained shrouded in mystery.

Natalie Howie (13)
The Bradbourne School

My Journey

'Ellie!' Mum called. 'We have to go early for the school trip today!'

I pulled myself out of bed and headed for the bathroom.

Mum called again, 'Do you want bacon and eggs for breakfast?'

I replied, 'Yes please.'

I went to my bedroom and got dressed and ran downstairs. I could smell the bacon cooking.

Mum was rushing around and getting ready. I jumped from the table and went and brushed my teeth. I went outside and sat in the car. Five minutes later, Mum jumped in. She turned the key. As the engine roared, she took off the handbrake and off we went.

The traffic was bad, as Mum was cursing the steering wheel. 'Come on, get a move on.'

We finally arrived at school. I ran into class and shouted, 'We haven't gone yet, have we?'

Mrs Smith replied, 'Not yet.'

I said goodbye to Mum and we got into the school coach. We were on our way to Bodiam Castle.

It was a long drive, but we got there eventually. We had a guided tour lined up. It reached 10am and we started the tour. I was walking behind my teacher, when I saw a tiny door. I went in; a bright light filled the room. I touched the light, it sizzled. Suddenly I was transported …

Laura Little (13)
The Bradbourne School

A Day In The Life Of Deryck From Sum 41

I decided to go and see the rest of the band and then suddenly, they were all sitting at a table and seeing people auditioning. I bellowed out, 'What's going on?'

'Ah, sorry, Deryck, but we've decided to get someone to take your place,' said James.

'But why?' I said.

'Because you suck. We hardly ever sing, it's always you singing, just us playing the guitar.'

'Fine, whatever, bye,' I said. I stormed out. I never knew they were like that. Well that's it, I'll show them. I'm getting my own band together.

The next day I saw my old band with a new member in it; it was Avril Lavigne. I went up to them and said, 'Hey, I used to go out with Avril Lavigne. Are you doing this on purpose?'

'No mate, she's a really good rock singer, like us,' said Mark.'

'Yeah, Deryck, you suck,' said Avril.

'Whatever - I'm going, bye.' I walked off and accidentally bumped into Adam from Blink 182.

'Hi, Deryck,' said Adam.

'Oh right, hi … um, James is it?' I said.

'No, no, no, no, it's Adam.'

'Oh my God, I'm so sorry,' I said.

'It's OK. Hey, I heard that you split up - well the others didn't, but you left and they have Avril Lavigne now,' said Adam.

'Yeah, it's true. Oh well, it doesn't matter,' I said. 'Well I know this is a bit soon, but would you like to join our band?' said Adam.

Emma Brereton (12)
The Bradbourne School

The Curse Of The China Doll

One day, a little girl called Molly was out with her grandma, when a little china doll caught her eye. 'Please can I get that doll, please?' said Molly.

'Yes my darling, you can,' said her grandma.

So they went into the shop, there was a little Chinese lady at the till. 'Hello there, what would you like?' said the Chinese lady.

Molly looked at the doll and pointed at it.

When they got home, Molly put it on her window sill. When night came, Molly went to sleep with her china doll. When Molly's grandma went to see her, she saw two red eyes looking at her. She turned her light on, but it was nothing. She went to her room, turned her light off and was just about to go to sleep. She opened her eyes and she saw the two red eyes looking at her.

Suddenly she saw blood on her bed. She saw Molly dead - the doll had stabbed her. They both lay there dead.

When Molly's mum went to go and pick her up, she opened the door and called their names. 'Molly?'

'Mum.'

She went upstairs. She opened Molly's door and saw blood on her bed. She saw it on the floor, it led into Grandma's room. She pushed the door open, blood was all over the bed.

Suddenly the lights went out. Something got her leg. She fell over, then she saw the two red eyes. Then she was dead.

The curse still lives …

Ellena Pitt (12)
The Bradbourne School

Have Fun In The Summer Holidays

I am writing to inform you that in the summer holidays we are having a two week activity school. The dates for the summer school are 26th July to the 8th August 2005. We will provide lunch, but only sandwiches, drinks, crisps, fruit, yogurt and chocolate. Teachers from the school will be taking part helping the children. Every teacher will have a group of between 8-10, this teacher will look after your child for the whole two weeks. Below is the itinerary for the two weeks.

- 26th - We will show the pupils around the school and meet some new friends.
- 27th - Fitness day
- 28th - Games, quizzes
- 29th - Day out to Eagle Heights
- 30th - Art
- 31st - Make a bird mask
- 1st - Dance for the day
- 2nd - Food technology
- 3rd - Science (explosion)
- 4th - Go and help with horses and have a ride for free
- 5th - Bring your pets to school (how to look after)
- 6th - Quizzes and games
- 7th - Trampolining
- 8th - Thorpe Park
- 9th - Leaving assembly

We hope all these activities outside, like Thorpe Park and Eagle Heights, the children will have permission from a parent or guardian.

I do hope your child or children will be able to attend these two weeks. It would help us and them with the new school and meeting new friends. We would also like the parents to attend the assembly where we will be showing pictures of what the children have been doing and have achieved.

Yours sincerely,
Alex Harradine.

Alex Harradine (113)
The Bradbourne School

The Girl Who Had No Friends

One day, Tina went to school as usual in the morning. As soon as she got in, Charlie, Keriena, Sophie and their friends started to bully her.

They accused her, sent her horrible notes, they ganged up on her, got other people to be horrible to her, pushed her, hit her, called her names and made funny faces at her and gave her horrible looks. They also sent horrible notes with her name on, talked about her and told lies about her.

This lasted for three weeks. During that time she told her form tutor twice, but she didn't do anything. Then she told her head of year (Mrs Brown) five times. She didn't do anything. Finally, she told her dad. He phoned in three times to Mrs Brown. She still didn't reply or deal with it. He told her to forget about it. She didn't forget about it. She wanted herself to be heard. It finally stopped, but did it … ?

Tamanna Miah (11)
The Bradbourne School

The Cabin

I was out on a Sunday afternoon with my mates, Luke, Emma, Lisa and Jo, when we spotted loads of smoke wafting up from the end of the road. It was so huge, it looked like a volcano, but we knew it wasn't. So we all jumped on our bikes and sped off down the road to investigate. We lost the fire and came to a public footpath leading through the countryside, so we all screeched our bike brakes and propped our bikes up on a nearby fence and walked down the tiny country path.

I had to run through a field of stinging nettles and no one helped me, even though I was wearing a skirt and was getting stung. We came to a dead end, so we came back, but just as we were about to leave we saw a man in a log cabin holding a knife. He then plunged it down. I turned away and heard a huge, blood-curdling scream. We ran to our bikes, through the stinging nettles and over a fence, and rode speedily down the road. But someone was following us. Luke saw a man holding something run into a bush and we screamed and rode off.

I don't know what happened after that, I just know I'm going back tonight …

Jasmine Hood (12)
The Bradbourne School

New House - Scary Surprise

Dear Diary,

Hiya! This is the first time I've written to you since I moved into my new house! Do you remember, I told you about it? Oh, OK, I'll tell ya again. We've moved from Surrey to the Kent area 'cause we had a well small house and were sick of it. Well actually, I really liked it - it was snugly and cosy! But I was being bullied, so I am glad we moved. The only thing is that I'm sure our new house has a curse, or even a *ghost* or something. I know, it's horrible to think about isn't it? Oh, it gives me the creeps.

It started on Monday, when we heard things crashing about in one of the spare rooms, and then on Tuesday, we were hearing footsteps and creaks of floorboards. And then on Friday, *Friday the 13th,* I was trying to get to sleep and then I felt something dragging me and then I couldn't breathe. I ran into my mum's room and she said it was nothing. But it was. I *know* it was.

On the next Monday, I decided to go to my new school, but it was just the same as my old one. The bullying started again, shouting names like 'four-eyes' and 'blonde bimbo' and loads more, but they're *really* rude so you don't really want to hear them. I ran home, I ran all the way and hid under my bed and cried. I thought I had got away from it, but then I heard a weird noise-like footsteps. But no one was there. No one could be there 'cause my mum was at work. Silently, I crawled from under my bed and looked out of my door. *Nothing.* I stared around my room and returned to looking out of my door and there it was, the most terrifying thing ever …

Georgina Poacher (13)
The Bradbourne School

Where Is The Light?

The pain was awful, but the feeling was great, just to feel one ray of light down on my face. Mum got angry at me for being awake during the day. She doesn't understand how I feel. Sometimes I just sit on the stairs crying, but then my mum comes along. She gets really angry when I wake her and she's trying to sleep, but nothing she does can be worse than being afraid of the dark and light.

This all started when I found out that I am allergic to light and my condition could be fatal if I stay in light for a certain amount of time.

I was eating my breakfast like I normally do, at 10 o'clock at night, when the house was burgled. I was so afraid, I didn't know what to do. I could have stopped him I guess, but he had a torch and I knew if he saw me, he'd shine it in my face. So I hid in one of the kitchen cupboards. Ever since then I've been afraid someone's in the house and I can't see them (because the house is too dark).

Someone asked me once, if I could wish for anything what would it be? I said, 'I wish I had a life.'

Sophie Brooker (13)
The Bradbourne School

Nothing To Say

'Talk, sweetie.'

I say nothing. I've never said anything, I don't think I ever will. Nobody understands. They all think I'm crazy. I'm not. They all think it's my fault … it's not … the doctors think I'm sick, very sick. I'm not … Mum's always getting angry. I can't talk. I won't talk. I'm scared to.

'Please, please talk,' Mum cries out to me as she sits on the sofa, rocking herself from side to side. She's the crazy one. Not me!

I've seen people to help me I mean, they don't help. Nobody can. My mind is blank, empty spaces. There's nothing there. I have a clear mind. I have a lot of time to think, but when I think I worry. I have to clear my mind of anything. It's like there's nothing inside me. Nothing at all.

I've been taken away to special homes, or that's what 'they' call them. They would just give me back to Mum. I was too much, they would say.

Mum's on the phone. I don't know who she's talking to. Probably Phil, the specialist. Mum calls him 'Help' when I'm being difficult. She says, 'I'm going to call 'Help' OK?'

But I would just pretend like I didn't hear her.

'He's not answering,' Mum says in a controlled panic. This scares me. I turn round and she's running out of the living room into the kitchen. I don't want to follow her. I always do though. This time I wait, just a little while, then I follow her. She's frantic, I'm so scared. She's crazy. Mad.

Mum is reaching into a cupboard, she turns around chewing something. She picks me up, rushes me to the sofa and sits down. Says nothing. And two minutes later, she's asleep. But she won't wake up …

Amelia Sharp (13)
The Bradbourne School

It's A Dog's Life!

Monday, 6.30am

Streeetch, 'Woof! Woof!' Let them know we need to check the garden out!

Anybody snuck in overnight? All clear …

Back in for breakfast, oh, only dog food. Yuck!

I'll sulk, grab a few zzzz, maybe chicken will appear?

8.30am

She's leaving for the school run, are we going too?

Yes, she's got our collars. Yippee!

Oh no, we're heading for the vets, no we've turned the corner
it's the park … phew!

We're here, I can't control this slobbering, it's embarrassing.

Let us out. Oh no, Polly the pain.

'Come on Daisy, keep your head down, run all the way, she can't keep up!'

9.30am

We made it! Back in the jeep. I'm in first.

No you're not, I'm in first. Ha, ha, beat you again.

We're home, there's the postman.

'Don't chase him Daisy, I'm warning you, *Daisy*!'

Too late! she's in for it when she comes back,

if she comes back.

10am

Now, about that chicken! It always works.

Mmm, yummy, time for zzz.

2.45pm

I see Daisy's back, she missed out on the chicken again
dumb dog!

If we sit here and eyeball her for a while
we'll get to go on the school run!

3.15pm

Yes, it worked. 'Come on Daisy, let's go!'

Jump in, ha ha, beat you again.

Waiting outside the schools, here they come,
hope they've remembered our treats?

Yummy, this slobbering's too much!

4pm
>Home again. Bored. That washing looks tempting on the line. Better leave it, chicken supper smells good!

6.30pm
>Master home, walkies time! 'Don't chase cats, Daisy, just try and behave *Daisy*!'
>Too late, she'll never learn.

8pm
>Phew, I'm exhausted. Zzzzzz.

Georgia Hart-Fisk (12)
The Bradbourne School

Gone Forever

It was a sunny day and it would have been the best - except!

It was called the funniest fair and everyone was talking about it. We all got packed up in the car; me, Mum and Dad. We had planned a day out at the funniest fair and it was going to be great! We got there and Dad gave me some money. I knew which ride I was going to go on - Haunted Dreams!

The man standing at the door looked a bit odd and I wasn't too sure whether to go on or stay away. After much thinking, I decided to go on. Bad idea!

I paid to go on and the man smiled. As I entered he shouted, 'And here you'll stay - forever!'

He slammed the door and as I flicked round, there was nothing! A blank, empty desert. I screamed, but no one heard. With nothing better to do, I started walking. After a while I remembered how hungry I was. My tongue was dry and I was hot. My head hurt and I realised it was useless, I would never escape. I fell down laughing to myself, though I had no idea why as there was nothing funny. But I couldn't help laughing. The heat had got to me - I was mad.

And that was when I gave up. I lay down and with a smile, I took my last breath!

Kiri Cramer (13)
The Bradbourne School

Blackburn Rovers Knocked Out By The Fantastic Gunners

The most exciting match of the season was just minutes away. It was played on Saturday, 16th April 2005 at the Millennium Stadium, Cardiff. It was Arsenal's last chance to win a cup this season.

Before the match all the players came onto the pitch and started to warm up. All the seats had been taken up by Arsenal fans, whereas the Blackburn allocation was not fully taken. Although the match started off very slowly, it got more and more exciting when Arsenal scored first, even though they were the only ones to score. Arsenal also went on to score another two goals which Robin Van-Persie scored beautifully.

The first goal was amazing. It was taken on the free kick position. The whistle was blown. He ran up to the ball and booted it into the top left hand corner. Every Arsenal fan stood up and cheered. It was a great atmosphere. As Van-Persie turned away to celebrate, a Blackburn player elbowed him in the face. Since we still are not sure whether it was accidental or not, it will be investigated by the FA. My personal opinion is that I don't think it was accidental, I think he did it on purpose.

The final score was Arsenal 3-0 Blackburn Rovers. Arsenal are now in the FA Cup Final to be played on the 21st May 2005. We won't know until tomorrow who their opponents will be.

The train on the way home was very boisterous. People were screaming, shouting and singing songs about the Arsenal players.

Chloe Brown (11)
The Bradbourne School

How The World Became What It Is Today

Many moons ago, a baby was born to Zeus and Athena. She had long, golden, flowing hair and shining blue eyes. She was named Athenia. As no one was protecting the sun, when she was old enough, it would be hers. Her older brother was protecting the moon. As men travelled to the moon and invaded it, he became angry. As the years passed he was known as Zook, the evil Moon God. Soon, Athenia was old enough to claim her title as Goddess of the Sun. She had healing powers and loved everything tidy.

As Keeper of the Light, she grew up giving the Earth its much needed light. People would see her for miles when she visited twice a month descending in a beam of light, her hair brushed and her dress spotless. She would clear up the litter, keeping the environment tidy, and heal the sick. She was hardworking, kind and brave.

Whenever her brother crossed her path and blocked the light, she would fight back with bravery and courage. Being young, she grew weak and had to give up. She would fight Zook for days and while she was busy, Earth would ignore her rules. They would discard her help and ill-treat the environment. She grew unhappy and that spread through the world. People began killing and making war. Athenia couldn't do anything, without happiness she was powerless.

Once the planet was lovely, now it was full of murders and wars. Athenia couldn't take the shame and poisoned herself. Man didn't know as they were busy doing wrong.

Without a leader we're hopeless.

Deborah Launchbury (11)
The Bradbourne School

Under The Tree

Summer was approaching and Tiger-eye was really excited. Although she was excited, she didn't want to do anything. But she did have her reasons - according to her.

'Tiger-eye.' Her mother had been nagging her for ages and ages. 'Please, please can you start stocking up?'

'No, not yet. I'm going to have a nap. See you later.' Tiger-eye walked off and said no more.

She found a spot under a tree where she could just relax. Tiger-eye ended up dozing off. She started to dream; the dream wasn't very interesting, then again, it wasn't boring. If anything, it was rather strange. Her dreams start as a big white mist, then go into a dream.

In this particular dream, there were three little girls, two of which were happy and playing in the sun and another one, who was rather sad. All sunburnt, bored, all because the little girl hadn't prepared for an enjoyable summer. Tiger-eye awoke with a fright and rushed home and started to gather summer essentials. She went to go and get some games for the summer.

When she arrived, all the games were gone. Nothing but a bottle of suncream. Throughout summer she was bored, had absolutely nothing to do. Basically, she wished that she'd been wise.

The moral to this story is that you need to think ahead to enjoy things to come. Not only in the future. Be in the know now.

Also, listen to your elders, don't just ignore them because you think you know best. People often are foolish and want everything to go their way.

Leanne Bashford (12)
The Bradbourne School

Knocked To The Ground

It was a cold winter's day. I, Laura Senetta, am fourteen years old and I was getting ready for yet another day of school at West Bridge High. Although I usually have a bowl of cornflakes, as I was running late, I just grabbed a cereal bar.

I ran out of the door kissing my mum goodbye, but as I ran out of the door and across the road, I heard tyres screech. I tried to run as I saw a car coming towards me.

Bang! It was too late, my fragile body had already hit the bonnet of the car and struck the ground. Although I was unconscious, I could hear sirens in the background and as I opened my eyes five hours later, I was in a hospital bed with an oxygen mask over my pale white face. I was wearing what looked like a blue-spotted nightie and my feet were bare.

The nurse came in and ran some tests and according to the results, I had a broken collar bone, fractured wrists and both my legs were broken. I also had many cuts and bruises and I felt so cold and shaky.

Three months later I was allowed home in a wheelchair. Unfortunately it's going to be that way for the rest of my life. So think. There's a lesson in this story. Always stop, look and listen before crossing the road.

Kirsty Brown (12)
The Bradbourne School

The Train Of Death

There I was, sitting on the train, it all seemed so simple at first. I was to get a train from Swanley to Victoria and then we were to meet to do business there. Johnny complicated things though, changed plans. That's how I got locked up, banged up for ten years. They'll let me out early if I behave, but I'm still looking at six to seven years. That's two thousand, one hundred and ninety days of my life. I wasn't meant to get involved, Johnny said he was going to give me some money to help me out. Somehow, I got locked up for being Johnny's accomplice to murder. Aiding and abetting the police called it.

As I was saying, it was all so simple at first. Then Johnny got on the train halfway through the journey. He said there'd been a big mistake and we had to cover up our tracks. I wasn't quite sure what he was going on about, but I followed him anyway. Gullible, I know.

Johnny stormed into her carriage, he grabbed her by the throat. I'd never seen him so mad, he was like a raging pitbull. I tried to block out the girl's scream as it pierced through my eardrums, filling my head until I felt like it was going to explode. I wanted it to end. I wanted it to be over.

There was a bump as the girl's body hit the floor. I stood there alone, with the blood on my hands. Who would believe I was innocent?

Alex Lynch (12)
The Bradbourne School

Dog's Trust

'Mum, I'm going in the garden,' Poppy shouted out to her mother. She put on her shoes and went off into the garden. Poppy had been going in the garden every day because next-door's dog Toffee had been sneaking under the fence and playing with her. He was a lovely golden Labrador. Poppy loved Toffee coming round because she didn't have many friend and she wanted Toffee to become her new friend. At first, Toffee didn't really enjoy going round there, he used to be a bit unsure of Poppy.

He went round the next day and Poppy came out with, 'Wanna go to the park, Toff?'

It was like he could understand what she said, as if they were two human beings talking to each other. Toffee barked and wagged his tail. She got to the park and from under the climbing frame came a group of bullies from school and started to walk towards her. 'Why are you here? You're not cool,' commented one of the girls.

'Neither are you. Shut up,' Poppy remarked.

At this point these boys and girls wanted to pick a fight with her! This one girl came towards her with her fist in her hand, the rest followed. They pushed her away and got out a knife. 'Come on, Poppy, if you want to get cocky.'

Poppy took a step back and the girl ran towards her.

'Gggrrrrrr!' Toffee had jumped in front of Poppy and snarled at this girl.

'Got your dog to fight your battle now, have you?'

'It's not my dog,' Poppy said in a fearful tone.

'Gggrrrrr!'

The girl chuckled to herself and walked closer with her knife.

Toffee jumped up at the girl, knocking the knife out of her hand and Poppy and Toffee ran back home. 'Toffee, you saved me.'

He scuttled back into his own garden.

She had no troubles the next day at school, the girls were pretty scared of her.

She waited in the garden that night for Toffee to come round. He came running out and jumped on Poppy. They ran around, played ball, played hide-and-seek and just cuddled on the grass. She had got really attached to Toffee and he had got attached to her.

'Toffee!' shouted Mrs Brown.

Toffee barked goodbye and ran to his garden. Poppy got in and about half an hour later, the doorbell rang.

'Hi, I'm Mrs Brown,' she said to Poppy's mum.

Mrs Brown came in for a cup of tea and said she had something to tell everyone. 'Me and Toffee are moving away.'

'What! But … but … you can't!' Poppy said with a tear running down her face.

Toffee walked in and twisted his head to the side in shock. Poppy ran to her room crying. 'He's my best friend,' she mumbled to herself.

Mrs Brown called her down. 'We are leaving tomorrow and I have a little something to give you.'

Poppy was upset, but also confused. What was she going to give her?

It got to next morning and Mrs Brown and Toffee knocked on the door. 'Here's your present, Poppy.' She put Toffee on a lead and gave him to her.

'You're … you're giving him to me?' Poppy said in amazement.

'Yeah, I know you have been seeing each other every day after school, and he hasn't been comfortable here, so here is your present.'

Poppy ran into the garden with Toffee and they rolled around in the grass. *'Thank you, Mrs Brown.'*

Laurie Monshall (13)
The Bradbourne School

Ghosts Forever

'This place is amazing,' said Lee.

'Yeah, I know,' said Lisa. 'Everyone is sleeping in my room tonight and we are telling ghost stories.'

'No you are not telling ghost stories tonight, you'll scare little Joe,' said Lisa's mum.

After dinner, everyone went upstairs to set up their sleeping bags. There were ten of Lisa's mates staying over: Lee, Hannah, Chris, Ashley, Darren, Hollie, Becky, Natalie, Tasha and Lawrence.

'Right, everyone, it's 11 o'clock, ghost story time,' said Lisa. 'Once, about 70 years ago, there was a family that lived in this house and they were really rich, and the oldest girl fell in love with the stable boy. Her father didn't approve of the relationship, so one night the girl sneaked out to see the stable boy, and her father followed her to find out where she was going. When he found out, he got his gun out of the shed and shot the boy in the chest, but the bullet went through the boy and into his daughter's heart. On full moons, you can hear her screams when the bullet went though her,' said Lisa.

'Oh, don't say that, it's supposed to be a full moon tonight,' said Hollie.

'You'll find out tonight if it's true,' said Lisa.

'If this is true, then make the girl turn the lights off,' said Lawrence.

'She's here …'

Stephanie Lee (13)
The Bradbourne School

The Diary Of A Soldier

Dear Diary,

I had a lovely dream last night. It was about the war, but it was over and everyone was happy. It's not like that here though. There's screaming and guns firing. The streets are littered with dead bodies and rubble. The sirens are sounding, telling everyone to take shelter.

I'm on a hospital bed at the moment. I got shot in the leg by a sniper and it really hurt. I'm OK now, I will soon be able to fight for my country again.

Someone's just been brought in. He's been bandaged round the head. I asked a nurse if he will be all right. She said she doesn't think he will survive.

I will have to leave it here. I'm feeling better now. I'll write in here tomorrow, if I'm still alive.

Helen Jenkins (13)
The Bradbourne School

Play Dead

Jo was always penniless, always in debt. I can't remember a time when she had money.

Yesterday, we both walked along the road and into the local shop, but just as we got there, Jo fell to the floor, tripped up by an old, crinkled-up paper bag.

'Hey, I think I bust open my knee.'

She had cut them both right open, but I was more interested in the bag. 'Jo, what's inside the bag?' I said, going to open it.

'Oh my God, I've never seen so much money before!' Jo said in astonishment.

'No, I bet you haven't,' I said, knowing perfectly well that she wouldn't hand it in. But before we could do anything, everything went quiet. You couldn't hear a sound …

A few seconds later, we could hear a small rustling noise, it was coming from the bushes on the other side of the road. The noise got louder and louder. Jo and I went cold. Slowly, we backed off. Jo was breathing heavily and I backed off even more.

As I walked backwards, I saw two bright circles in the bush. I was scared, but not half as much as Jo. She was holding the money, and the lights looked as though they were staring right at her.

Then a deep, sharp voice said, 'Play dead!'

Sarah Fleet (12)
The Bradbourne School

Pitch-Black

It happened again, I woke up with images flashing in my mind, cold sweat running down my face. I could only remember parts of the dream. I know it's going to happen, it's happened before and it's going to happen again.

Every so often I have these dreams, dreams that feel so real that they fill me with fright and fear. Fear for my life, fear for my best friend's life. Only a week ago I dreamt my best friend was involved in a car crash, she couldn't even drive! She'd taken some drugs and felt on top of the world, she then decided to go for a spin in her friend's car. She lost control of the car and skidded off the road. Then I saw images of her in hospital and I woke up petrified and shaking like a leaf.

A couple of days later I got a call from her mum, my friend was critically ill in hospital, and now it's happening again. I see images, disturbing images. Images of fire and burning bodies. A big building gone up in flames and there's me standing there, watching it burn down. I make no attempt to help put the fire out or help anyone trying to escape, I stand there motionless but then I collapse and it all goes black, pitch-black.

Rosie Cooper (13)
The Bradbourne School

A Day In The Life Of Samantha Harper

Samantha was 11 when she moved to Alabama. She'd moved there from England - but not out of choice. Her dad had a new job abroad so she had to leave her beloved family and friends behind, including her Westie - Fifi. It was only for a year but she still didn't want to leave all the same.

She left on the Friday, the end of March, at around 7am. Her family and friends were at the airport waving her off. As the plane took off, she felt a sense of fear and rage. Sam was scared of the fact that she would have to start a new school and angry at her dad for making her do this.

They arrived in America on a Saturday morning, the first day of April at 7am. The journey took exactly 12 hours and Sam hadn't slept through any of it.

'Well here we are Sweetie,' announced Dad. 'This is our home for the next year,' he triumphed, his hand on her shoulder.

She couldn't believe it, she wasn't in England anymore, Sam wanted to cry.

Sam's first day at school was terrible. Her new classmates teased her because she was English. She was also very clever and pretty - they were jealous. At lunch, no one would sit with her so she sat on a toilet, locked the cubicle door and ate her lunch from a tray on her lap. She was so lonely, when Sam got home, she sat and cried.

Amy Ashworth (13)
The Bradbourne School

The Dancer's Best Dream

One hot summer's day there was a young girl named Lisa, she was beautiful. Lisa was a dancer and was wondering which dream she would have that night. Lisa used to wish that she could be the best dancer in the world when she grew up. Her best friend Katie was also a dancer and had been dancing longer than her which made her even more anxious.

Lisa lay down ready to fall asleep, she counted sheep for a while then finally drifted off. Lisa was in a deep sleep and had just starred in the best dream ever. She was on a stage in front of a huge audience who were cheering and clapping. Everyone was saying, 'She's fantastic, unbelievable.'

She was still in the dream but instead of being on stage Lisa was standing in front of a mirror in a dressing room. When Lisa looked in the mirror she was shocked, she was ... older. Lisa immediately thought, *am I still in my dream?* because it seemed so real.

Minutes later Lisa awoke from her dream shouting for her mum, 'Mum, Mum, come here! I've just had the best dream ever.'

She jumped up out of bed after getting no response from her mum. She looked over the whole house but couldn't find her. There was nowhere she could be except the bathroom.

As she entered it, she looked in the mirror, with surprise she had to take a second glimpse, then screamed, *'Mum, help I've grown up! I'm older.'* Lisa was so scared that she was all alone without her mum and dad. But she was happy that she was older. Lisa was so excited and from that day onwards Lisa became the best dancer in the world and everyone enjoyed her dancing.

Charlotte Hazard (11)
The Bradbourne School

Hut Horror

It was a Wednesday when it happened. Stupid, stupid Becky! Why? If I was smart I wouldn't let Jessica take me down to Bracken Lake with all her friends on that sunny afternoon.

The small brown hut across the lake was meant to be haunted but really I didn't believe a word of it. But there I was, standing like a total idiot waiting for Jessica to say, 'Truth or Dare?' I chose 'Dare' because well, there's a lot of things I don't want to tell the truth about … like where I put my old bright green pjs.

'Now this is a double-doctor-doughnut dare!' said Jess. 'Swim across the lake and tap on the door of that hut.'

And like the stupid idiot I am, I did it. I swam across that dirty lake and went up to the door. In the tree above me there was a magpie. A thought flashed in my mind, *one for sorrow*. It cawed once and flew away. I looked back to Jess and she just nodded. I went up to the black door and knocked. There was a sound of thunder, a flash of red, a blood-curdling scream … then it went black.

Laura Powell (12)
The Bradbourne School

A Day In The Life Of Megan Hallmoss

Hiya! I'm Megan Hallmoss. I wake up at 7 o'clock and go downstairs to eat my breakfast. Then I go back upstairs to get dressed. I clean my teeth, pack my bag and put my hair up. Watch TV until 7.30am then I go to the bus stop to catch the bus to school. I get to school at about 8.30am because I live in Edenbridge.

When I get to school, I go to my locker to get my books for my lessons. Then I talk to my mates and when the pips go, I go to my form room. My form tutor takes the register, then I take it back to the office. We wait until the pips go for the next lesson. I have six lessons a day and three homeworks a day.

After the first two lessons, I have a break of fifteen minutes. Then I have two more lessons then it's lunchtime for an hour. Then I have two more lessons and then it's home time. I go to my locker to get my bag then wait for my bus to arrive. I get on my bus and go home.

When I get home I get out of my school uniform, then do my homework. Then I go out to play with my mates and at 5 o'clock I go in for my tea, then I play on the PlayStation or watch TV until 8.30pm when I go to bed.

Zoë Duffey (12)
The Bradbourne School

Trapdoor

Creak! Thud!

The trapdoor swung open, the darkness rising up like a deep well. The girl picked up a stone and dropped it into the square hole. The darkness swallowed it up, although there was a strange hiss; exactly what she was looking for.

'Wow!' she gasped, 'I've found it!'

Another girl swung down from a nearby tree.

'Are you sure it's the real thing?' she whispered.

'Yes. The snake pit is in the correct place and the rope net has been activated.'

'Good. Now you had better jump down first.'

'Why me?' the first girl, name of Joanne, moaned.

'I'm the leader so I decide what you do and don't do!' The second girl whispered.

'Oh fine!' muttered Joanne. She tied a piece of rope to a tall, strong pine tree and slid down the rope into the hole.

'It's okay! You can come down!' Joanne yelled up to her companion, Jade.

'Are you sure that rope is secure? I don't want to break a nail.'

'Oh ha, ha, very funny. Just come down!'

'Okay.' Jade slipped down the rope, landed on the net and every single one of the snakes hissed.

'Here … ' Joanne pressed a stone which was clear of moss, plants and debris; the stone slid back to reveal …

'It's a tunnel!'

'Right then Jade, seeing as you're the leader, you'd better go first!'

'But, but, oh fine! You'd better cover me from the back just in case the snakes come up!'

Then …

Bang! Thump! Crash!

'Jade? Hello!'

There was no answer …

Megan Haysom (11)
The Bradbourne School

A Day In The Life Of A Cat!

Hisss! Miaow! No they're at it again, can't they stop that for five seconds? *Hiss!* I will take that as a no, after all Sooty thinks the garden can only be used by him. Ah well, time to get up.

Being fed can be the best part of the day or the worst part, but anyway today it's good. I've got beef. I think I might end up with some sliced ham for lunch, I usually get ham for lunch.

Miaow, *puurrr* - yes I've finally been let out of the window now, this is the funniest part of the day - playing. Me and Fluffy, Sooty and Kati have to purr and miaow cutely just to get out of the window.

*Bang! O*h great, it's back. Annoyed Heather has returned from school, take cover! The world will never be the same. Oh well I'll just have to go under the sofa.

When it was finally clear Katie came home. I like Katie she feeds me, but because I hid from Heather for too long, *I missed tea!*

Oh well, I can't always win but I promise I will never miss bedtime, but Sooty has taken my seat. Now I'll have to fight for it!

This was very unexpected but he let me have my seat! Oh well, I really wanted to fight Sooty, because if I beat him I would be the Kitty Cat ruler. Oh well, time to go to sleep!

Hazel Ewens (12)
The Bradbourne School

A Day In The Life Of Abbey

Every Saturday my friend Kate and I go to Theatre Train, whereas my brother goes to a football club.

Theatre Train takes place at Wilmington Grammar School, although there are other Theatre Train groups all over the country, this is my nearest one.

The class runs for three hours each week, it consists of three sessions, dance, drama and singing.

Theatre Train is the place you would go to boost your confidence and have fun without being pressurised into taking exams.

I like going to Theatre Train because I think I'm good at all three sessions and would like to be part of something to do with dancing, singing and acting when I'm older. Many people go to Theatre Train, boys and girls from 6 years old to 13.

I've been going for a year and a half. I have been in three operas, the club's show at the Dominion Theatre and this year we're doing a James Bond show/performance in Drury Lane Theatre.

The annual shows we have to do are very exciting. We've lots of different dance moves and song words to learn. We only have the band call before the actual show, so we have to know every tiny bit to get if perfect. The rehearsal is held in St Albans and lasts all day. The other Theatre Train groups are there as well. Each year the show is held in a top London theatre, it is an amazing experience to perform to so many people in such a huge theatre.

I never thought I would be able to do anything like this.

Abbey Warner (11)
The Bradbourne School

Winnie The Pooh Robs A Bank!

Winnie the Pooh caught robbing Barclays Bank in Maidstone.

Yesterday at 12pm the clock struck outside Barclays Bank in Maidstone. But yesterday there was a difference, after the clock had struck the bank started making a loud beeping noise.

The police got a phone call from Mrs Richards, saying that she could hear the bank's alarm going off and she could see lights flashing. When the police reached the scene, they looked inside and saw a small bear with a red T-shirt, emptying the tills. It was a chase to get the bear but when they did they realised that this bear was Winnie the Pooh! They took him down to the station to be questioned.

All Winnie the Pooh would say was 'I want some honey'.

We talked to Police Constable Jones and he said, 'I cannot believe that a bear like Winnie the Pooh would ever do something like this. I don't understand why he needed the money. He was rich enough from the TV programmes, books and teddies'.

Today, Winnie the Pooh was sent to prison for a month for stealing. In this situation Winnie the Pooh has been very stupid in taking too much and being very greedy. He didn't need that money and it wasn't his to take.

Maybe Winnie the Pooh isn't who we think he is.

This is Katie Foreman reporting for The Sun. Have a great day. Goodbye.

Katie Foreman (12)
The Bradbourne School

A Short Story!

As the summer passed, elderflowers grew and surrounded the hut, leaving a crisp red colour scattered across the field from the tree that grew beside it.

As I walked through the carpet of redness, I couldn't help but look at the abandoned hut. My heart ached at the sight of it, but in my head it was saying, 'It's made by magic, if you go in there, you will lose your life forever!'

Before I knew it, I was walking towards it. As I got closer I could feel it was enticing me in with power. Suddenly I could feel my head throbbing and it felt like it was spinning. I ran from the hut. It was so overwhelming but somehow it was trying to tell me something.

When winter finally came, the crisp snow lay down. The wind started howling and whistling. I could see the hut; I saw a lady, a daughter and a son, all playing in warm rays of the sun. I could hear this little whispering voice saying … 'This is just a warning, if you stay any longer then you will suffer a pain which you have never felt before!' As the sun was setting, you could hear the screams of the mother trying to prevent the clasped hand circled round her neck and her daughter and son dropped down on a rope, *hanged!*

I realised I should not have witnessed this scene; it would drag me in with its power!

I hope no one ever goes in there.

Chloe Checkley (11)
The Bradbourne School

The Spooky House

I was strolling to school. On my way I came to a halt to see right in front of me a huge house. Sophie thought to herself, *I'm not scared of that place, I'm going to go up there after school. Lily is going to come with me even if I have to drag her there myself.*

As soon as Sophie got to school, she sprinted to find Lily. 'Lily, Lily, guess what? You've got to come with me after school. I have to show you something, it's so important,' Sophie yelled.

'Okay, okay, calm down. I'll meet you after school,' shouted Lily.

When the bell went for the end of the day, they both ran out of the school doors and to the house. When they got there the door just opened by itself. They both ran in as quickly as they could and the door shut behind them. They both screamed. They both clung, arm in arm, terrified. They started to walk around the house, thinking to themselves, *let's go.*

Bang!

'What's that?' Sophie said. They entered the dining room, they both looked around and saw the table laid for 12, there was a shudder from the level above. Lily was wondering what was going to happen. They ran out of the dining room and into the kitchen and just froze, because in front of them stood a zombie . . .

Find out what happens in the next issue.

Megan Johnson-Hodges (12)
The Bradbourne School

A Day In The Life Of Tanya Littlewood

I never look forward to hearing my alarm in the morning. I hate going to school. Since I was in Year 4, a nasty gang of girls have been picking on me. Although I don't like to show it, what they do, really gets to me. whether it's raining, snowing or perfect sunshine, they are always there waiting for me. That's why arriving at school is the worst.

Whilst I was gazing out of the school bus window, I wondered what today had in store.

On arriving at school, they were there, waiting. Luckily they hadn't seen me. I crept around the back of the school, hoping they wouldn't notice. Too late, they were sprinting after me. Although I was running as fast as I could, they caught up with me. My legs were quivering and I felt as if I had a beating drum in my chest instead of a heart.

One of the girls yanked my pretty pink hair-tie out of my long, wavy hair and threw it to the ground. I shouted at them to stop but that seemed to make them want to persist. Finally they got bored. A teacher noticed I was crying and enquired about what was wrong. I told her the problems I was going through. Later I saw the bullies in the head's office.

From that day I could go to school with ease. Now I like my alarm in the morning.

Lisa Surry (12)
The Bradbourne School

Bank Becomes Bankrupt!

The Bradbourne Bank in Sevenoaks has been robbed! By? We don't know! When? Tuesday 4th September. The robbery was in the early hours of the morning. It was between 1.30am and 3.10am. What has been stolen? The robbers have taken £98,744,623 from the bank!

The bank is a new bank, therefore the builders hadn't even installed CCTV cameras. Bradbourne Bank had only been open since last Thursday.

We have some comments from the local public in Sevenoaks. Here are a few of them: Jenny Clark from Riverhead emailed us saying, 'I'm very disappointed in the citizens who have created this mess! I hope the police catch whoever is making Earth such an inappropriate place to live I honestly don't know what this world is coming to!'

Louise Cooper from Dunton Green, says, 'Whoever stole from the bank is affecting everyone else, for the old bank was moved, so this was our new one. The Bradbourne Bank is now not being opened again until 29th December. So me and many other people have to drive so far, just to go to the bank!'

Jack Jones from the town centre texted us saying that 'The builders should have put up the cameras as soon as they had decided the date that the bank was going to be opened! They just think it's what some people do. Well I say that they shouldn't give them a chance to steal and get away with it! I think they need to think of everything when building, especially the safety and security rules!'

Ryan Church from Bat and Ball said, 'They shouldn't have such easy access in and out of the bank. I mean they must have put up some alarm or even security on the doors. They shouldn't even have to think of that, it should have been a natural thing to do. For goodness sake, it's not rocket science!'

If anyone saw or heard anything at all, please call this number 09477 3685 44.

Please don't be afraid to call. We won't give out personal details!

Olivia Williams (12)
The Bradbourne School

A Day In The Life Of Katie Ray!

On a Tuesday morning I wake up at seven o'clock to get ready for school.

Although I wake up early on Tuesday's it is the best day of the week for me because I go street dancing after school, (seven o'clock till eight) also most of my favourite subjects are on a Tuesday, such as drama, ICT, dance and maths.

As all my favourite subjects are on a Tuesday, I am looking forward to street dancing throughout the day. I think that I enjoy my day at school even more than usual.

As I get home at half-past four, I quickly have something to eat before I getting ready for street dancing. But before I know it, Emma (Ella's mum) is knocking at the door ready to take Ella and I to dance.

When we arrive at Goodmans we give Louise (our dance teacher) five pounds for our lesson.

Ella invited me to go dancing with her four weeks ago and I have been dancing ever since.

Street dancing is very similar to pop dancing because the routines and movements are similar.

As it is street dancing, we learn lots of different movements from dances in the background of pop music and videos.

I enjoy street dancing because we don't do it at school and I can spend time with my best friend.

Even though I have only been dancing for four weeks, I am learning a difficult dance to a song called 'Switch' by Will Smith.

I really enjoy street dancing and it is something that I would like to keep doing for as long as I can.

Katie Ray (11)
The Bradbourne School

Locked

Chase and Zoe made their way through the garden, the grass was long and patchy, covered in rubbish. Empty bottles lay scattered over the garden and newspapers were torn into pieces and flung across the ground.

The house which this garden belonged to had been empty for years. On the outside, all of the windows were smashed. Above them you couldn't see the walls because they were covered in graffiti. The house had certainly passed its sell by date.

Chase and Zoe reached the door, which was open a fraction. They had been dared to go inside by their friends. Everyone said that the house was haunted and that an old lady had died inside! Chase didn't believe anything that they had said but as he pushed the door open, a shiver ran down his back.

Inside wasn't much better. Empty cans lay motionless on the floor.

'This isn't so bad,' murmured Chase as he cautiously stepped through all of the rubbish. 'Let's go upstairs!' As Chase reached the upstairs he turned and looked at Zoe, he could see that she wasn't sure. 'Don't worry,' he said and took her hand.

Upstairs there were three rooms, a bathroom and two bedrooms.

In the bathroom the sink had been pulled off the wall and moths had nibbled away at the curtains. The bedroom has been badly vandalised, the mattress had been ripped apart and a smashed TV lay in the corner. 'Come on let's go,' pleaded Zoe. 'It's easy to predict what the next room is going to be like.'

'No wait. Just one last room,' said Chase and he went through the bedroom door. Zoe was left alone, she walked over to the window and looked out. Suddenly there was a small cry from Chase.

The door of the last room flung open and standing in its frame was Chase, his face was as white as Zoe's top.

'What's wrong?' asked Zoe.

Chase turned to his side and there sitting in an old wooden chair was a lady! Her face was rosy and full of life, although her body was motionless. 'She's dead!' whispered Chase.

Zoe stepped into the room, her eyes transfixed by the woman.

Suddenly the door behind them banged shut and cracked as its key turned in the lock. Chase rushed to the door but there was nothing they could do, they were locked in.

Sophie Kelly (12)
The Bradbourne School

Mixed Up Worlds!

Daisy was fast asleep one night when suddenly something landed on her bed. She thought it was the cat Molly, but when she opened her eyes she saw it was Bart Simpson!

She looked up at the poster by her bed and all that was left was his skateboard. 'What! I don't understand,' she stammered.

'No need to Daisy, I'm just visiting one of my biggest fans,' Bart replied.

Daisy looked around to see if her sister was awake but she was fast asleep.

Bart spent the whole night with Daisy playing 'The Simpsons' Monopoly' and Top Trumps and all sorts of things. Her sister never woke up nor anyone in the house for that matter. It was like they were all unconscious. Bart explained how he visited all of his fans, a different one each night and tonight was Daisy's turn. He promised to return one day.

She must have drifted off back to sleep because when she woke up Bart was back in the poster on the wall. She stared at the poster for a long time and then she thought she saw him wink at her.

The next day she didn't know whether to tell anyone at school, she thought they might think her mad, but her friend Holly was crazy about Bart Simpson, so she told her.

After she had told Holly, Holly asked her something very strange. Holly questioned, 'Did Bart wink at you?'

Daisy answered, 'Yes.'

Daisy Hook (11)
The Bradbourne School

A Day In The Life Of Annie

Hello, I'm Annie Edwards. Here is a story about the most embarrassing day of my life.

When I got on the bus in the morning, everyone laughed at me. I then realised I had picked up my brother's Action Man rucksack, I was so embarrassed!

When I got to school, everyone was pointing at me. Some girls thought I liked Action Man, they said I could have their old ones! I thought the day couldn't get any worse, but it did!

Because of the rucksack, I didn't have any of my books so in most lessons, I had a detention. I had to stay in at lunch, pulling chewing gum off tables. I heard a commotion outside, everyone was crowding around some boys, who were selling something. I ran out to see what was going on.

I found out the boys had been through my bag and found my diary, which my brother had obviously taken. They had ripped the pages and sold them all for £1.

As I walked towards them everyone turned to look at me. I started to hit the boys with my fists, I then ran around the playground collecting all the pages. When I had them all I ran back into the classroom. I was devastated. Suddenly the bell went, so I then walked to my form room.

When I got home, my mum told my brother off, he was grounded for a month! But I think I would rather be grounded than have such an embarrassing day!

Emily Maddox (11)
The Bradbourne School

Basement Terror

Bang! This was the third time this week we had heard strange noises from the basement. I sat up at the top of my bed scanning the room for anything unusual. My heart was pounding like the beat of a drum. Things began to heat up as the fear inside me grew. Beads of sweat drizzled down my face as I breathed intensely.

I swerved round my bed, dropped my feet on the floor while tucking them into my slippers at the side of my desk. Taking deep breaths, I stood up ready to find out what the mysterious sound was. Step by step I kept close watch around me. Wiping the sweat off my face, I came to the door reaching out for it, heart racing so fast. I had no idea what was in store for me and I didn't think it was going to be good but I had to find out the noise-making vandal, before it found me …

When the time was right, I turned the doorknob, wishing I hadn't. I began to walk in the hallway across the creaky floorboards. It was pitch-black, terror filled my mind. While keeping a slow pace, I soon reached the stairs, clinging onto the banister. We had a hostile person on our case, I didn't know what to do!

As I walked down the stairs there was another bang! This militant person or creature was trying to make a point, but what was it?

Before I knew it the basement door was facing me, staring obsessively, with great apprehension, I turned the handle. Quivering, I made my way down the next stairs. Tension built up. As I hit the concrete floor a feeling of nausea crept over me. Two blood-red eyes penetrated me, peering behind a box. It was out to get me, coming closer, closer, closer …

Shani Collins (12)
The Bradbourne School

Beowulf: Travelling Towards The Monster

Boiling with anger, Beowulf screeched.

'We're lost!' he declared. The icy cold wind drove his hoarse voice into the snow-capped mountains.

The boisterous blizzard forced the troops back; the snowflakes felt like knives cutting their frozen skin, biting at their arms and legs and slicing their determination into a thousand shards of glass.

They trekked through the snow for what seemed like days. They came across enormous claw marks on a tree.

'We must be getting nearer,' Beowulf gasped.

'I can't go on!' Keekah whispered, collpasing in the snow, sinking in its cobweb-like texture.

'No!' Beowulf's voice echoed.

The troops' souls had been crushed like a bear trampling on eggs. With each fearsome footstep they were growing closer to their worst nightmare …

In a distant cave a hideous beast was sleeping. The smell of rotting bodies filling the air. The warriors were oblivious to the danger ahead …

'Legolan! Help me shift this boulder,' Beowulf called. They heaved the massive boulder from the entrance to the cave. As the soldiers trudged forward the boulder slowly rolled over the edge of the cliff. There was a dull resounding thud as it hit the mountainside below.

'Hurry, in here!' Beowulf yelled above the noise. The soldiers rushed forward but too late! Icicles fell, slicing everything in its way. The soldiers screamed. Beowulf, Legolan and Ookah were trapped. They gasped in terror at the bright patches of red seeping through the ice wall in front of them. A deadly silence filled the air …

Natalie Price (12)
The Grammar School for Girls Wilmington

A Victim Of War

It was early morning when I had opened the door to see William's mother Margaret standing before me with a sad look shadowing her face. My first thought was William. She spoke the words that I had dreaded. He was injured. Warm salty tears trickled from my eyes.

The days passed as I waited for Meg. I hated the hospital and longed to play football like the boys through the window. As the nurse's gentle hands washed my face I wondered if these were to be the only hands to touch me again. I would never feel the girls' warm hands or small waists as they treated me as though I had a queer disease.

The strong antiseptic smell in the hospital caused a sickening feeling to rise in my stomach. I walked through a maze of long, empty corridors to a large room filled with soldiers. There he sat held up by pillows. I stood shocked, my mouth to dry speak. He was limbless!

I could not stand her pitying stare. I had never thought about her reaction on seeing me but now I wished that I had. Anger rose within me as it had been for her that I had gone to war and now all she could give me was pity. That was when I knew our relationship could not last.

Why did he treat me like this? I fled from the hospital with tears streaming down my face. Why did he not love me anymore? He would always be in my heart no matter what happens.

Laura Spitter (15)
The Grammar School for Girls Wilmington

Beowulf

As they trudged through the thick, sludgy brown snow an overwhelming smell over powered the trembling warrior's senses.

The monster was waiting. She could feel every breath they took, ever step they took. She knew they were coming. She was ready.

Suddenly she sprang from her cave like a coiled spring.

'Run!' yelled one person in the group.

'No,' growled Beowulf, 'we must stay here and fight!'

Beowulf stood his ground in front of the monster. He got out his sword and tried desperately to kill her, but with no avail.

The beast strode over trees and lakes, to her enormous, gloomy, damp lair. Beowulf stood stunned. He had been sure he could defeat her. But he wasn't about to give up now.

Then out of nowhere his prayers were answered. A magnificent golden eagle landed softly beside him. It winked with its big brown eyes and lifted Beowulf onto its feathery back. They took off in a cloud of dust, soaring over whole lakes and forests.

Beowulf could see a field mouse scurrying along below them. The eagle swooped down like lightning. Beowulf clung on for his life until his fingers went numb, but he just couldn't hold on. He fell through the air and landed in a ravine, with a loud *crash!*

He stood up, shaken. He began prowling round the ravine, looking for a way out. He knocked on every stone until suddenly one opened up. Beowulf shouted with joy, and then began to crawl along the tunnel …

Alysha Bennett (12)
The Grammar School for Girls Wilmington

Beowulf

Trudging along through the forest, barely able to see for the blizzard, Beowulf and his men continued their journey. They reached a clearing, surrounded by fir trees. A roar was heard below.

Beowulf silently beckoned the men forward. They picked their way towards the trees on the other side. They never arrived. Halfway across, they fell into a deep hole. Beowulf scrambled up and became aware of the monster standing before them. With a mighty roar, it threw his baton onto the men, killing one. Howling, the monster kicked Beowulf around the pit. Whipping its hand around the men's heads, he killed the rest.

Years passed, the monster had sat in his gloomy cave since, with Beowulf's men's decaying corpses for company. Many more men had tried it that far - and died. Nobody knew about this beast down in the forest - but they knew no one who went into these eerie woods would return.

In the village where Beowulf had started his journey, a team of archaeologists planned to solve the mystery.

After miles of travelling through the forest, a roar was heard.

The men cautiously clambered out of their mountain buggies, walked to the clearing and slipped along the edge. The monster heard them, leapt out of the pit and kicked them down - to their death. All but one man, the monster had not noticed. He soon did. The man had no escape - the monster was leaning over him. He did the only thing possible. He jumped.

Claire Martin (12)
The Grammar School for Girls Wilmington

Shendal

The warriors begin their quest. Shendal sat in her cave, waiting. She knew they were coming.

In the forest Beowulf and his men halted.

'We must rest, it's dark, Shendal will be waiting,' Beowulf shouted over the howling wind.

Suddenly they heard a horrific, high-pitched squeal. It was Shendal.

'Run!' Beowulf yelled to Koda and Keda.

'I'm not leaving you to fight alone,' Keda shouted. He pushed his brother into the undergrowth drawing his sword. Shendal roared throwing Keda into a tree. He fell unconscious.

Koda grabbed Keda's sword. He ran behind Shendal and stabbed her tentacle. She squealed, like a stuck pig and ran.

'Where has she gone?' Koda gasped.

'Not far enough,' Beowulf whispered.

'We should move,' Koda said.

'Keda is unconscious, we cannot carry him tonight, we'll wait for morning.'

'If she returns?' asked Koda.

'She won't, she's injured. We'll leave at first light,' Beowulf reassured the young warrior.

When they awoke, Keda didn't have memories of the fight. They ate, they needed their strength.

'How are you feeling?' Koda asked.

'I've had better days.'

The men laughed. They packed up camp. They made their way silently. After following a trail of blood and broken branches, they found a clearing. It was Shendal's lair. Beowulf led the way.

'I'm going to slay her while she sleeps. If I don't return, set fire to the cave then go as far away as possible.'

They agreed and waited outside. Beowulf looked at them, and then disappeared into the cave …

Paige Smith (12)
The Grammar School for Girls Wilmington

The Cottage

There was an old lady that lived alone except for her dog. One night she felt very tired so she decided to go to bed. That night she woke up because she heard a scratching noise. She checked to see if her dog was OK, but the strange thing was he wasn't there.

She went downstairs to see if he was there and she heard the scratching at the door. She answered the door and her dog ran inside. The dog was very shaken up and very pale so she made the dog a drink of warm milk. He had been outside for about two hours. She tried to put him into bed but he wouldn't go in, so she let him sleep in her room with her.

About two o'clock she heard the scratching on the door again. She got up and was terrified when she found her dog wasn't in her room. She was really freaked out so she went downstairs, opened the door and he came in. She sat down in front of the television and tried her hardest to keep awake but she finally drifted off.

She woke up suddenly as she heard a dripping noise and a squeal. She crept into the kitchen and checked the taps but they were all tightly screwed on. She went upstairs quietly and went into the bathroom and there behind her was her little dog hung up by his hind legs. Written on him was the message, 'I'll be back for you'.

Katie Dodsworth (12)
The Thomas Aveling School

Hell Of The Horror Cornfield

There are so many people that tell ghost stories, and I've got one to tell that happened when I was 23. That was 64 years ago now.

I was with my best friend Paul in our car. We were going on a vacation, to a mansion. When we were on our way I saw it, I didn't know what it was. We finally arrived at the mansion.

As we walked in, it felt like a person was staring at me behind the bushes. We walked in the creaking door and I went up to the room I was staying in. Out of my window, behind the mansion was a forest then a cornfield with a little cottage in the middle.

That night I went to sleep. Just as I was dozing off I heard a scream. I jumped out of bed and looked out of my window. It sounded like it came from the cornfield, in the cottage.

I woke up with Paul screaming. I told him what happened. We both put our coats on and then went outside the mansion. It was dark and rainy. The wind was whistling at me, telling me where the scream had come from. We walked through the forest onto the cornfield, the scream was getting louder.

We knocked on the cottage. Something answered and let us in. We asked it what the scream was. It said, 'Sit down …'

Well the scream was … You'll never find out, no matter what you do to the thing, how much you hurt it, it will never leave.

Jodie Fraser (12)
The Thomas Aveling School

The Kids In The Tree

In November 2002 two kids called Chippy and Barry were the best of friends. They both dared each other to go in the off-limit field. They climbed through the metal hole in the fence and through the bushes they got to the middle of the field. The tallest tree they had ever seen was there. They climbed it. As time went on it became dark.

Then they climbed down out of the tree and started to walk to the fence when Chippy stepped on something mouldy and smelly. It was a *hand*. As Barry ran away to be sick, he saw loads of other bodies everywhere. Then the tree started wobbling. Chippy walked over to the tree and at the top was an egg. It started to hatch and out came a flying Devil with wings. It was gooey and it swooped down and picked up Barry and ripped off his head.

Chippy ran out of the field and down the street. He saw it coming closer as he knocked his door. Suddenly it swooped down and grabbed him.

'You bloody pranksters,' said Chippy's mum.

Craig Evans (12)
The Thomas Aveling School

Staring Through The Window

This story happened many years ago, in the admiral's house down in the dockyard.

A young girl once lived in that house. She lived with her parents and her fiancé. He was a sailor in the Navy. He was often going off on courses and training for war, but this was the real thing. She was very worried but had faith that he would return.

Before he left she broke the news that she was pregnant. Her fiancé swore that he would be back in time.

Months passed and still no sign of him. Then one stormy night came the news of his death.

Once she had the baby it was taken away by her parents. You see, in those days if you didn't have a husband and you fell pregnant, it would be taken away as soon as it was born. She was so upset. She got locked in the attic and wasn't allowed to speak to anyone.

She kept thinking about her fiancé and her baby. One day she got so upset that she tied a rope around her neck and the stair rail then jumped.

It wasn't for some time that her parents found out she had hung herself.

Now she sits at her window waiting for her fiancé to return but on every Wednesday at exactly 3.50pm you can hear a scream falling from the stairs, then it stops and all you can hear is a rope swinging.

Kirstin Bicker (12)
The Thomas Aveling School

The Little Drummer Boy

Many years ago, on a peaceful night, two young men, Paul and Jack, were just finishing working at the dockyard. They started to walk up a long winding road.

'Paul, what are you doing tomorrow night?' asked Jack.

'I'm staying at home with the family. I can't wait till tomorrow because it's pay day,' shouted Paul.

A while later Paul and Jack started shouting at each other about money and how much each other earned. Jack saw a little drum on the floor all the while they were shouting.

Suddenly Jack pushed Paul on the floor and started to fight with him. It was getting out of hand now.

'It's for your own good!' cried Jack, as he stabbed Paul in the neck.

Jack had killed his best friend. He didn't know what to do with the body. 'I'll chuck the body in the river.' Then he remembered his brother telling him that heads float on water. That's when he had a great idea. He ran to the little drum and ripped it open, then cut Paul's head off and stuck it in the drum. So Jack went and dumped the body in the river and hid the drum in an abandoned factory.

30 years later they knocked down the factory. All the while the builders heard drumming. They then found a drum with a head in it.

I know this because I am Jack.

Amy Dettmar (12)
The Thomas Aveling School